PICTURES AT ELEVEN

ROBERT PLANT

ALBUM BY ALBUM

MARTIN POPOFF

WP
WYMER
PUBLISHING
Bedford, England

First published in 2024 by Wymer Publishing, Bedford,
England www.wymerpublishing.co.uk Tel: 01234 326691
Wymer Publishing is a trading name of Wymer (UK) Ltd.

Print edition (fully illustrated): **ISBN: 978-1-915246-51-6**

Edited by Agustin Garcia de Paredes.

Printed and bound in Great Britain by Halstan, Amersham, England.
A catalogue record for this book is available from the British Library.

Typeset/Design by Andy Bishop / Tusseheia Creative.
Cover design by Tusseheia Creative.
Front cover photo © Jarle H. Moe / Gonzales Photo / Alamy Stock Photo

Table of Contents

Introduction

Welcome one and all, back to another book in our *Album by Album* series, this time concerning the baffling and wonderful solo career of Robert Plant. You might've noticed that I've written a bunch of books in my time, including one on Led Zeppelin, but this is the first on that band's golden god of a lead singer and lyricist. And you know what? This has been on my bucket list with respect to these casual and conversational panel books that I cooked up and have been executing, for a long time. There's actually three: I've been pondering one of these on the likes of Robert Plant, Kate Bush and Peter Gabriel for years, even if I was going to have to publish it myself.

From a purely logistical and pragmatic point of view, Plant's catalogue is pretty much the ideal length, in terms of number of albums, to make one of these canon examinations not too short, not too long, not too hot, not too cold. But more importantly, Plant is legendary for his mood and stylistic changes, which often includes shuffling personnel in and out at a dizzying pace. This result is a body of work inside of which the records zig and zag, shaken and stirred, now and zen, a band of joy. And that right there makes for zesty discussion chapter upon chapter. There's always some fresh new sound to discuss, some crazy sub-genre addressed, some connection to Plant's pageantrous past, ambivalent or cheeky.

So yes, as a bit of background, I started doing these for Voyageur Books a bunch of years ago, and then that company closed down their music book division and the idea then lay dormant for quite a while. The idea at that point was to get celebrity panellists, as notable as I could possibly get, which culminated in Sir Paul McCartney joining me to talk about Queen.

But in the ensuing years, myself and a few buddies put together a YouTube channel called *The Contrarians* where we basically talked about our favourite and least favourite albums seven ways to Sunday. As the concept evolved, we started doing these "dark horse" panels in which we would include in the powwow Patreon subscribers that wanted to give it a go. Those dark horse panels quickly became my favourite show theme, and what was most notable was that I even enjoyed talking about albums I figured I knew inside and out, or at least had closed my mind as to what else there was to learn about them or other ways to appreciate them. I was emphatically proven wrong night after night when what I call our "wise music swamis" taught me new ways to look at records by Judas Priest, Black Sabbath and Rush, with the odd howler of disagreement along the way, but for the most part, suppositions well-argued.

And so, what happened was that for the second book in the series, I decided to try one on a band I knew way too ridiculously completely. That band was Blue Öyster Cult. Initially I thought there was no way I could stomach doing another book on those guys after the traditional biography, *Agents of Fortune*, a detailed timeline book called *The Visual Biography* and then a wacky occult conspiracy thing called *Flaming Telepaths: Imaginos Expanded and Specified*. And then after hearing dozens of cool things Zoom call after Zoom call, my suspicion was confirmed that I could come up with something fresh on a band like this that I'd blabbed about so much, if I more or less stood aside and moderated.

And that's what these books are: moderated Q&A discussions on every studio album in chronological order, by a given band. But what I've also learned is that in tandem with hearing so many fresh ideas about these bands, a bunch would spontaneously blossom in my own head. All of a sudden, these one-on-one Zoom calls became back-and-forth conversations where I'd be having, much to my surprise, a bunch of new ideas that I'd fire back at the guy whom I was supposed to be interviewing. This is really important, because what I discovered while doing *Dominance and Submission: The Blue Öyster Cult Canon* is that I had a convenient place to stick in my own opinions, and that's by letting my moderator's role expand, by letting the questions breathe with context. And it actually takes less effort to leave my own thoughts in rather than remove them, because really, I'm just including more of myself that was already in the transcript, whereas earlier on, I might have spent more time editing out my own remarks. In other words, I've become more part of each chapter, each album analysis, than I had originally intended. And so slapping my name on the front of the book started to feel more comfortable, whereas, say on the first title, *Wild Mood Swings: Disintegrating The Cure Album by Album*, it felt gratuitous.

So yeah, to reiterate, what you're about to embark upon is a deep-tissue-massage deconstruction of every Robert Plant album with a revolving cast of characters who each had been asked to bear down on three albums, and then maybe do a few minutes on a fourth or some cleanup later. And like I say, I'm jumping right in there saying my piece as well.

Let me also venture a few words about Robert Plant right here in this introduction, if I may. Being sixty as I write this, of course I went into Plant's first album, *Pictures at Eleven*, super-excited and already a Led Zeppelin fan. I loved the album, but then, swear to God—and I'm sure I'm on record saying this on a whole bunch of video shows, *The Contrarians* and otherwise—I spent probably from about 1983 to 1995 calling *The Principle of Moments* the greatest album ever made, or my favourite album of all time, take your pick. That's how enamoured and obsessed I was by what Plant had put together for a team and a collection of songs with that hallowed record. I was also privileged to see that tour when it rolled through Vancouver, at the Pacific Coliseum, with, of course, Phil Collins grounding and pounding—and often dishing; that's the word that comes to mind—behind the guys.

And then after that, Plant kept challenging us, fully delivering a shock with *Shaken 'n' Stirred* and then becoming a regal aristocrat for a few records before deciding he would become a reverent historian of the roots of rock 'n' roll, while weirdly becoming some kind of hipster (that's not the last time you're going to hear that). And of course along with the thorough dive into Americana is a whole range of world music addressed, and all of it while simultaneously exploring sound and production to a feverish extent unlike any heritage act kind of guy. What emerges is a life lived fully, a rock 'n' roll career that is both distinguished and extensive, and all of this after leading the charge of another band of pickers and grinners you might have heard of back in the seventies.

Collaboration is a huge part of what Plant does as well, and the spirit of that is all over this book, even if we're not going to be looking at the albums he did with Alison Krauss or as part of Page Plant, or for that matter the EP from The Honeydrippers. So yeah, what follows is 11 chapters, one each on every studio album beginning with 1982's *Pictures at Eleven* through to 2017's *Carry Fire*.

I'm still buzzing about how well the Blue Öyster Cult book of this series turned out, and I really feel that if you are inclined to like that band, you are going to love and appreciate them much more after reading that book. Same thing here with Robert Plant. The things these guys say about these albums and songs, and the detail involved, should make you run back to these records for another few spins, very much like a really good liner notes essay might do.

Ultimately that is the hope with this book and pretty much any rock book that I've written, no matter what the concept or brief (and there have definitely been a few different ones), namely, to get you to appreciate on a deeper level these albums that you paid good money for, whether that's LP, CD, digital download or through your Spotify subscription. In the modern day and age, I guess one might define my goal as making you carve out more time for Robert Plant at the expense of the literally thousands or tens of thousands of other artists you might be inclined to burn brain cells on.

Of course, what Robert would probably ask of you is, hey, don't listen to this old dog mumbling away. Me and my Sensational Space Shifters covered this song so you would go seek out the original and realise how great this music was from sixty or seventy or eighty years ago. The irony of this whole exercise is that you might think that me and my assembled cabal are a bunch of music nerds, but none of us could hold a candle to how enthusiastic and knowledgeable Robert is about the music he loves.

Anyway, hopefully with this book you'll learn a bunch of stuff, about Robert Plant's records and then, through extension and expansion, a much wider history of rock 'n' roll and the blues. All right let's get started.

Martin Popoff
martinp@inforamp.net; martinpopoff.com

Pictures at Eleven

"He was lovely, Cozy was; he was a really nice bloke, but he just came along and played the drums. We had already gotten what we were going to do sorted out. Jason Bonham had been helping us, and Jason was only a kid then. He was about 13, but he was a phenomenal drummer (laughs). And Cozy'd just come along to put it down. Because Cozy's timing was absolutely solid, rock-steady. He was the closest thing you could get to John Bonham, which was what Robert was always looking for, ever since the day John Bonham departed. But Cozy couldn't do all the stuff; he couldn't do the 'Pledge Pin' kind of playing, so we got Phil in to do that, who was dangerous. Scary. On the case, totally professional, brilliant and a really nice bloke. And a good laugh down the pub over a pint of Guinness. Yeah, one of the best drummers I've ever worked with."

"As for Robbie, Robbie is my best friend, and he still is, and I see him all the time. I talk to him on the phone, and he moans at me and I moan at him. He's very, very quiet, very private, lives a reasonably underground life, plays the guitar all day every day. Well, he's one of the best guitarists in the world, without a doubt. He likes to go down the pub for a pint. And he'll go up and play if somebody wants him to and they'll pay him (laughs)."

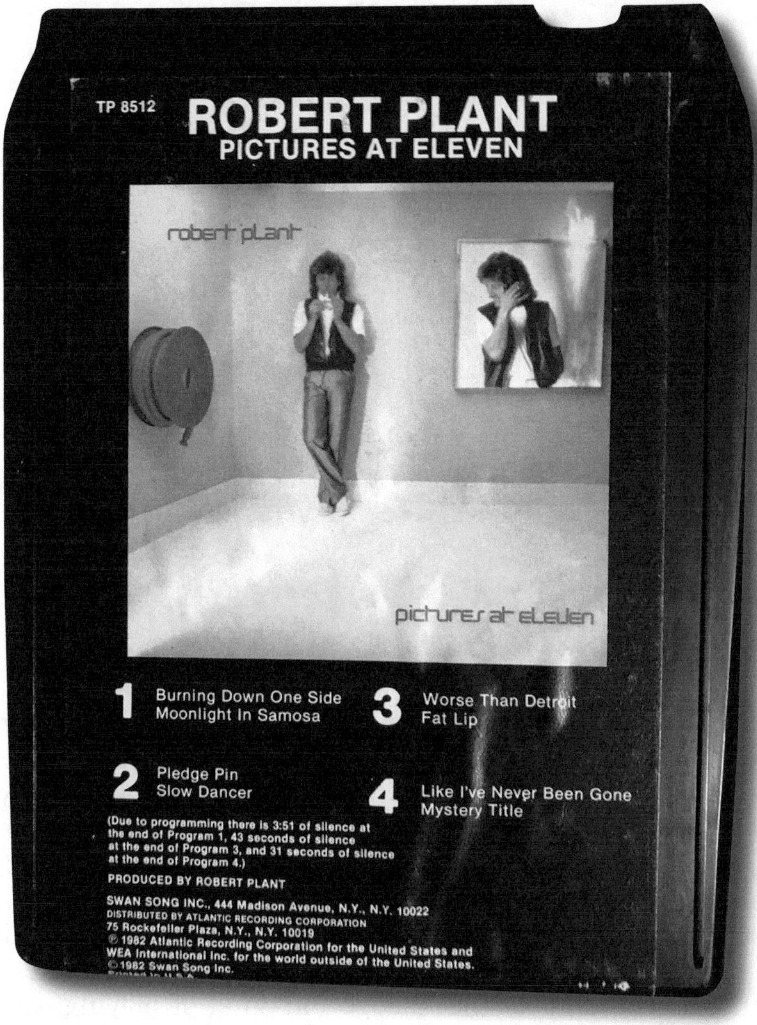

TP 8512
ROBERT PLANT
PICTURES AT ELEVEN
robert plant
pictures at eleven
1 Burning Down One Side
Moonlight In Samosa
3 Worse Than Detroit
Fat Lip
2 Pledge Pin
Slow Dancer
4 Like I've Never Been Gone
Mystery Title
(Due to programming there is 3:51 of silence at the end of Program 1, 43 seconds of silence at the end of Program 3, and 31 seconds of silence at the end of Program 4.)
PRODUCED BY ROBERT PLANT
SWAN SONG INC., 444 Madison Avenue, N.Y., N.Y. 10022
DISTRIBUTED BY ATLANTIC RECORDING CORPORATION
75 Rockefeller Plaza, N.Y., N.Y. 10019
℗ 1982 Atlantic Recording Corporation for the United States and WEA International Inc. for the world outside of the United States.
© 1982 Swan Song Inc.
Printed in U.S.A.

Printed in U.S.A.
Swan Song
ROBERT PLANT
PICTURES AT ELEVEN   TP 8512

"But really, Robert was in charge of everything. I tried to get him to give me some lyrics once, to write some music to, and he wouldn't have it that way around. It always went the other way around. You write the music and I'll put the words to it. Because he can't play any instruments. He can play a bit of guitar but not enough to write a song. The first album was quite a rocky album, wasn't it? It was rockier than *Principle of Moments*, more guitars, more grungy sounds. And it had that Eastern thing, didn't it? 'Slow Dancer'... I remember Cozy pushing all the sliders up on the desk, of his drum kit, right to the top, and he turned up the monitors as loud as they could go, and it was kind of like, this is what happens after Led Zeppelin."

Jezz Woodroffe

Credits

June 25, 1982
Swan Song SS 8512
Produced by Robert Plant
Engineered by Pat Moran
Recorded at Rockfield Studios, Monmouth, UK
Personnel: Robert Plant – vocals, Robbie Blunt – guitars, Jezz
Woodroffe – keyboards, synthesizers, Paul Martinez – bass, Phil
Collins – drums on all tracks except "Slow Dancer" and "Like I've
Never Been Gone" which feature Cozy Powell.
Key additional personnel: Raphael Ravenscroft – saxophone on
"Pledge Pin"

Side 1
1. "Burning Down One Side" (Plant, Blunt, Woodroffe) 3:55
2. "Moonlight in Samosa" (Plant, Blunt) 3:58
3. "Pledge Pin" (Plant, Blunt) 4:01
4. "Slow Dancer" (Plant, Blunt) 7:43

Side 2
1. "Worse Than Detroit" (Plant, Blunt) 5:55
2. "Fat Lip" (Plant, Blunt, Woodroffe) 5:05
3. "Like I've Never Been Gone" (Plant, Blunt) 5:56
4. "Mystery Title" (Plant, Blunt) 5:16

A *Pictures at Eleven* Timeline

October 1976. Black Sabbath issue their seventh album *Technical Ecstasy*. Providing keyboards on the album—and on the tour for the record as well as the tour for 1975's *Sabotage*—is Gerald "Jezz" Woodroffe, who will figure prominently on Robert Plant's first three albums.

1978. Stan Webb's Chicken Shack issue an album called *That's the Way We Are*. It's guitarist Robbie Blunt's last stop before showing up as Robert Plant's right-hand man for his first three solo albums. Prior to this he was on the band's 1977 album *The Creeper* and earlier on records by Bronco, Silverhead and Broken Glass. Also on *The Creeper* is bassist Paul Martinez, who will similarly serve on *Pictures at Eleven*, *The Principle of Moments* and *Shaken 'n' Stirred*.

August 15, 1979. Led Zeppelin issue their eighth and final album, *In Through the Out Door*. It is Robert Plant's last stop before beginning his solo career.

November 14, 1979. Little Feat issue *Down on the Farm*, their last album before a reunion in 1988. It's the last significant stop for drummer Richie Hayward before he shows up to put his stamp on Robert's *Shaken 'n' Stirred* album.

September 25, 1980. John Bonham dies, effectively ending Led Zeppelin.

December 4, 1980. Led Zeppelin issue a statement, reading, "We wish it to be known that the loss of our dear friend and the deep respect we have for his family, together with the sense of undivided harmony felt by ourselves and our manager, have led us to decide that we could not continue as we were."

September 1981. The Michael Schenker Group issues their confusingly titled second album, *MSG*. It is the last stop for drummer Cozy Powell before he appears on two tracks on the high-profile first solo album from Robert Plant, although he is also banging away on that band's February 1982 live album, *One Night at Budokan*.

September 1981 – 1982. Robert Plant records tracks slated for his first solo album.

September 18, 1981. Genesis issue their *Abacab* album. It's the last stop for Phil Collins before he gets well stuck in with Robert Plant and the Led Zeppelin singer's first two albums. A month before Robert's first album hit the shops, Collins would find out that *Abacab* had just gone platinum in the US. Back in February of '81, Phil had issued his first solo album, *Face Value*. That record had certified gold by June, but its smash success was slow burning and still a few years away. Bottom line, Phil would soon be part of three certifying albums all jumbled together under three different band concepts.

June 25, 1982. Robert Plant issues *Pictures at Eleven* in the US, followed by the UK launch on July 2nd. Interest in Robert is heightened when a Led Zeppelin rarities record called *Coda* is issued in November. The album reaches No.5 on the *Billboard* 200 chart, No.2 in the UK and No.5 in Australia. It eventually certifies silver in the UK, gold in Australia, platinum in Canada and platinum in the US.

August 27, 1982. *Pictures at Eleven* reaches its US gold certification, for sales of over 500,000 copies, going platinum in 1990 for sales of over one million copies.

September 1982. "Burning Down One Side," backed with "Moonlight in Samosa," is issued as the first single from *Pictures at Eleven*. It peaks at No.3 on the *Billboard* sub-chart Top Tracks (now called Mainstream Rock), stalling at No.64 on the main Hot 100 chart and at No.73 in the UK. The UK 12" single adds the non-LP "Far Post."

November 1982. "Pledge Pin" is issued as the second single from *Pictures at Eleven*. It is backed with LP track "Fat Lip." "Pledge Pin" reaches No.11 on the Top Tracks chart.

January 1983. "Far Post" manages to become a moderate hit in the US, rising to No.11 on the *Billboard* Top Tracks chart and reaching No.74 on the Hot 100.

Martin talks to Ralph Chapman, Tim Durling and Rick LaBonte about *Pictures at Eleven.*

Martin Popoff: Okay, so here we go: the very first Robert Plant solo album, *Pictures at Eleven*. Can you set up for me how we get to this point?

Tim Durling: I don't think Robert ever wanted to stop making music—he just wanted to put aside Led Zeppelin when John Bonham died. I don't think he ever said, well, right, I'm going to retire and become an accountant now and just live in the hills, although there's probably a part of him that wanted to do that, that just wanted to get away from it all, because not many bands had the hyperintense career that Led Zeppelin had. Success followed them wherever they went. It was huge success, way outside the success of any other rock band of the era. They've got four diamond-certified albums now, and that's out of eight records. And the counting continues in the streaming age, and I notice the first album isn't far behind. Yeah, no other hard rock band of that era—Deep Purple, Black Sabbath, Uriah Heep—can compete with that. Led Zeppelin were just always something else. And I've heard James Hetfield say the same thing, that when Cliff Burton died, he's like, "There is no band now; it's just three guys." And I think Robert's thinking that, along with the idea that he still wants to make music, but doesn't want to play the commercial game, even though he turned out to be very smart in the way he navigated the eighties with his solo career. But no, I don't think he ever wanted to put out albums that would sound like Led Zeppelin albums with his name on them instead of the band name.

Ralph Chapman: When I first heard the record in the summer of '82, I wasn't even aware that it was coming out. It was one of those moments where you've got your alarm set to play music to wake you up, and what I woke up to was "Burning Down One Side." And what I immediately knew when I heard that was, I don't know who's singing that, but that's Phil Collins on drums. Because I was in the height of my Phil Collins obsession, and I could immediately hear his style; his sound, it was unmistakable. And then I just waited for the DJ to say, "That's the new Robert Plant song, 'Burning Down One Side.'" And it's like, oh, that's cool. I obviously knew who Robert Plant was, but I wasn't into Led Zeppelin.

So *Pictures at Eleven* is actually my doorway into Led Zeppelin. I was a dyed in the wool progressive. I was a Beatles and Genesis fan really, but always knew of Led Zeppelin. So that was really interesting to me and extraordinary to me that Phil Collins was all of a sudden playing with Robert Plant. And I mention that story not because I love to talk about my past as much as I think in a sense that Robert Plant, if you step back, Led Zeppelin had broken up in December of '80. I know he'd done a pickup band-type thing with Robbie Blunt, but he hadn't gone back into the music industry. People maybe forget that Robert Plant was a human being who saw the dissolution of Led Zeppelin, the breakup of Led Zeppelin, from a friendship level. I'm sure he was shattered by Bonham's death. Bonham was thirty-two, and they were best friends for years.

But also, in the lead-up to *In Through the Out Door*—I've read various interviews and maybe you have as well—that he was conscious of being in his 30s and of feeling out of step, not wanting to be written off as an old fart, all those kinds of things. And then Led Zeppelin did *In Through the Out Door*. Jimmy Page was kind of fading with heroin addiction and heroin-based apathy, possibly, and John Paul Jones steps in the breach and *In Through the Out Door* is arguably their most contemporary-sounding record in the sense that Rush and *Permanent Waves* is a real shift to where you can hear all new influences. I don't want to make this all about *In Through the Out Door* but it's an important part of the context. It's recorded at Polar Studios, the Abba Studio and whether you love it or are indifferent to *In Through the Out Door*, it's a very distinct-sounding record.

Rick LaBonte: *Pictures at Eleven* is an important album to me because I was born in 1970, and by the time I started getting into Zeppelin the band is dead. I'm ten or 11 when I got Led Zeppelin one. So to me, Robert Plant is the surviving member that kept us intrigued with and remembering the Led Zeppelin saga. So by this point I was watching every move Robert Plant did. Jimmy Page and John Paul Jones weren't that busy, so all eyes were on Plant. What a big challenge it must have been for him to go out under his own name. Firstly, when he'd do interviews, he's well-documented as saying he could never picture himself as a solo act. He's on record saying that. And then now you gotta go out there and you don't want to be reminded of the past. If he was gonna play Zeppelin songs, they would have carried on without John Bonham, right? He wasn't in that frame of mind. And it was Phil Collins who nurtured him and helped him find his own identity.

Again, he was aiming to be very modern, which makes sense because *In Through the Out Door* was a modern record for that time. That was the sound of '79. It may not have been the heavy rock Zeppelin fans wanted, but Plant is very aware of his surroundings. Musically he's up to speed. He wouldn't be like Jimmy Page and go, "Eddie Van Halen who?" Not knowing him after like five albums. Plant knew who was up-and-coming. He would follow *Billboard* and go to talk shows and be on *Rockline*. He made a point of being out there and in the clothes and fashion of the eighties and it's all resonating in this music too.

Tim: You're only three years removed from *In Through the Out Door*, and that album, was a change for Led Zeppelin anyway, with a lot more keyboards. I love the album, actually. It's probably my favourite Zeppelin album because it is so different. And certainly Robert's vocal timbre is similar because, again, you're only three years removed. So he's still singing for the most part in his Zeppelin voice here. And I think the production is even similar, and also similarly not dated. It holds up well today, where a lot of eighties productions don't.

Martin: Before we get to Phil Collins, how does Robert wind up with Robbie Blunt in the all-important guitarist role?

Ralph: Well, Led Zeppelin breaks up because Bonham dies in September of 1980 and I think Plant was vulnerable. First, I think that's why he looked to someone like Robbie Blunt, who he knew, who was from the same part of England and had a certain pedigree himself. Not with bands that were big, but a band like Silverhead's pretty cool with Michael Des Barres, and Bronco. So that was familiar to him, although nobody knew who Bronco or Silverhead were. There was a huge expectation put on Robert Plant that if he was going to come back, he had to come back with more than just coming back. Or at least he felt that way.

Rick: Robbie was an old mate of Robert's and they were playing rockabilly stuff and covers prior to this album. He's bluesy but he manages to put in a very modern performance on this album. I figure that Robert was trying to find people and personalities that weren't going to pressure him, and he just so happened to find a really good songwriter. He just lucked out. I honestly believe he just lucked out.

Tim: With Robert re-entering the studio for the first time after losing John Bonham, who was a childhood friend, it probably felt right to have people he knew and trusted by his side. He's a long way from farming out jobs to unknown musicians. And at the risk of incurring the wrath of millions of fans all over the world, Robbie Blunt strikes me as a less sloppy version of Jimmy. You know, this is how the notes are supposed to go. I think Robbie ends up doing some really inventive things on guitar, far from obvious and always fitting the songs.

Martin: And Ralph, what does Paul Martinez bring to it? You interviewed him. What else did he tell you that was interesting about this?

Ralph: He had a lot more to say about *Principle of Moments* when I spoke to him. My understanding of how *Pictures at Eleven* came in is that Robert always had Blunt as his collaborator, and then he put the band together. So they had done a substantial amount of songwriting and pre-production and then picked players as it went along. So Paul was very much a hired hand to an extent, I think, not knowing whether this project was going to continue. And by the time it ends, and it's received well, that's when Robert tells them that he's going to stick around.

And so, with *Principle of Moments*, the songwriting changes and Martinez is a much bigger part of the songwriting on *Principle of Moments*. Here he just strikes me as a hired hand. He did say that he was amazed at how quickly he was able to lock in with Phil immediately on *Pictures at Eleven*. But I don't think he necessarily sticks out in the way that he sticks out on *Principle of Moments* and *really* sticks out on *Shaken 'n' Stirred*, where all of a sudden, on a song is like "Little by Little," he's a huge part of the focus of that song. *Pictures at Eleven* has a very dense, for the most part—"Fat Lip" and "Moonlight in Samosa" being the exceptions—unrelenting sound to it.

Martin: And how and why does Robert get involved with Phil Collins?

Ralph: Well, if I can go back to Paul Martinez, he alludes to the idea of why Phil was the perfect choice. First of all, Phil was an acolyte or a follower of John Bonham. If you listen to tunes like "Squonk" from *Trick of the Tail* or "...In That Quiet Earth" from *Wind and Wuthering,* you're hearing a guy who definitely can do Bonham. I know this is a dicey area, because no one can play like John Bonham, which is true. John Bonham is certainly one of my favourite drummers, so I never undervalue what an extraordinary player he was. But Phil could do that. He could emulate John pretty convincingly. And I don't mean aping him but honouring him and recognising that for a song like "Squonk" on *Trick of the Tail*, this calls for John Bonham. He used to say, "I'm going to put my Bonham hat on." And he used to go see Bonham play in the late sixties, I believe, when Bonham was playing with Tim Rose. He loved John Bonham. John Bonham was a hero as much as Bill Bruford and Roger Powell from The Action. Anyway, so Plant was observing that Phil could honour John, could play like John, could invoke that sense of power and subtlety that was such a huge part of Bonham.

But also, Phil was an extraordinarily versatile drummer. So back in '81, he had already played with Eno, he had Brand X, he had played with Rod Argent, he had played with Pete Townsend, doing some really experimental stuff with Raphael Rudd, who did the brass arrangement on "Rough Boys." He had an incredible pedigree, Phil. People dismiss Phil, and that's usually an indicator that they're complete shitheads. But in many ways, Phil was like a British version of Jim Gordon or Jim Keltner or Steve Gadd, not because he played like them, but he had the ability to play a myriad of styles convincingly, efficiently, creatively. I had interviewed Rupert Hine, and he said the same thing, that Phil could just reinvent himself for whatever kind of session. I don't know how much Robert knew about Phil, but Phil had a reputation, obviously, having played with all these people. So that's one side of it.

But I think the other side, just going back to the idea of Plant being vulnerable, is that back in '81, where he would have gotten Phil, Phil had certainly come into his own as the frontman of Genesis. Plus *Face Value* had come out and made an extraordinary splash. But he wasn't enemy No.1; he was still seen as one of the top British artists. He was showing up on *The Old Grey Whistle Test* and being interviewed and he was a legend. He wasn't the guy who had done ballads. He was in that really cool, pre-"Against All Odds" moment where he was just an amazing musician, who happened to come into his own as a singer and a songwriter.

But he was a drummer first and foremost, and he was successful, and he had a reputation for being incredibly efficient, energetic and knowledgeable in the studio. And to have Plant recognise that

I can get a guy… because there's going to be a lot of people paying attention to *Pictures at Eleven* from a drumming point of view. That's my belief, that the Zeppelin fans, when they got it, they would demand that either consciously or unconsciously it was like, "Who's this fucker got to play drums with him? And he better be good, because you're replacing our John."

Martin: Which brings us to Cozy Powell, who drums on two songs. I suppose "guests" would be the word.

Ralph: I think that was Robert's initial impulse, to get someone like Cozy Powell, who is not even a tenth the drummer that Phil Collins is. Still, he's a great, great player, but he really is more of a traditional school. I love Cozy, but when he joined Emerson, Lake & Powell, and I saw him and Keith Emerson being interviewed, Keith Emerson talked about how in order to tour ELP, they had to rearrange a lot of their material to suit Cozy Powell. Because Cozy had a very specific type of playing.

With Phil Collins, you wouldn't have had to do that. He could play Carl Palmer and he could play Cozy but Cozy was Cozy. And the great part of using Cozy at first is that he invoked that kind of tub-thumping, British, heavy, familiar sound, that Plant I think was drawn to for his first record; I think he couldn't help but be drawn to that. I don't want to come out with a record that, not just from a drumming point of view, but from a vision and from a tone and from a songwriting point of view, that is too much of a departure from Led Zeppelin. I can't lose my legacy, what I built, but I need something new; I need a direction to go so I'm just not being a Zeppelin pastiche act.

Cozy I think would have taken him closer to that pastiche. I'm speculating, but I think Plant, having been with John Bonham, knew he had to have a guy. And this bears itself out through the rest of his career. Phil was just the first in a bunch of drummers, especially in the later part of his career, who are incredible players in terms of, again, versatility, and who can invoke Bonham but then invoke like these Moroccan percussionists.

I think Cozy was never going to be the answer. And it's interesting. Again, when I spoke to Paul Martinez, he mentioned that a lot of drummers vied for that seat. Word got out that Plant needed a drummer. So, you had guys like Simon Kirke and Carmine Appice and I think even Roger Taylor, all vying for that. But I think they were all closer to that Cozy idea. And Simon Kirke was a big friend of John Bonham's. But I could imagine Robert said, "Thanks but no thanks, because you don't actually know what I need."

Martin: So, it's Phil Collins who fitted his thought process best, I imagine?

Ralph: Yes, he's thinking, what I need is a guy who's going to point me forward creatively and rhythmically. He's thinking, I'm re-entering the biz—am I an old fart? And you're gonna get a guy like Phil Collins who is gonna say, "You're a fucking legend. You have an incredible voice. I'm in the same position you are, in terms of stature. So, you can trust that I know what I'm talking about. Oh, and we're signed to the same label. We know the same Ahmet Ertegun-type people." And I think Plant really leaned on Phil for emotional support at the same time.

Looking at the pre-production of *Pictures at Eleven*, my understanding is they completed a lot of the pre-production demos, which are different from demos, with Jason Bonham, who's like a 15-year-old at that point. So, they had all these tracks, the remaining tracks that Cozy wasn't part of, and I imagine that the great thing about Phil is Phil worked, certainly in those days, incredibly fast. So, Robert sent him those tapes. And he was composing drum parts, knowing that he probably had three days in Wales where they recorded. And he just laid them down and they were perfect. They were exactly what the songs needed. And I think that was also energising to Plant: not only is he all these things, but he can play and I need him to play. He's a star and I need to lean on him, but he's fucking efficient, and we can get this done. And it will sparkle and pound where it needs to. And I can deliver it with confidence to the record company because I got this guy, Phil Collins.

Martin: But he's not really helping from a production standpoint, is he?

Ralph: No, because Robert Plant is clearly the producer. And Pat Moran gets the only engineering credit, who has got a long history; I believe he played with Paul Martinez as well. That may be Paul's connection to Robert. But I'd say Phil came in as a session player who also knew this is how you make the sound—he had opinions, which added credibility. He wasn't just a session guy. And God bless someone like Cozy Powell. But Phil had a pedigree of hits, of success, of knowing what to do to tweak those songs. And not to beat it to death, but he was renowned. He was beloved by producers, producers who I've spoken to, who say, "You get Phil and you get more than just a drummer—you get an artist." That was a huge thing. "Not only am I laying down these drums, but this is what you should do, and you should listen to me."

Rick: It's not exactly producing, but I feel like Phil served a little more like a musical director instead of just a drummer. He's coming from Genesis, he's going to make sure everything is tight, no sloppiness, no loose ends. I think he inspired the situation to be running like a tight ship. Plant is not used to managing a band. I don't think Robert Plant was in the driver's seat here. Sure, he's the boss and is doing the lyrics and trying to find his voice and trying to find the song and maybe involved in the sequencing, the running order. But as far as the musicianship goes, he had a lot of help. I think there were a lot of people saying, "Robert, we can't let you not make this work." But it's a balance. There's an expectation, and so there's some Zeppelin-esque vibes to the record and even some very Jimmy Page-like licks from Robbie. But he's also got to be aware of what's out there at the time—Foreigner is out; Journey is out. All of these bands had big guitar moments. He knows he needs a guitar hero or at least a strong guitarist on the album, because that is the trend in the market at that time.

Then again, I'd say Robert was a bit more in the driver's seat with *In Through the Out Door*, along with John Paul, because Jimmy was a little bit out of commission, so to speak. And then it's interesting that *Pictures at Eleven* sounds like a follow-up to that record. Plant wanted to be relevant. He wasn't about going back to the past. It's almost like, if people forgot where I was, that would be fine because it's just a haunted memory. Let's face it, his last few years with Zeppelin, they weren't exactly buddies because they were all in their own world and dealing with their own issues. Other than John, who was now dead, they weren't there to nurse his feelings when his son Karac died. It wasn't a family at the end; it was more like a business with co-workers. So he needed somebody like Phil Collins who had a lot of opinions and was a go-getter and would kick the legs out from his chair and say, "Don't worry, you're doing the right thing." He needed a coach, someone who had good advice. "Just because you were the voice of Led Zeppelin, that's not who you are."

But yeah, all those players are fantastic. They even eventually get Bob Mayo to join them on guitar. He's actually the keyboard player/guitar player for Peter Frampton. You hear him when Peter Frampton does that, "Do you feel like I do? Bobby on piano—Bob Mayo." That's the same guy. He's playing guitar and a little bit of everything on tour, but he's not on the record. So, the rest of the band other than Cozy Powell will be following them on tour for the next two albums. And they're really good players. And all people from Birmingham, all people that lived in a neighborhood—they would meet at the pub. And that's why he didn't do a lot of auditioning. He was hanging around with people that were close to him.

Martin: Okay, so *Pictures at Eleven* shows up in the record racks. What do you make of this title and album cover?

Rick: That title, you'd get that on the American news at the time: "Oh we got a news story and pictures at eleven." So, they're saying that we've got film to back it up. And so what's the news about Robert Plant? Well, we've got the story, and pictures at eleven, so to speak. I like that. What was shocking for a kid though was seeing him smoking, lighting a cigarette. Like, you're the singer—and you're smoking?! That was a shocker, that he did that. But once you see the song titles, it's like, *Burning Down One Side* would have made more sense for the title. Anyway, this is a Robert Plant for the eighties. His hair is shorter. You don't get the bare chest, he's not wearing bell bottoms, he's a different man than you saw just five years ago. This cover is almost like a facelift. And give credit to Peter Grant: Swan Song is operating still but just barely, and *Pictures at Eleven* is on Swan Song, although Robert would have to start his own record label when it comes to the next album.

Tim: Yes, after this he had his own label, Es Paranza. At this point it's Atlantic, with the boutique label Swan Song used only this one time for Robert Plant. It's really interesting that after that he broke away from it. The only other album that came out on Swan Song after this was the self-titled from Wildlife, which was Simon Kirke and a couple guys that went on to FM, the Overland brothers. They put out an album in '83 that was on Swan Song and the last Bad Company album with Paul Rodgers, *Rough Diamonds*, came out on Swan Song two months after *Pictures at Eleven*.

As for the front cover, yeah, he's got the slightly shorter hair at this point. It looks like a Hipgnosis cover, the way it tells some kind of obscure story. But it's not; it's Michael Hoppen, who I don't recognise. I find that the font they used for the credits on the inside is terrible; it's really hard to read. But yeah, you've got this fire hose on a reel, but on the back, the hose is coming off the reel by some invisible hand, I guess. And really, nothing bears any relation to the title. Which, oddly, Robert does that quite a bit with his song titles, coming up with some extra words that aren't part of the lyrics.

Martin: Once past the cover, the record starts with "Burning Down One Side," which, again, I could picture tucked into *In Through the Out Door* no problem, from the guitar licks down through the drums.

Tim: Sure, and I'm not sure what the title means, unless it's referring to the front cover where he's literally got fire on one side of him. I don't understand that album cover. This was, I think, quite successful at rock radio, and it's a good song, well-produced. I will say that his vocals sound a little overwhelmed by the instrumentation. It's really hard to tell what he's saying, but it sounds great. And one of the things I love about his first two albums is that you really get to appreciate Phil Collins as a drummer. You're not distracted by the fact that it's his song, his singing, his band, his album, but you just get to hear Phil Collins, the drummer, incredibly musical on this song and most of the others that he plays on—very frisky. This is as good a song as any to pick as a single to announce the project. We're up and running, and it's not that far removed from something like "In the Evening." And it introduces the world to Robbie Blunt, great guitar player, master of many guitar sounds. It strikes a balance as a more traditional rock-sounding song without really sounding like a Led Zeppelin leftover.

Martin: Further on the title, not only is it not mentioned in the lyrics, it really bears no relation to the story, although there's a vague mention of fire at the end.

Tim: He does that a lot, especially on these first two albums. At least there are no songs with ellipses. It's like the title provides a bit of extra room for him to put his thoughts down. And the downside of that is, if you're trying to introduce someone to his solo work and you say, "Yeah, you remember that song, 'Burning Down One Side,' or

'Big Log?'" "No, how does it go?" You read these titles and you can't picture the chorus.

Anyway, love this song, and while it's also a great introduction to the solo career, it's also a great introduction to Phil. You get the beautiful snare sounds and the fills—no pun intended—where you don't expect them, but always just in the right spot. It's never flashy, never showy, and almost like a more analogue version of his *Abacab* drum sound, which is maybe one of the best recorded drum sounds ever, right? It's tough to beat. But playing with a completely different artist, it just works so well. As we know, he doesn't play on all the songs—Cozy Powell plays on a couple of songs on here. My understanding is that for a very, very brief moment, there was a consideration that he would replace John Bonham had Led Zeppelin continued. Obviously, that didn't happen. But it's interesting enough that I have to wonder if he was the first to come along, and then Phil Collins became available. I'm not sure how they ended up working together, but it just works very well. And it leads to how good this album sounds too because you've just got that punchy, crisp drum sound underneath it all.

Ralph: I heard that "burning down one side" is actually a euphemism for smoking a joint wrong or something like that. Lyrically, it's familiar, comfortable territory that has that evocative poetry of Plant and that peerless phrasing where the words almost don't mean anything. But you're just amazed at how melodic and how seamlessly this guy can weave words around a melody, which was one of his stock-in-trades. I think at times he was a profoundly superb lyricist, but the irony is you could hardly understand the fucking lyrics a lot of the time.

Rick: I remember seeing the video for "Burning Down One Side," and it's just as abstract and hard to follow as the words. But it's a catchy tune and I agree—the drums sound fantastic. I like all those stop-and-go moments here, although you get a lot more of that on *The Principle of Moments*. And I appreciate the arrangement, where you've got a simple keyboard part, simple guitar solo, guitar, bass, drums and vocals. It's proggy and still accessible, like Asia was doing at the time. They were bringing poppy songs but have prog elements in the arrangement. Phil Collins brings that to the table, including his bright and tuned tom-toms.

I also think this is the first time you started seeing the gated vocal and vocal plate that Robert Plant was using, where it compressed his voice. In some ways it's good; in some ways it's not. "Burning Down One Side" is so compressed, it's missing some of the nuance that you can definitely hear live. You can hear the dynamic and the stretches in the voice live where here it's not like that. You know why? Because that's a Phil Collins vocal plate. That's what he used in his songs, and it gave him that same recipe or format. And that's why people can't make out some of the words Plant is saying. It's not like that in every song. "Like I've Never Been Gone" has more definition and more dynamic. You can make the lyrics out.

Martin: Where else can you hear this vocal plate effect?

Rick: It's on any Phil Collins album. In fact, there are vocal plates that are literally built… you buy digital delays for vocalists, and it has that Phil Collins vocal plate that they would commonly use in the eighties. But I think you can hear it in all of his solo works, his solo records, especially "In the Air Tonight." On here, "Burning Down One Side" plus I think "Mystery Title" has some of that. It's a compression that takes out some of the dynamics. And Plant wasn't used to singing that way. That would never work with Strange Sensation. I'm not saying it would never work, but it's not what he does with Strange Sensation. He'll go so quiet with the whispering and then he'd yell, and he wants that dynamic. He doesn't want everything to be the same volume.

Martin: Next is "Moonlight in Samosa," which is a little more conventional, more steeped in the romance and mystique of Robert, less perky and new wave like the first song.

Tim: "Moonlight in Samosa" is interesting because right away he gets very mellow. Beautiful guitar work from Robbie Blunt in this one. Yeah, I remember hearing this for the first time and thinking wow, it's not commercial. Or it's not pandering commercial. But it's very melodic. And I have to think that this must have been under consideration for a single at one point, but it would probably have to be edited for length. Yeah, just a gorgeous song. And kind of right away, we learn that this is not going to be Zeppelin light. It's going to be something different.

Ralph: If you look at songs like "Pledge Pin," "Fat Lip" and "Moonlight in Samosa," for me, those demonstrate that Plant has found in Robbie a composer that will not jar the listener but take them to an adjacent place. Blunt is obviously a great composer of music, but also, he was an amazing slide player and acoustic player. "Moonlight in Samosa" is a tune where I think Blunt is really instrumental. That and "Fat Lip" really point the way forward.

Now I guess what pulls me back from calling this an imagined Led Zeppelin ballad is Phil's drumming, because it's so laid-back. It's him and a singer-songwriter. It reminds me a bit of his drumming on *Grace & Danger*, the John Martyn record. It's a singer-songwriter approach, like a Russ Kunkel thing, not heavy-handed at all, which can't help but feel like new territory for Robert Plant, which he explores later, while he explores so many other things as well.

Martin: To me, "Pledge Pin" is like the next new wave step beyond "Burning Down One Side," more playful in parts but also more melancholy in parts. There's a wildness to the expanded range.

Rick: Yes, and another strange title. When I was a kid, I didn't know what a pledge pin was. I love that saxophone solo right in the middle of it, and I love when they bring it down to a simmer and then pick up again and the horn starts wailin'. I literally remember feeling the hair standing up on my arm as a kid. I'm like, wow, that's really cool. Plant never had a saxophone on an album before. It's very eighties to do that but it sounded really cool.

Tim: Very much so. "Pledge Pin" got a lot of airplay. As Rick says, one of the things that you notice right away is it's the first time you've heard Robert Plant's voice with a saxophone, played by Raphael Ravenscroft, who's probably best known for "Baker Street" by Gerry Rafferty—that's a pretty well-known saxophone break. If you just heard the bed track of this, you wouldn't necessarily expect to hear Robert Plant's vocals on top of it, but he's selling it. If he ever had any doubts about what he was doing with the solo career, he never lets it show.

Martin: I get a Police vibe from this one, with a bit of jazzy Andy Summers guitar and then of course the busy yet quiet drumming when we get to the verses. Heck, even the herky-jerky drumming at the beginning.

Ralph: I don't really hear it, although the sax might cause one to think of *Ghost in the Machine*, which is the same era. I don't necessarily disagree with you. "Pledge Pin," has got this quasi-reggae rhythm, and it's got the rim shots and "As the cavalcade begins to thin" (laughs), you know, that piece in particular. What's interesting about "Pledge Pin," in that interview I did with Paul Martinez, he said that Phil was really instrumental in that arrangement. So, I would owe that to Phil as much as I would Plant. As for the guitar, I don't think Blunt is being dragged along. I think Blunt was only starting to get dragged along when Plant's fascination with technology and Euro-pop textures happened on *Shaken 'n' Stirred*. That's where you see those two guys kind of drift from each other. But here on this album, they're very connected and going to these areas quite confidently.

Martin: Side one of the original vinyl closes with "Slow Dancer," like the fourth track on side one of Deep Purple's *Who Do We Think We Are* is "Smooth Dancer"—never been able to shake that thought since I took this album home from the record store back in 1982!

Rick: Funny, yeah, well, we've got Cozy Powell playing what is obviously the most Zeppelin-like song on the album in "Slow Dancer" and then also "Like I've Never Been Gone," which is pretty Zeppelin-like too, only that's more down to Robbie Blunt's chord changes and total Jimmy Page-like guitar licks. To me, if they were to carry on, he was the right guy to be behind the kit. So yeah, obvious "Kashmir" is a touchstone, and it's got the "oh-oh" part, which is a signature we'll hear in a lot of Robert Plant solo song choruses. Cozy plays it with so much drama and power. Anybody who was worried that Plant would go commercial, that song served as an anchor.

Tim: It's got that Eastern modality to Robert's vocal and that Page-y swagger to the riff. Plus, those big drums—boom, whack, boom, whack. It's almost like you gotta give the masses one song that they can latch onto. I'm really surprised, for that reason, that it didn't get more radio play, because it's a calling card, an invitation. It wouldn't surprise me to learn at some point that Atlantic wanted to make it the album opener.

Ralph: As incredibly delicious as "Slow Dancer" is, and "Like I've Never Been Gone," the two Cozy Powell songs, "Slow Dancer" almost veers to pastiche in the sense that it's got the chant and the very Middle Eastern vibe to it, and the really thundering bass drum. It strives for the exotic but because you can read the motivation, it becomes kind of a static song from a stylistic and progressive point of view.

Martin: With "Worse Than Detroit," we're back to a jumpy, nervy new wave place, a bit frivolous, I guess until you notice the Led Zeppelin blues underpinning, especially in the vocals.

Rick: Being from Windsor, across the border from Detroit, I never liked that title (laughs). Why was it worse than Detroit? I don't know how people in Detroit welcomed that title. Anyway, I love the tune now. It's a great rocker. I remember him playing the Prince's Trust Rock Gala and doing that song in a supergroup with Pete Townshend. It's one of the encores and it was really done well. It's a song that starts one way and then stops and then there's a whole new epic tail-end to the song, just like "Pledge Pin." There's the first four minutes and then there's this jam at the end that is all about performance, even though there's not much for Robert to do. But man, you can't have that album without that in it. It's kind of a guitar hero moment but they needed it.

Martin: You also get another title that has nothing to do with the rest of the song. At the music end, I hear a bit of a shifting, shuffling *Presence* vibe, like in "Hots for Nowhere" but also "Royal Orleans."

Tim: Sure, so I guess it's a Zeppelin nod, but less obvious than "Slow Dancer." But it's good—you just want to keep listening, keep it going.

Ralph: Well, "Worse Than Detroit," to me, is probably Phil's most direct homage to Bonham, with where he puts the high-hat lifts and how he uses the bass drum pattern on that. But there's something about that song—and it might be in the arrangement—that doesn't invoke Led Zeppelin to me. Sure, it's a reminder that Plant's foot is still very much in this quasi-heavy sound, for lack of a better term, but it's on his terms.

Martin: Well, I still think it sounds like the mean median average of like five songs on *Presence*.

Ralph: Yeah, you know what? I can't argue with that. "For Your Life" has a funkiness to the break that I can somewhat hear here. Yeah, especially the break on that song. But my thing about "Worse Than Detroit" has always been it's just a great song. It's an extension of the prowess of Robert Plant from the Led Zeppelin Robert Plant to the outside world, this new world in the eighties. The new songs are just as extraordinary, as hooky and as heavy. But it's this weird combination of... what did they used to call Led Zeppelin? It was a magazine title—tight but loose. It was the idea of something being heavy yet supple and subtle. Listen to Phil's bass pedal work and where he puts those lifts. But also while invoking Bonzo the most, it's also the best display of Phil's talents, along with "Burning Down One Side," obviously.

I also want to mention that Plant makes the decision—which I think is really important—not to tour *Pictures at Eleven*. He doesn't have enough material and he doesn't want to go on the road as, like again, a pastiche or trading on Zeppelin, which I think was an incredibly brave move. Like, he's got to do another album before he can go on the road.

But you get a glimpse of what that could have looked like. As Rick mentioned, about a month after the album comes out, he does the Prince's Gala. He's got Phil on drums, and he's got Robbie Blunt on guitar. So, it's three of the main dudes playing this show, and they play "Worse Than Detroit." There's also the house band. So, Pete Townshend is there and Gary Brooker and Midge Ure and Mick Karn and it's an incredible band. But the core of it is Phil, Robbie, and Robert. And you get a sense of how exciting that tour might have been. But in the end, you think how shrewd it was of a plan to say, you know what? I need to do another album. But watching Blunt live, he was an exciting guy to watch. He was cool to watch. He had his own style and magnetism that was just different because he was not Jimmy Page. But it wasn't like maybe what Plant fell into later in the eighties of trying to invoke something. There's no invocation with Blunt. Blunt was his own man. He had his own pedigree and his own style. But he wasn't famous. So again, that goes back to Phil. I think Plant acknowledged that Blunt wasn't a celebrity, but he was more than worthy as a partner, at least in this part of his career.

Martin: "Fat Lip" delivers what is essentially the second ballad of three, but there's a twist.

Rick: Yes, we get a drum loop, signature eighties sampling, which actually you'd hear a lot on Phil Collins records. It's catchy, but another strange title. But as a singer myself, I like the way the vocal comes first: "I can't believe," and then the music kicks in. There's very good vocal phrasing. It's almost like he's creating a call-and-response with the guitar. Interesting delivery. But yes, very eighties. Don't forget, it's not too long after that he puts a break-dancer in the "In the Mood" video. So, we get those eighties contemporary electronic beats. I think the aim was to create a pop song with a fresh pop sound. But it's a beautiful song. Robbie Blunt is his own guy and he's an amazing player. But you hear him in Silverhead and Bronco and it doesn't seem like he would fit. But he seems to be able to plug in and play in any style and situation Robert wants to pursue.

Tim: With Phil not in on the writing credit for this one, maybe you can rule out him having anything to do with the programming. He programmed his own stuff on his solo albums and with Genesis. Then again, this is one of three where Jezz gets a credit, and we know he's a synthesizer whiz. It was the flip side of "Pledge Pin" and if I remember correctly, it got some airplay on its own too.

Ralph: That's a big moment for Plant because he's not even got a real drummer on there. It's programmed, and I'm pretty sure that was Blunt. For a long time, I thought, oh, that's Phil, because one of Phil's adages was, "You'll hire me and I'll do what I think belongs there. And sometimes I don't even belong there." So, for a long time, I thought that was Phil's choice. But then, in talking to Paul Martinez, he seemed to think that it was Robbie Blunt. If it was Robbie, either way it's impressive, because if it was Blunt, that's a very forward-thinking move to sit back and say, "I know it's a Robert Plant song, but we don't actually need drums. This actually creates the atmosphere we need."

So then when you go to *Principle of Moments*, and all of a sudden Robert throws in Simmons drums, this, to me, is the first moment of that, the drum machine on "Fat Lip," which is exciting. Again, if you're a Zeppelin fan and you want thunder, this seems limp. But as you see the arc of Plant's career, it's not limp, it's bold. Some of the boldest musical statements on *Pictures at Eleven* are also some of the most subtle musical statements, be it the Raphael Ravenscroft sax on "Pledge Pin," or what sounds like a Roland 606 machine or something like that on "Fat Lip," or how laid-back Phil is on "Moonlight in Samosa."

Martin: You get to "Like I've Never Been Gone," and it's interesting to hear what Cozy does with a ballad.

Rick: Yes, but as a singer, I'd say that "Like I've Never Been Gone" is the masterpiece here vocal-wise. It's a song where he just shows who he is. When he holds that note so long on "sunshine in your eye," that's a Robert Plant thing to do, like he does in "Kashmir." And instead of going for the stars, he holds that note nice and long and it's ear candy. It's a pretty song. There was a trend in the eighties where every rock band had to have their ballad. But this wasn't a sell-out ballad. It's got that Led Zeppelin power. It's almost a tribute to the dramatic type of vocal that he'd been known for. Definitely one of my favourite tunes by Robert as a singer's showcase.

Tim: Here's another one that could have been a single. And it's also interesting that it's one of the few songs where he actually sings the title line in the song. I guess he does in "Slow Dancer" as well. But yeah, it's interesting that he's put these two grandiose ballads on here, this one and "Moonlight in Samosa." Again, Robbie Blunt on guitar; no one ever talks about him as a great guitar player, but then again, we never saw him again after *Shaken 'n' Stirred*. But he sure was the perfect foil for Robert on at least the first two albums, a connection to their shared past.

Ralph: Yes, Robbie Blunt was a perfect partner for him, who, again, could trade on what made Plant famous, but still make it sound fresh. They had a history together, but what I find really interesting about Robbie is that the closest he gets to trading on Page—and this is perhaps unfair—is the solo on "Like I've Never Been Gone." That really does invoke Jimmy Page in richness and melodicism.

Martin: All right, we've come to the end of the album with another one that invokes *Presence* for me—in the same way as "Worse Than Detroit" did and with the same five songs, all of them except "Achilles Last Stand" and "Tea for One" (laughs).

Rick: Sure, it's a rocking tune with a weird country twang to it, maybe even a bit of progressive hard rock for the end of the album. And it's a crazy way they end the song too, with a flourish. It's a good song but not the strongest song. I think it fitted really well at the end. "Mystery Title"—I guess they didn't know what to call it.

Tim: You hear this one and in retrospect realise there's a bit more Zeppelin on the album than you thought. "Mystery Title." Like, why? Why wouldn't you give it a title? Even as someone who more than most writers likes to use that title space to cram in more lyrics, here he gives up! It almost seems like they got to the very end and he thought, "Oh, I don't know; just call it 'Mystery Title.'"

Ralph: Although I love it, it's kind of a doodle of an idea. It doesn't really go anywhere, that song, in some ways. But it's a perfectly fine closer. You know me; I'm obsessed with sequencing. And I love how this record is sequenced. And I do like his choice of ending it with "Mystery Title," which invokes the idea of making what you want of it as a listener, of where's this gonna go now? And when we get to *Principle of Moments*, you see a huge—I think—substantial leap. He's gotten his feet wet with *Pictures at Eleven*. He's assuaged some of the concerns he had where he was going to reinvent himself to the point of tossing his history. As an album, it's just a really poignant, powerful, but conservative statement about where he was at in that moment—with signs of departure.

Martin: Nice. And what does anybody have to say about "Far Post," our one non-album B-side?

Rick: It's got an interesting, affected vocal approach. I had heard it only because *Rockline* played it during an interview. I taped it to a cassette because I wanted to keep it, although I would get it later on. I like it because it's such a weird, different vocal for him. It didn't fit on the record because of that, honestly, even though the music does. I just think the vocal approach was so different. I like it more now. To me it's one of those gems that I look forward to because I didn't hear it to death. Did it need to be on the album? Like I say, I don't think so. It's a long album, so you'd have to remove something. What would go? "Fat Lip?" I would have a hard time. Maybe that's reason they left it out. I don't know, the vocal sounds like it wasn't done in the same studio.

Tim: Yeah, non-LP, but it's on the remastered version. "Far Post" got a lot of airplay in its own right on the *Billboard* Mainstream Rock Charts and probably a lot of the rock radio stations. I would have put this one in place of "Mystery Title," or in addition. There's only eight songs on the album proper. I don't know why he didn't just make it a nine-song album.

Martin: Well, we're already at a little over forty-two minutes.

Tim: Maybe that's why. I suppose it was pushing the limits of the technology. I know that for a fact, because I own it on eight-track. This was the only Robert Plant solo album to come out as an eight-track for retail. The record label made the conscious decision to put the tracks in the actual order that they appear on the album. But there's one program that has a lot of extra space at the end of it. So, at the end of program four, there's like a minute-and-a-half of space you had to fast-forward through in order for them to get the songs in order. So, in a way, yes, you're still dealing with those space issues. Ironically, they probably could have put "Far Post" at the end of the eight-track and had a bonus track. But that's just a funny observation. Fortunately, with the remasters, the record labels usually do a pretty good job at collecting those extra songs.

Martin: And what happens next?

Tim: Well, that's the interesting part. As Ralph says, he didn't tour this album. He didn't tour until the next album because he wanted to have enough of his own material. He didn't want to go out and play a bunch of Zeppelin songs. He resisted playing Zeppelin.

But fortunately the album doesn't sound dated, so it was fine to wait. For example, it's better produced than the Asia stuff, which I know you've mentioned as an interesting comparative. I don't think that Mike Stone's production aged particularly well. *Pictures at Eleven* in comparison is a little bit more high-fidelity. It's not dated, and yet it's also not seventies-sounding at all. Some seventies artists that continued to make music into the eighties, when they put albums out in 1980, '81, '82, they didn't sound as fresh. If you look at the *Billboard* charts from that time, it takes a couple of years for a decade to realise it's a new decade. That's not the case here. *Pictures at Eleven* sounds very current, up with the times. And even years down the road, it doesn't sound stapled or nailed to that time, which is a really, really hard thing to do. Robert's an artist at this point that definitely wants to participate in the world, and without a hint of nostalgia.

Martin: Nice, I like that. Ralph, any closing thoughts?

Ralph: Well, okay, I just want to reiterate that with Phil Collins, Robert got an incredibly versatile player. With Phil you also get a sound. You get a sound that's at the vanguard of drum production. And obviously building that into *Pictures at Eleven* gives it a distinct sound. But again, that's why I told that initial anecdote about how I thought it was a Phil Collins record when I first heard it as my alarm went off. Because it had that barking tom-tom sound and that feel that he has on the high-hats that is like no other to me. That's a weird combination of jazz and Billy Cobham and Ringo and Bonham, like a melange of influences that sums Phil up.

Martin: And as Tim says, they somehow managed to make a record that doesn't sound linked to any of the worst vagaries of the eighties.

Ralph: Yeah, well, that's the upside of conservatism, right? You can put on a Big Star record that was recorded in 1972 and it sounds like it could have come out in '85 or '96 or now. And yeah, you're right. And that works politically too. People like conservatism because it's familiar, because it trades on the same emotions that humans have had ad infinitum. And you can see why by the time it gets to *Shaken 'n' Stirred*, things are much more difficult, and people complain about that record being dated, which I think is horseshit. But I don't believe in dated records. Unless you want to say, well, Phil Collins' sound is dated, his drum sound is dated. I'd argue, not really. I still hear that sound. I can listen to a Jonathan Wilson record and hear that barking tom sound from an album that came out three or four years ago.

I'll close with this. People, I think struggle with understanding what *Pictures at Eleven* is, or the triumph of *Pictures at Eleven*. From my point of view, the triumph of *Pictures at Eleven* is that he did it. They actually did it. It's not about launching into new frontiers, which is more the purview of some of his other records, like *Shaken 'n' Stirred*, which is, as you know, one of my favourites, one of the more provocative and adventurous records that he did. I don't think *Pictures at Eleven* is adventurous. In many ways, it's quite conservative. And why that is, I think, was that Robert, after all the tragedy he'd been through, needed to be eased back into making music again.

8-Track
CARTRIDGE
Mfd. by RCA Music Service under License
6550 East 30th Street, Indianapolis, Indiana 46219
ROBERT PLANT
THE PRINCIPLE OF MOMENTS
Atlantic Recording Corp.
75 Rockefeller Plaza
New York, N.Y. 10019
S162228
RCA

The Principle of Moments

"*The Principle of Moments* is my favourite, definitely, with 'Big Log.' That's the one (laughs). That's the one that saved the day. Robert was on a kind of spiritual quest, is the best way of describing it. The nucleus of all of that was Robbie and me and Robert, and it was a very special time. We were very close, and we were having the most fabulous fun. And when we went out on the *Principle of Moments* tour, it was like going on a pilgrimage. We had that lovely little private plane, that old Vicand, and we just rolled around America in that going 'Mmm, this is nice' (laughs). On one of those Canadian gigs, John Paul Jones came up and played. I've played on stage with him a couple of times, Bristol in England and there."

"And so yeah, *Principle of Moments*, Robert gave me a copy of Roxy Music's *Avalon* and said, 'I want to do an album like this.' And you'll notice a lot of the keyboard textures and jangly guitars and stuff had the certain vibe of that album. I spent hours analyzing that, so I could get out of it what I wanted. As for Phil Collins, he was just called in at the last minute, down to Rockfield Studios. He was only around for a week for *Pictures at Eleven,* and about two weeks for *Principle of*

Moments. So he really didn't have any musical input, but he did play the marimbas on 'Big Log.' That album is Robbie's finest hour, and he'll tell you that as well. He still thinks it was. And that's sad, really, because my finest hour is *Shaken 'n' Stirred*. But I love *The Principle of Moments* too, especially 'Messin' with the Mekon,' which was a great live track. And 'Thru' with the Two Step,' that's my swan song, isn't it? Because those keyboards are all over that from the beginning."
Jezz Woodroffe

Credits

July 15, 1983
Atlantic 7 90101
Produced by Robert Plant, Benji Lefevre and Pat Moran
Engineered by Pat Moran
Recorded at Rockfield Studios, Monmouth, UK
Personnel: Robert Plant – vocals, Robbie Blunt – guitars, Jezz
Woodroffe – keyboards, synthesizers, Paul Martinez – bass, Phil
Collins – drums on all tracks except "Wreckless Love" and "Stranger
Here… Than Over There" which feature Barriemore Barlow.

Side 1
1. "Other Arms" (Plant, Blunt) 4:20
2. "In the Mood" (Plant, Blunt, Martinez) 5:19
3. "Messin' with the Mekon" (Plant, Blunt, Martinez) 4:40
4. "Wreckless Love" (Plant, Blunt) 5:18

Side 2
1. "Thru' with the Two Step" (Plant, Blunt, Martinez) 5:33
2. "Horizontal Departure" (Plant, Blunt, Martinez, Woodroffe) 4:19
3. "Stranger Here… Than Over There" (Plant, Blunt, Martinez, Woodroffe) 4:18
4. "Big Log" (Plant, Blunt, Woodroffe) 5:03

robert plant
in the mood
robert plant
Big Log (Edit) 3:44
Aus dem Album "The Principle Of Moments"
robert plant big Log
robert plant
big Log

A *The Principle of Moments* Timeline

July 15, 1983. Robert Plant issues *The Principle of Moments*, his second solo album. The first single is "Big Log" backed with "Messin' with the Mekon" in the UK and "Far Post" in the US. "Big Log" reaches No.20 on the main *Billboard* chart, the Hot 100. It also reaches No.11 in the UK and No.6 on the *Billboard* Top Tracks chart. The album itself reaches No.8 on the main *Billboard* chart, along with No.7 in the UK. Besides reaching platinum status in the US, the album also goes gold in Canada, Australia and the UK.

August 1983. Robert and Maureen divorce, after fifteen years of marriage and three children.

August 13, 1983. Despite not being issued as a single, "Other Arms" manages to become Robert's first No.1 on the *Billboard* Top Tracks chart. Robert asked that the song not be issued as a single, worried about being pigeonholed as a hard rock act, but Atlantic promoted the song anyway, asserting its potential.

August 26 – October 1, 1983. Robert conducts his first solo tour, a North American campaign, beginning in Peoria, Illinois and ending in Vancouver, British Columbia, with the author attending that show.

October 1983. Swan Song Records ceases operation. Its last four albums, in order, are *Pictures at Eleven*, followed by Bad Company's *Rough Diamonds*, Led Zeppelin's *Coda* and the self-titled from Wildlife.

October 17, 1983. *The Principle of Moments* is certified gold in the US.

November 19, 1983. "In the Mood" is issued as the second single from *The Principle of Moments*, with the main B-side being "Horizontal Departure."

November 22 – December 24, 1983. Robert and his band play the UK, in support of *The Principle of Moments*.

January 1984. "In the Mood" reaches its chart peak in the US, hitting No.39 on the *Billboard* Hot 100. It also reaches No.4 on Top tracks but stalls at No.81 in the UK.

January 12, 1984. *The Principle of Moments* is certified platinum in the US.

January 22 – February 29, 1984. Robert and the band play Australia, New Zealand, Japan and Hong Kong.

May 1984. "Other Arms" is issued as a single in Japan.

September 24, 1984. Robert, Jimmy Page and a bunch of buddies, under band name The Honeydrippers, issue a five-track covers EP called *Volume One*. It certifies platinum in the US and triple-platinum in Canada, on the strength of two singles, "Sea of Love" and "Rockin' at Midnight."

December 15, 1984. Robert Plant appears on *Saturday Night Live*, performing "Rockin' at Midnight" and "Santa Claus Is Back in Town."

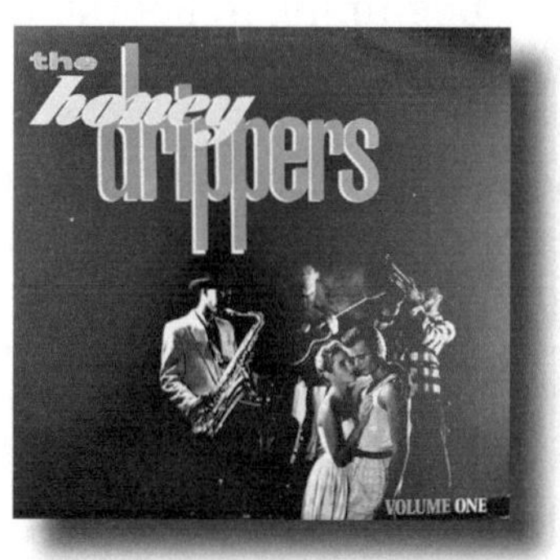

Martin talks to Tim Durling, Chad Green and Douglas Maher about *The Principle of Moments.*

Martin Popoff: All right, so to begin with, how has Robert advanced his cause with the second album? We know he doesn't tour the first one and also Phil Collins is back.

Chad Green: Yes, and he makes one of his best albums, in my opinion. It's not my favourite, but my favourite albums are not always necessarily the artist's best work. He's had a chance to settle into this solo role. Led Zeppelin's well behind him at this point but it's still there in his mind, fresh somewhat. But he's found himself a little bit here. The quality is good, the musicianship is amazing and lyrically, again, I don't know if he's referring to his relationship with his spouse who he's ending it with and has probably been in the process of ending it with her for a while, or if he's talking about girlfriends that he's had or has. But the theme is relationships, although you'd never gather that from the inscrutable titles.

Martin: And Doug, I always appreciate your industry perspectives. Where does this album sit in the environment of the times?

Douglas Maher: I always kind of label this album as a *Plantacab*, if you will. Part *Abacab*, part Robert Plant, right? I'd say *The Principle of Moments* is Plant's most deep dive progressively, as far as prog, if you will, obviously with Phil Collins having some influence into that musically, even though he's brought in basically to drum. I have these kind of warring armies of thought, if you will, with regards to this record. Thinking about this as I approach 50, when people look at Robert Plant and his catalogue of the eighties, they tend to always think of how Robert Plant was in the sixties and seventies. So I try to be objective in that and say, okay, well, it's kind of like how Rush was looked at in the eighties, versus those who grew up with them in the seventies.

And the thing I appreciate about what Robert Plant does on *Principle of Moments* is that he's taking a leap into the eighties. But at the same time, he's putting kind of a new signature stamp on it, that we're not going to get the bluesy Robert Plant, although it does pop up in spurts. We're gonna get a more modernised, early eighties sound. You do have that prog feel, but I also think that this is very much Robert Plant meets The Police as well. I sense a lot of that and always have. And that was an attraction for me. I was young, but I got into rock because my brother was four years older than me. So everybody that I was around was much older because of his friends. And that was the kind of neighbourhood I grew up in—everybody hung out with everybody. So I got introduced to Rush through *Permanent Waves*, and I was only six years old.

And where I was living in Florida, MTV had come in pretty much about six months after its launch. There are people around the country and the world that can't relate to those things. Because MTV didn't come into their market. When "In the Mood" and "Big Log" were played pretty much every ninety minutes or every two hours, that was a big thing. You weren't seeing Led Zeppelin videos on MTV; there was no cutaway of clips or anything like that. So Plant had the media ability at that point to be introduced to a younger generation. And I looked at Robert Plant as just being Robert Plant, the solo guy. I wasn't looking at him as some guy from Led Zeppelin. I barely knew the Zeppelin stuff, because I was still young. Another interesting thing. There was no tour for the first record and the tour for this record was a month essentially, September '83. You had a couple or few days left in August that he did one or two shows, and he did one show in October. So the singles became more important than usual, which we'll get to.

Martin: Yes, thanks, let's do that. Tim, opening thoughts?

Tim Durling: Well, I'd say that *Principle of Moments* is a more fully realised version of *Pictures at Eleven*. Everything just works better here. It's quite possibly his finest statement as a solo artist, and actually one of the best albums he's ever been involved with. It's basically the same players as the first album. The only difference is instead of two tracks having Cozy Powell on them, you've got Barriemore Barlow from Jethro Tull. But again, Phil Collins is back on drums and he's even pictured, just like one of the guys. It's important to note too that his solo career was just getting underway. Somehow he found a way to do this album and even tour it, despite a second solo album in '82 and a big Genesis album coming out basically as he's on tour with Robert.

Martin: What kind of statement does the album cover art make?

Tim: First thing I notice, they brought forward that same very distinctive font that they used on the first cover. And like the first one, this cover doesn't make any sense. There's this absence; it looks like something's been very crudely erased out of the picture. But again, it's Robert leaning against a wall and not looking at the camera. I suppose it puts across the idea of a moment, with this quick flash vibe.

Martin: Plus you get those pastel colours. I remember getting a T-shirt at the show in Vancouver and it was light grey with those colours.

Tim: And I think that's by design, too. He didn't want it to look like your typical rock concert shirt. "Yeah, man, I went see Robert Plant last night—check out this black T-shirt with a skull on it." That could be a Human League or Simple Minds shirt. or something like that. The message is that he wanted to completely distance himself from the hard rock aesthetic.

Martin: And you know what else that looks like? The *Abacab* album cover, right? White, with the graphics squared in the middle, abstract.

Tim: Totally, yeah it does (laughs). With those sort of characters that aren't letters, per sé. Yeah. That would have been cool if he'd done the different coloured cover variants like they did with *Abacab*, or what they did with *In Through the Out Door*, for that matter.

Martin: Okay, as we drop the needle, so to speak, we're hit with "Other Arms." Kind of thumping, thorny, wiry. It's always evoked reggae for me, although it's not following many reggae rules.

Chad: Yes, which possibly emerges from the drumming. I'm interested in this dynamic between Robert Plant and his band, and Phil Collins, because I have a suspicion that it didn't really entirely fit, him and Phil. Robert does talk about it in one of his podcasts. He talks about Phil Collins being pretty forceful and take-charge, but he says it in a very nice way. And of course Phil Collins went on tour with him after this album, so things must have been pretty good, although making the albums, perhaps there was some tension. Great guitar hooks on this one, bright production and the drums take centre stage.

It's a plea to lay down your arms. That opening salvo tells you everything about the song, really. He's saying I want this conflict to end. He's talking about a woman. And I think by the end of the song, after looking at the lyrics, and even in the sound and tone of the song, he's liberated by her departure. She clearly didn't share his perspective and she took off. She clearly didn't share his perspective that she was the problem. She probably decided that he was the problem and she left on her own accord, I'd say. So, they both move on and the song ends kind of triumphant and jubilant, like a celebration. Therefore, it's a good breakup song, I guess (laughs). So yeah, the common theme of seeking harmony, or perhaps it's better stated as conflict avoidance, as the song is narrated from the protagonist's perspective. The conflict ends when Robert is liberated by her departure and their release of each other, basically.

Douglas: From a business perspective, "Other Arms" was the battle song, if you will, with Ahmet Ertegun at Atlantic Records, the whole thing where they wanted this Led Zeppelin frontman, the rock god, if you will. They wanted him back front and centre, commercially speaking. And that is the song that represents that. And it's funny; that song is still on classic rock radio today in a lot of markets, and there was no video. But what really makes it interesting is that's the song that the label wanted him to start off with, and Plant was saying, "I don't want to be defined as that anymore. It's a great piece of music, but I want to approach the market my way"—which was "Big Log," which was "In the Mood."

And interestingly enough, in its popularity later in 1983, it took out "Every Breath You Take" at the No.1 spot, okay? At least on the Mainstream Rock chart. That is a remarkable achievement, when you consider not only the popularity of that song, but just the state of music in general. At that point in 1983, it was video that made your song successful. Video broke your song, made you popular. So those album-oriented rock charts, third, fourth, fifth deeper tracks and what have you, radio markets would hold onto those songs, even if they weren't doing well, but were requested well. But that was something of a marvel, for it to chart as high as it did, going No.1, and being his first No.1 of any sort as a solo artist.

Martin: So, I guess Plant got his way then, because "Big Log" is the first single, with "In the Mood" following after the tour ends, right?

Douglas: Correct, yeah. Plant said, I'm calling the shots here. He was extremely interested in video-making, in storytelling and presentation, okay? And you saw a little bit of that in *The Song Remains the Same*, with this kind of mystical storytelling approach. Plant was really fascinated with this. And being able to apply this on a 24-hour music channel and other video shows that started popping up—*Friday Night Videos* and things like that—he was able to establish himself and be able to stand along the other rock artists at the time who might have been newer, not having been out over a decade already. It's very important that Plant did that. He developed a relationship with MTV. But early on you had Atlantic radio reps that were out there behind his back that were pushing "Other Arms" without Robert's knowledge. The instinct of Ahmet, when he heard "Other Arms," was, that's the hit. And that wound up becoming a much bigger song after the fact. So, you had these A&R reps that were going around and pushing that song underneath the sheets, if you will.

Tim: "Other Arms," fantastic opener. Right away you hear a really tasteful drum fill. It sounds like it's tailor-made for rock radio in the eighties. But it's not hard rock. Robbie Blunt presents a very clean guitar sound but it comes off tough because the drums have so much weight behind them. This might not make sense, but to me it sounds like a top-shelf Eric Clapton track. It's British but it's in some middle zone where it's neither hard rock nor pop; it's just rock. But it's the type of thing that could do quite well at rock radio.

And the word "arms" appears in the lyrics a lot, but he never says, "other arms." As for "Lay down your arms," it could mean your arms, like physical arms, or it could mean weapons or trying to resolve an argument. I don't know how much of this is personal, but I do know that he and his wife Maureen finally divorced in 1983, right after this album came out.

And you and I have talked about this before, the fact that years later, Sammy Hagar would do a song on his *Ten 13* album, "Protection," that literally starts off with him singing "Lay down your arms" and even similar music and vocal phrasing and melody. You told me the story about bringing that up with Sammy and Sammy being surprised and saying he'd gladly send Robert some royalties (laughs). Robbie Blunt, again, I love that little descending part that he does at the 1:56 mark. And the drums are just perfect there too. That song is just a great way to start the album. You're just like, all right. Just like "Burning Down One Side," except the vocals are nice and clear on here. You can hear what he's saying.

Douglas: "Other Arms," as far as my visceral reaction, with the presence of Phil Collins in there, it could have been on *Coda*. These riffs that are on this record—and this goes on really throughout Plant's catalogue, I would say up to *Fate of Nations*—you arrive at the opinion that Robert was intentionally selecting guitarists who weren't Jimmy Page, but could play like Jimmy Page. It's a standout track any way that you look at it. It's just got that driving, hard, punchy riff, but somehow you're instantly taken aback. You're hearing an artist outside of their main band and you're a bit disoriented.

Martin: Next is "In the Mood," and look, for all those years *The Principle of Moments* was my favourite album of all time by anybody, I also thought "In the Mood" was the greatest song ever constructed by anybody, although that's silly, or at least sillier than ranking full albums. But I still think so!

Tim: Funny, yeah, well, of course it's brilliant—and completely objectively, right? Beautiful, beautiful pop song, with fresh, different drums from Phil. Everything is just in its proper place, with the fills not coming in where you expect them, but you are so glad they are there. Beautiful high-hat work too, gorgeous melody and hooks, and I love the keyboards, which don't sound dated despite being so prominent. It's actually quite complicated, but effortlessly so, where a musical novice can tune out any of the progressiveness. Like, I say, where Phil throws in those tom-tom fills, it's never overdone— everything is in its place. It should have gone even higher on the charts because it's got such a strong, refreshing pop melody. The video got a lot of play too. It's a simple song lyrically, almost as if a super-literary lyric would be too much to handle, given how perfect and polished the music is. I can see how it got a lot of radio play. It's a metaphor for taking all of the elements of *Pictures at Eleven*, and improving on them, making more successful songs.

Martin: It's a masterpiece. It's one of those like "Ballroom Blitz" or "Walk This Way" or "Bohemian Rhapsody"—yes, even Pantera and "Cowboys from Hell"—where I like to imagine the song being played in the boardroom down at the label and just jaws hanging down to the floor.

Tim: Oh, yeah, absolutely (laughs). Atlantic Records would be going, "I smell money." Yeah, like "My Sharona" too, right? How can radio resist this? When I saw Robert in 2019, this was the only song from the eighties that he did. It was a little bit different, but people were singing along because he kept the melody the same. People love this song.

Martin: Yeah, with this album in general, I feel like the only artist who is at this hallowed place creatively at the time is Peter Gabriel.

Tim: Yeah, but I find it's a bit more accessible. Peter Gabriel had a certain amount of weirdness about it that you either got or you didn't. I feel like you could play *The Principle of Moments* to a random group of people and they'd go, "Hey, what's that? That's pretty good."

Martin: Paul Martinez gets his first of what are fully five song credits on the album. What do you know about him?

Tim: He's a session guy, but when I hear his name, I mostly associate him with Robert. But he's got quite a discography. He even played on one of the Tom Cochrane and Red Rider albums. He played on the Honeydrippers EP and Paice Ashton Lord's *Malice in Wonderland.* He played on a Bernard Purdie album, Cat Stevens, Renaissance. Yeah, he's a British studio musician and songwriter. And actually, he was also the bassist when Led Zeppelin had their ill-fated reunion set at Live Aid.

Martin: It's almost like half these guys Robert gets in his band are like secret agents. They're these super musicologist guys that nobody knows about.

Tim: Yeah, it's not like he's got the Toto guys coming in that have been on a million albums. I never understand why more people aren't saying, "Hey, I want the guy that played on that Robert Plant album. I want him to play guitar on my album." It just never seemed to happen. Nobody went on after Robert to become a household name.

Martin: And Robert definitely had no problem calling for fresh blood in his bands.

Douglas: No, in '85 after Live Aid, at the end of his tour in '85, he fired everybody and wanted to start new. This is the fascinating thing about Plant that I was unaware of until maybe ten years ago. I didn't know he shopped songs. I didn't know that he used you know, Diane Warren-esque writers that he sought out for melodies, and for catchy songs and things like that. But he worked with publishing houses, which was shocking to me. This is later, not on this record. He would poach artists who he would hear on publishing house recordings. He would go, "I like the way that sounds. I love this guy's approach." He'd bring a guitar player or a keyboardist in and he wouldn't say, "Play these Zeppelin songs." He would just say, "Play me a few songs." He would say, "I want to hear what you're doing now. Give me an idea of where you've been and where you're going."

And when I heard that, I thought, well, that's safe. You know, can this guy hang musically? Or is he going to be stock? Is he going to be a basic guy that's going to come in and say, "I could play the chords; I could throw out some solos here and there." Plant was looking for people who understood the history of music in general, dating back to the fifties, even the forties. And doing that, it was a security blanket for him, that he was going to be able to create music that was satisfying to what his soul was requiring. I know it just sounds like a bunch of entertainment bullshit and it probably is, but okay, I found it very shocking. That he was poaching artists that way and that he was poaching songs in general. I know when Johnstone came in, that was a publishing house guy. And Robert Plant had said, "I'm hearing this and I need to meet this guy and see where this goes."

Chad: I agree with Tim that there's nothing overly deep about the "In the Mood" lyrics. He's basically stating that he's an entertainer. He's in the mood for a melody, although I think that comes with a bunch of things. He's in the mood to give of himself, to serve people, to serve his talents up to people and to entertain. Thematically, it reminds me of that old Scott Joplin ragtime thing, "The Entertainer." Phil's prog rock-styled drumming in this song is well-suited. It's got bright, clear, production and all the instrumentalists are well-heard. It all kind of comes together and it's catchy, enthusiastic. But Robert's relying on generating a mood rather than serving up really deep lyrics. He achieves what he wants here.

Douglas: Okay, so "In the Mood," No.4 AOR track, No.39 on the Hot 100. I think this is Robert Plant's best song that he's ever written as a solo artist. It's got this dreamy, floating sound that's analogous to the imagery of the video. Robert's kind of in and out of focus. You're in open fields and you get the leaves and the trees and everything. He's in this like small house somewhere, where this video is taking place. It captures it perfectly. Because "I'm in the mood for a melody/I'm in the mood for a melody/I'm in the mood."

I want to say however, I'm generally not impressed by Robert as a lyricist. To me he writes a lot of scratch lyrics, with a lot of oohs and aahs, and he touches way too often on similar themes. But on "In the Mood"—and I attribute this more to the musicians who wrote the actual music on the song—he takes you to this dreamscape. There are these floating melodies that drift in and out across this sound wave pulse. But you're taken on a journey, and then also in the video, which is very hard to do. Phil's drumming is legendary too. You could call this song and much of the album progressive, but usually when you say that you talk about whether it's too progressive or not enough. But here they just catch it before it goes too far. A lot of these progressive-leaning bands attempt to write these hits.

Anyway, back to the lyrics, Robert Plant has a tremendous ability to sing, harmonise and create melodies. He's blessed with that gift no matter what song he's playing. So, in that light, it doesn't matter what the song is saying lyrically, with his catalogue. Not really. And I'd say there's no message that Robert Plant is ever trying to push forward, at least until much later in the nineties and 2000s. He's absolutely created much more substance, lyrically, later on.

Martin: You know, I get to "Messin' with the Mekon," and I'm really feeling that concept Tim just articulated, that these are just better songs that could have been on *Pictures at Eleven*.

Chad: I love this song. It's a breakup song and basically, it's saying, "Stop bugging me." He's over some previous relationship arrangement that just ended and despite repeated themes, she wants him back. There's some repeated requests and he's just not interested in resurrecting that relationship. Maybe it was dysfunctional, where they were both getting some of their needs met. I think that's what happened. Maybe he was in a dysfunctional relationship where they were getting their needs met, but it just wasn't sustainable. It's gotten to the point where it's not worth it anymore, that overlooking certain things is not working for him anymore. I think that's what he's thinking about. And as we know, this album was happening in the heat of his divorce. But I think he also transforms anguish into affirmation here and makes a good justification for moving on. At the music end, like "In the Mood," there's a strong melodic backbone but there's also complexity.

Douglas: A couple things about "Messin' with the Mekon," one, it reminds me of "Darlene" from *Coda* and two, the drumming is Phil Collins meets Peart meets Stewart Copeland—in a word, proggy. I find it to be more Yes-sounding than Genesis which is surprising considering who you have in the room. To me, this song represents a situation where the label is working in concert with Plant and trying to see, okay, you're still in the infancy of a solo career here. What is going on? Zeppelin had some out-there moments, but this one is particularly progressive for Robert, among the solo songs.

Tim: "Messin' with the Mekon;" again, he's using the title as extra space for lyrics that he couldn't fit in the song (laughs). Musically, with the really trebly guitar and some of the synth sounds, it reminds me very much of what Rush would end up doing eventually on *Power Windows* or *Hold Your Fire*. I've got to think those guys were continuing to pay attention to what Robert Plant was doing. They looked up to him. But yeah, not sure what he's singing about, but it's catchy and I find myself bobbing my head. But it's still tricky stuff, musician's music, including a hint of reggae. As a matter of fact, on the reissue of this album, there's a live version of them doing Bob Markey's "Lively Up Yourself." So it makes sense that a little bit of that would seep into the music.

Martin: Closing side one of the original vinyl is "Wreckless Love," which is the closest this album ever gets to Led Zeppelin, and even then, it's not as connected to the past as "Slow Dancer" or "Like I've Never Been Gone." There's really nothing conventionally arranged on *The Principle of Moments*.

Douglas: No, although weirdly, "Wreckless Love" reminds me of "Gallows Pole." Mostly though, you're hearing the Middle Eastern music that will define Plant's future albums essentially in the nineties and 2000s. Also, here's the first of two with Barriemore Barlow from Jethro Tull on drums, and what we get is a halting, geometric pattern, acoustic but with electronic toms and some other drum machine-like touches. It definitely doesn't sound like what

Phil might do. And again, lyrically, I don't find there's a whole lot of substance to work with here.

Chad: The bass line really stood out to me here, plus cool synth, guitar and drums—very enjoyable. He's infatuated with something good and yet bad here. Could this be a mistress? That's the reckless love, although he sticks a "w" in there, when wreckless is not really a word.

Tim: It sounds like he's having fun with this one, the way he sings it. And as Chad says, he's spelling reckless with a "w," although I'm not sure why. I like the mix of acoustic and electric drums; it's rare to have that sound this palatable, especially in 1983. It's a long song, contributing to us only getting eight songs on the album, just like last time.

Martin: Over to side two, I could imagine "Thru' with the Two Step" on *In Through the Out Door*. It's in the ballad zone, which is visited twice on *Pictures at Eleven* and twice here. As well, Robert's fairly Zeppelin-like with his vocal stylings.

Chad: When I first heard this album, this was my favourite song on the album, and I think it might still be. It's got the sense of a waltz, although it's not in three-four time. I think the music and the lyrics support each other and that's intentional. He's through with this relationship again. He's breaking out—it's a breakup song. He's through with this relationship where he's sneaking around and cutting it close. He may be referring to some kind of tryst. There's the sense of an arrangement that's just no longer working out and so he's delivering that message. Like I say, it has this waltzing pace and even says, "You waltzed into my life" and of course it references dancing in the title. I can picture two people dancing to the song even though it's not a very nice song to dance to because it's about ditching somebody. So yeah, it's not exactly a waltz but it's got that steady, rhythmic, swinging dance quality. I like the way it's composed. When Robert does the slower material like this, I think it's when he's doing his best work. Maybe I'm getting more mellow with age.

Douglas: On "Thru' with the Two Step," at the 2:05 mark, I know it's just a brief fill, but Phil Collins gives us the future opening of "I Wish It Would Rain Down." I'm always a sucker for hearing artists who way back when were doing something and then you're like, I've heard this before. I think Phil Collins really owns this song, and really, Martin, if we're being honest here, I think Phil Collins owns this record. The drums define this record. And then I would probably say the keys and then Plant's vocals. Yeah, it's just a dominant on this record. The song has an "I'm Gonna Crawl" vibe to it, in the drunken drowsy keyboards right off *In Through the Out Door*. As you said, I too could imagine this song on that album. If you close your eyes, you can almost picture this on one of the early Peter Gabriel albums. I totally forgot just how open-minded Plant was during this time. I can also picture this on a 1980s John Hughes film soundtrack. It just has that feel to me.

Tim: I don't know if this is him saying goodbye to the seventies, because to have a ballad open side two, that's a bit of a statement. I'm not sure of these keyboard sounds but there are some beautiful melodies, nonetheless. It's a headphone song, beautifully produced. The vocals are very upfront. But it does sound like he's saying goodbye to something in his life.

Martin: With "Horizontal Departure," I'm struck again just how similar a good chunk of this album is to the debut.

Tim: I get huge Police vibes from this. Phil Collins is doing that frantic thing he does, playing quick snare fills. Again, the beat is never where you think it's going to be until it gets to the chorus and the chorus is that "Whoa, whoa" thing, so Police-sounding. But most musicians in the eighties at this point, you could not escape The Police. They had a huge influence on Rush. They were on the radio everywhere with that reggae/ska thing mixed in with the guitar chords in the chorus. I don't think Robert Plant would ever be so cynical as to say, "Let's write a song that sounds like The Police." But he'd say, "It sounds like something that would be fun to play." That's what I get out of the song. And again, here comes another title that doesn't have anything to do with the lyrics.

Chad: "Whoa, that's why you have to leave me all alone." That's all I can hear in my head now, from yet another relationship song. He's like, you found another fool in me and I'm all done with this. Like he's ending it. He's kind of frustrated and heated up in this song and I guess in all of them. For some reason, I'm really feeling Robert's heartfelt personal feelings in this one. It's like a sincere sampling of his thoughts about himself. He's opening up; you can feel it.

Douglas: How is Phil Collins not paying Stewart Copeland royalties on this track? The vocals are phenomenal here. It's got a great vocal or echo delay on it with a Billy Squier "In the Dark" kind of feel to it. That was commonly used around that time. There's a very Mark Knopfler-esque type solo, pretty much to a tee. But the rest of it is more like Andy Summers. Rush's Alex Lifeson was also drawing from Summers and The Police at that time, all the way through *Grace Under Pressure* and into *Power Windows*. So, these prog guys loved The Police.

Martin: Speaking of prog, our next track is part that, some neo-prog, and part pointing the way toward the stilted rhythms of *Shaken 'n' Stirred*.

Chad: "Stranger Here… Than Over There;" I love that title. It's stranger here than it is over there. It's like everything's weird but if you want weird, come over here—this is the weirdest. And this is happening within the context of relationships again.

Douglas: This song could have been taken from any early eighties, cheesy horror movie soundtrack. I'm trying to be kind with it, but it sounds almost like Tony Banks walked in the room for ten minutes. Remember everything that was going on in the '83 *Genesis* album with "Mama" and "Home by the Sea," all the weird songs? I don't want to call them dated sounds, because they were just sounds at the time, but it's a forgettable song, an absolute waste of time. It sounds like an unfinished demo. The lyrics, again, just seem to be a bunch of scribbled crap about lost love, finding love, chasing love. Jesus, it just goes on and on.

Martin: All right, the album closes with "Big Log," a huge hit for Robert and the guys. It's a beautiful song, but not the master class in songwriting that "In the Mood" is. I guess this one falls between the other ballads so far and "Fat Lip."

Tim: Yes, like "In the Mood," immaculately written but more of a pop song. It's effortlessly enjoyable by anyone who has ears. I just don't see how you can listen to this song and not go wow, that was really good.

But it's got the drum machine; it's just that beat all the way through. Probably programmed by Phil. I always found it interesting that even as a drummer, he had no problem using drum machines, like, "I don't need to play the drums. I just I like the way this sounds." This'll get to No.20 on the main *Billboard* chart. It was his highest charting song as a solo artist. Gorgeous guitar from Robbie Blunt, like Mark Knopfler and that really clean Stratocaster sound. Just a gorgeous ballad.

In that "Should I rest for a while at the side" part, there are these keyboard swells that just come in at the right place. And man, Robert Plant is the only guy I know that can take a lyric like "My love is in league with the freeway" and make it commercial-sounding. Because that's kind of the hook of the song, along with the "Leading me on" part and the gorgeous background vocals there. It's a well-deserved hit single and it must have lent him an increased feel of competency. He's had two Top 40 singles. It probably felt like he was on his way now.

I wonder if there was ever a time when they tried "Big Log" with live drums and just said, you know what? I think I like it with the machine. Maybe they wrote it on the drum machine as a demo and said I like it better with the drum machine. Because it's like "In the Air Tonight." It's unrelenting because an actual drummer could not sit there and keep that beat. They'd go crazy.

Douglas: I always loved the story of the title, "Big Log." I remember learning this as a kid. It's as simple as when they were recording this in the winter, and it was cold and snowy and freezing. And they had fireplaces in the studio, and they used the biggest tree that was there to keep them warm. But these trick titles, he does that on every record, especially in the eighties and nineties. By the way this one was written at Roy Harper's house, from "Hats Off to (Roy) Harper," the Zeppelin tune. He later ended up writing "I Believe" there as well. But yeah, great guitar solo and great overall mood.

The video was constantly on. It was shot in Vegas and California. Car breaks down and Plant, again, goes on about being on a journey and you start getting into his search for love, lost love being the journey. There's being on this journey and also arriving at the destination, but also taking those moments in when his car breaks down. All of that imagery is there to make you think about the moment that you're in, while you make this journey. That's why that car breaking down is in that video, why that metaphor is there. Beautiful song and one of his biggest hits ever, in the solo career.

Chad: I see "Big Log" as a song about the going part of the coming and going, which he in fact alludes to in his podcast. I love the video. He breaks down on this desolate stretch, at a gas station with no one around to help and he starts to reflect on the journey. And then it gets a little more esoteric. But he's definitely departing some previous relationship. I think his journey is the departure of some relationship, or someplace in life that he's moving on from. And it's not without some trouble along the way. But he overcomes the trouble; the tow truck comes and gets him. And then the funniest thing, along comes this beautiful woman breaking down at the same gas station just right behind him after he leaves. So maybe that's the love of his life that he just missed. It was so close, but didn't happen. I don't know if that's the metaphor they're trying to convey but that's what I took from it. I think it's probably because I'm in my late forties and I'm dating after getting divorced. It's just a series of close calls. I don't know. But I really enjoyed the video.

I wonder how intentional all of this is when he's writing. I think, Robert, if anybody, would write with intention. There's definitely recurring themes, and almost by definition, recurring themes underscores intention. And then the music fits. Even though he's not playing the guitar, he's not playing the keyboard parts, he's not doing any of the instruments, it all pulls together into an aesthetic you associate with Robert. And even the video's telling a story. I think he's very involved. I don't think he's just letting some corporate record label types and video directors make all the decisions for him and his work. He's got influence and pull because he's Robert Plant. He was in Led Zeppelin. He's bought himself some freedom, right?

Anyway, such a good album. And maybe it's so good because of his divorce plight during the making. Maybe it's similar to *Rumours* by Fleetwood Mac, where they were going through all these real relationship problems, and that inspired them to produce some really great music. There's some really hard-won truths and that got poured into the lyrics.

Martin: Actually, Chad, I made the *Shaken 'n' Stirred* chapter a solo thing, because Ralph turns in an epic lecture there (laughs). But to go off topic for a minute, what did you think of that record as a follow-up to *The Principle of Moments*?

Chad: It didn't resonate with me. It's poppy, quirky, and definitely has the stamp of 1985 on it, I'd say. In the podcast, Robert, who can be self-deprecating, which I appreciate, he quipped that he made a rash entrance into the eighties. And I get the sense he means this album and not the first two when he says that. I know that when he talked about "Too Loud," he says there was a Talking Heads influence. Anyway, the production is really good and bright; everybody's instrument, including Robert's voice, shines through.

But I think that first song there, "Hip to Hoo" serves as a metaphor for the album. It's frenetic, erratic, quite synthesizer-dominated, complex and busy in its own way, and again Robert is focused on his romantic relationships. He's basically telling a girl that he can't handle any more drama, that this isn't working for him. It's a good song but it's different; I can see why it's lost on a lot of his normal fans.

And then "Kallalou Kallalou" reminds me of *Miami Vice*, with the synthesizer in it and also the bass line. And that's right in that timeframe. Of course, "Little by Little" made it onto the *Miami Vice* soundtrack. Maybe everything sounded like *Miami Vice* in 1985. Lyrically he's like, "Please don't go, please don't go, don't go breaking my heart." Again, that relationship theme runs through this whole album. This is now two years after his divorce.

Martin: What do you make of how Robbie Blunt's role changed from *The Principle of Moments* to *Shaken 'n' Stirred*?

Chad: Well, he's barely noticeable on the first couple songs (laughs). It reminds me of the narrative in Rush at the time, with Alex Lifeson feeling like he was edged out by Geddy Lee and his synthesizers in the eighties. Robert's still the great collaborator, but I suppose here it's more so with Jezz Woodroffe. What's really profound about that man is his ability to inspire. When you listen to his podcast and how he describes himself, he's a bit of a mediator, an orchestrator. Like I say, he's not playing the guitar or the bass or banging on the drums. How does he get these songs done? These musicians are autonomous beings and they come up with their own creative ideas, but he does talk about being very involved. I'd love to see him in action. I'd like to see if he's nice about it. I think he probably is super-nice about it. I don't think he's a tyrant.

But yeah, I think the Police influence continues from *Principle of Moments* onto that album. On "Trouble Your Money" you've got the rim shots on the snare drum and the prominent bass line and even the rainy, jazzy guitar—I could picture all three of those guys making that music. I'm a huge Police fan and I just love that sound. If it's a direct influence, it's done tastefully.

I really like "Sixes and Sevens," really melodic, more typical of Robert's solo style on *The Principle of Moments*. He's just pacing himself, singing along moderately, heartfelt, to this steady but pretty slow rhythm. Great way to end off the album. Lyrically he's taking time there to pause and reflect on his actions and conduct, not just his actions, but the actions and consequences of actions within relationships. Because in relationships you get that. You get responses, right? Somebody does something and then there's a response and that goes back and forth. It either holds together or it falls apart. I think that's what he's referring to in that one. He's pausing and thinking about what he's experienced. When he says, "Am I at home?," I think he's wondering and questioning, am I happy where I'm at right now and where I've been? And what am I going to do next?

I won't go through all of them, but yeah, the big song there, "Little by Little," gives us more of The Police, but only for the introduction. It persists but it becomes more subtle. The keyboard really shifts the song along. Lyrically, there are themes of coming and going and lost and found, kind of like "Big Log." It's definitely got that poppy sound of the day, but it stands out as a distinct Robert Plant song. But I can see why it was the only successful single from the album, and probably the main reason the album went gold. Still, if you're coming from the Led Zeppelin era, yeah, you might not like *Shaken 'n' Stirred* very much. Yeah, "Doo Doo a Do Do" definitely, with that "boing" bass sound, it sounds almost a bit silly. I can see that one not resonating very well with the old fans. It's one of those that contributes to the album being misunderstood more than anything. But misunderstood or not, he definitely lost some fans along the way, which really wouldn't have been the case with *The Principle of Moments*.

Tim: I agree with Chad, and I like how he put it, that *Shaken 'n' Stirred* didn't resonate with him. And he's right about its effect on the old fans. I was the same way. But *The Principle of Moments* is, of course, a more than solid album, maybe his best. Before we close, I also want to mention a song called "Turnaround," which ended up on the expanded version. It's a decent song, but I have to think that it probably didn't end up on the album because maybe it's a little bit too close to Zeppelin. I hear echoes of "Heartbreaker," but really, very little. Also a bit of the "Houses of Holy" guitar sound. Glad they released it, but like "Far Post" with the debut, I wouldn't have replaced anything on the album with it. Although at 39 minutes, you're at a number where they could have added it in.

Shaken 'n' Stirred

"Robert, in 1983, wanted to be modern. He wouldn't touch any of his roots or where he came from or do any Zep songs. He wanted to be modern and I wanted to rock. But all the guys in the band were great. It was a deep culture shock living in England and being the only Yank in the band. But as we started to progress into the record, after rehearsals and everything, they treated me good. It started to grow on me. Like a wart. No, it was good. It was a lot of fun. Benji Lefevre was getting really great drum sounds and it was a lot of fun to do. There were five Simmons mixed in with my kit. I had to incorporate them somehow to make Robert think we were being modern, so... I tried to get modern. It was recorded in the room they'd recorded *Sgt. Pepper's*, but it had all been redone. It was in Kensington or something. I couldn't find it now if I had to."

"On tour, we were playing huge places, The Forum and what's that big hatbox in Dallas? Anyway, the big hatbox in Dallas. Lots of stuff like that. He's not used to seeing empty seats, so it would be like ten percent short of a sellout and he would get depressed. Ahmet Ertegun loaned us his G1, and then I guess Mo Ostin wanted to use it or something, so we got a propeller version of the same plane. That was the only time I've ever been in a private plane (laughs); it was nice."

robert plant
Mfd. by RCA Music Service under License
6550 East 30th Street, Indianapolis, Indiana 46219
ROBERT PLANT
SHAKEN 'N STIRRED
Atlantic Recording Corp.
75 Rockefeller Plaza
New York, N.Y. 10019
S154215

S154215
ROBERT PLANT
SHAKEN 'N STIRRED
Programs
1 Hip To Hoo
   Doo Doo A Do Do   10:39
2 Little By Little
   Kallalou Kallalou
   Too Loud (Beg.)   10:39
3 Too Loud (Concl.)
   Trouble Your Money
   Pink And Black   10:39
4 Easily Lead
   Sixes And Sevens   10:39
© 1985 Robert Plant
℗ 1985 Atlantic Recording Corporation for the United States and
WEA International Inc. for the world outside of the United States.
Produced by Robert Plant, Benji Lefevre and Tim Palmer.
WARNING: Unauthorized reproduction of this recording is prohibited
by Federal law and subject to criminal prosecution.
Es Paranza Records
Distributed by
Atlantic Recording Corp.
75 Rockefeller Plaza
New York, N.Y. 10019
A Warner Communications Company
Printed in U.S.A.

PARANZA
That Side
This Side
HIP TO HOO (4:51)
KALLALOU KALLALOU (4:17)
TOO LOUD (4:07)
TROUBLE YOUR MONEY (4:14)
PINK AND BLACK (3:45)
LITTLE BY LITTLE (4:43)
DOO DOO A DO DO (5:09)
EASILY LEAD (4:35)
SIXES AND SEVENS (6:04)
STEREO
79 02651
Q
ROBERT PLANT
SHAKEN 'N STIRRED
Produced by;
Robert Plant, Benji Lefevre and Tim Palmer
Songs written by; R Plant, R Blunt, P Martinez, J Woodroffe, R Hayward
Songs written by; R Plant, R Blunt, P Martinez
Songs written by; R Plant, J Woodroffe
Songs written by; R Plant, P Martinez, J Woodroffe
(ASCAP)
MANUFACTURED AND DISTRIBUTED BY/FABRIQUE ET DISTRIBUE PAR WEA MUSIC OF CANADA, LTD. 1810 BIRCHMOUNT RD., SCARBOROUGH, ONTARIO
A WARNER COMMUNICATIONS COMPANY

"What I remember most was Jezz on the tour, because he was so gullible. It was funny. Like, we got off the plane in Phoenix and he looked at all the sand and he said 'Where's the beach?' And we pointed west, you know? It's over that way. And Benji told him in Australia that there were these special kind of weird animals in Australia called drop bears. They were like koalas but they were really violent. And they would drop out of trees on tourists and beat the shit out of them."

"And in Japan, we had him walking up and down the length of the bullet train at 170 miles an hour looking for the bath car. Like sure, there's going to be a bath car in a train going 170 miles an hour. But we were in the club car and he went the length of the train and he came back and said, 'I couldn't find it.' And I said, 'Yeah, man!' Robbie was going... Robbie called him Toby, because he had a thing about Jezz. And he said, 'Yeah, it's there, man. You missed it! Go again.' He did— three times."

Richie Hayward

Credits

May 20, 1985
Es Paranza/Atlantic 90265
Produced by Robert Plant, Benji Lefevre and Tim Palmer
Engineered by Tim Palmer and Benji Lefevre
Recorded at Marcus Studios, London, UK, Rockfield Studios,
Monmouth, UK and AIR Studios, London, UK
Personnel: Robert Plant – vocals, Robbie Blunt – guitars and
synthesized guitars, Jezz Woodroffe – keyboards, synthesizers, Paul
Martinez – bass and guitar, Richie Hayward – drums
Key additional personnel: Toni Halliday – backing vocals

Side 1
1. "Hip to Hoo" (Plant, Blunt, Martinez, Woodroffe, Hayward) 4:51
2. "Kallalou Kallalou" (Plant, Woodroffe) 4:17
3. "Too Loud" (Plant, Blunt, Martinez, Woodroffe, Hayward) 4:07
4. "Trouble Your Money" (Plant, Blunt, Martinez) 4:114
5. "Pink and Black" (Plant, Blunt, Martinez, Woodroffe, Hayward) 3:45

Side 2
1. "Little by Little" (Plant, Woodroffe) 4:43
2. "Doo Doo a Do Do" (Plant, Blunt, Martinez) 5:09
3. "Easily Lead" (Plant, Blunt, Woodroffe) 4:35
4. "Sixes and Sevens" (Plant, Blunt, Martinez, Woodroffe, Hayward)
6:04

A *Shaken 'n' Stirred* Timeline

May 20, 1985. Ending a two-year gap, Robert issues a new solo album, called *Shaken 'n' Stirred*. The album reaches No.20 on the main *Billboard* chart, the Hot 200, and at No.19 on the UK charts. Lead single "Little by Little" hits the top spot on the Mainstream Rock Tracks chart, staying there for two weeks, while "Sixes and Sevens" reaches No.18.

May 22, 1985. Robert Plant appears on *Late Night with David Letterman* to promote the new album.

June 10 – August 5, 1985. Robert Plant and his band conduct North American touring dates in support of *Shaken 'n' Stirred*.

June 15, 1985. "Little by Little" enters the main *Billboard* chart, peaking at No.36 and thus becoming Robert's third Top 40 single. The US picture sleeve single is backed with album track "Trouble Your Money." The song features in a *Miami Vice* episode called "Junk Love."

July 1985. Issued as the second US picture sleeve single from the album is "Too Loud," backed with "Kallalou Kallalou."

July 18, 1985. *Shaken 'n' Stirred* achieves RIAA gold certification.

August 1985. "Little by Little" is issued as a single in the UK, backed with "Doo Doo a Do Do," but available in various versions, including remix.

September 8 – 24, 1985. Robert and the band play a handful of European dates.

November 8, 1985. Mikhail Baryshnikov and Gregory Hines movie *White Nights* debuts in theatres. The soundtrack album to the film includes Robert Plant solo B-side "Far Post." The hit song from the album was "Separate Lives," a duet between Marilyn Martin and Robert's old drummer, Phil Collins.

March 11 – 15, 1986. Robert plays three UK dates, the last of which is benefit concert Heart Beat 86, staged to raise money for the Birmingham Children's Hospital. Robert Plant and the Big Town Playboys performed three Honeydrippers-like selections, "She Walks Right In," "Come On" and "Mellow Saxophone."

robert plant
shaken 'n' stirred
INCLUDES THE SINGLE
LITTLE BY LITTLE

robert plant
pink and black

Robert Plant
Little
By
Little
Remix

PB-1034
NOT FOR SALE
SHORT VERSION
LITTLE BY LITTLE
リトル・バイ・リトル
robert plant
ロバート・プラント

Martin talks to Ralph Chapman about *Shaken 'n' Stirred.*

Martin Popoff: Well, what do you think of *Shaken 'n' Stirred*?

Ralph Chapman: Thanks again, Martin, for having me on. It's a pleasure to talk about these records, especially these records from my youth. I was a teenager when *Shaken 'n' Stirred* came out, and I bought it on the release day. I had been following his career since he became a solo artist. I was probably too young, in many ways, for Led Zeppelin. In the early eighties, I discovered, well, first it was The Beatles but then I went into this whole prog thing and became enamoured with the drums and specifically Phil Collins.

So, as I had mentioned, I remember waking up to go to school, and you'd have the alarm come on with the radio and the song that came on was "Burning Down One Side." So this is 1982. And I instantly recognised that was Phil's drumming, unmistakably, his tom sound and everything else. And that kind of awakened my interest in Robert Plant and then Led Zeppelin. That's what got me into Robert Plant—through Phil Collins, which is probably a very strange road for a lot of people out there, but that's how it went. And then a year later *The Principle of Moments* came in and I share your extreme passion for that record. And again, it was mostly Phil on drums with Barriemore Barlow, one of the greatest drummers ever to pick up the sticks in my opinion. And then Robert came to Toronto with Phil on drums; I think it was September of '83. So I was right there; I got tickets right above the drum kit. I'm gonna get to *Shaken 'n' Stirred*, but this is a little context for what is maybe quite an unorthodox view about this record. And I was in heaven for that show. At the same time, I had bought up the Led Zeppelin catalogue, so I was all in with Robert and Led Zeppelin at that point. Seeing Robert with Phil on that *Principle of Moments* tour… that was my first apex of my love for him. So I couldn't wait for the next record to come out.

But what did come out was that EP, by The Honeydrippers, with "Rockin' at Midnight" and things like that. And for me, immediately, I knew there was no Phil. And, of course, pre-internet, you do some research and it seemed like Paul Shaffer was involved and maybe Ahmet Ertegun. I obviously knew who Paul Shaffer was. But it was such a huge departure from *Principle of Moments*. The record really, really confused me. And he showed up on *SNL* and it was like my parents' music; it was the quiet generation, even though it was probably just skirting the line of boomer and quiet generation, but it was not what I was interested in. I wasn't mature enough. Of course, now you listen to the Honeydrippers EP, and it's exquisitely produced and played and you respect it and you understand it. But at the time, I was baffled by it, and I didn't know where he was going to go at that point.

And so, what happened is, come 1985, I'd heard the rumours of it, that a new album was coming out. And I knew Phil wasn't going to be on it, which was a drag. Richie Hayward was going to be the new drummer. I didn't know who Little Feat was, and I certainly didn't know who Richie Hayward was when I was nineteen. And in many ways, that's the joy of being nineteen as you're just discovering these things.

So, the record comes out, and I have to digress for a second. I may have been one of the few people who liked Robert Plant's solo material at that point as much as Led Zeppelin. So, I used to get a lot of friction at high school for that. Like oh, you know, it's somehow derivative because Jimmy and John Paul weren't there, and obviously John Bonham wasn't there. But to me, it was all one narrative. As I said, I got to Led Zeppelin through progressive rock. I saw Led Zeppelin as a progressive rock band, I didn't see them as a hard rock band or a blues rock band. I saw them as progressive, which still rankles the odd person. It's kind of like Rush. I see Rush as a prog rock band, but man do I get in trouble from a lot of fans out there about that. Anyway, it was all one beautiful melange with Robert Plant back then.

So, the album comes out. I knew it wasn't gonna have Phil and I put it on my parents' old stereo and the first thing is "Hip to Hoo." First track and there's a female vocalist, and there's a huge swath of synthesizers, and I knew this was going to be a record that was going to confuse me and my 19-year-old mind. And I have to admit, I listened to it maybe three or four times at that point, and it left me completely alienated. To me, it had nothing to do... well, it has nothing to do with The Honeydrippers, which was good, but I could not hear continuity. At that point in my life, in my young life, between *Pictures at Eleven* and *The Principle of Moments* and this, it had some of the earmarks of at least *Principle of Moments* in the sense that—and I knew immediately, even on that stereo—the production was out of this world. It was huge-sounding. And it wasn't just the kind of reverb on the drums. It was the way those songs were recorded, how they were layered and arranged etc. And so I scanned the credits and Tim Palmer was there, who I didn't know but I assumed that he was a huge part of this, to be generous, more evolved sound.

But this record was not immediate for me. The one record I think of is Paul McCartney's *Pipes of Peace*, which is another record that I almost hated. And then I evolved, started to understand where artists go, what kind of artists I like, and what they tend to do through their career, which is make changes. Not that *Pipes of Peace* necessarily is a reflection of that, but it's an off-the-wall record in terms of one that is largely loathed by the populace, but one where its charms revealed itself later in life.

So, with Robert, now we're going back to 1985 and the album did very little for me. I went to the tour, and I gotta say, it was so loud; it was at the CNE stadium, and they opened with "In the Mood." I remember that. And, again, I didn't know much about Richie Hayward. All I knew was he didn't play "In the Mood" like Phil had played it at the Gardens. It wasn't as good in my mind. And then Jezz Woodroffe did this keyboard solo that was so loud, I have to tell you, it was so loud that the blood ran down my face. I was in the 14th row floors and that place just shook. It was painful. It was almost negligent in my mind, that they had that thing. So that was part of that whole *Shaken 'n' Stirred* experience for me. It was disappointing. It was married to a concert that wasn't as good as the Gardens September '83 show with Phil. It had a woman singing on it and had all these baffling elements that were just alienating for me.

So, you would have thought a few years later—I'll get back to this one—*Now and Zen* came out and you would have thought I'd be relieved. But what *Now and Zen* did—within my mind, so now I'm twenty-two—that comes out and I've developed quite a bit. Perhaps I should have been excited. Remember, I was one of those crazy teenagers who was sitting with my friends watching *Johnny Carson* one night, July 11, 1985. And we looked at each other because the news had broken that Led Zeppelin is, as much as they can, reforming at Live Aid. And Phil was going to be one of the drummers. So, we got in my friend's Mazda GLC and we drove down to Philadelphia and picked up some scalper tickets and we went to Live Aid, ostensibly to see Robert with Jimmy and John Paul, and Paul Martinez as I found out.

Anyway, so I won't go on—Live Aid is a totally separate story disconnected from *Shaken 'n' Stirred*. But the main thing is I waited in the hot Philadelphia sun, and then finally this reformation takes place. Jimmy has come out and slammed the performance and he seems to be not right through that performance. But it was one of the greatest things I'd ever seen, that short set. I think they did "Stairway," "Whole Lotta Love" and "Rock and Roll." But the interesting thing about that, for me is as much as I was elated, I had a sense of because Paul Martinez was on stage, I missed Robert's solo band. Part of me didn't like him going back to the past, even though I didn't detect any of the poor performances or anything like that they talked about later. I thought it sounded fine; absolutely fantastic. Tony Thompson with them as well.

There's still part of me that thought, ah, this is a nostalgia trip. And I was nineteen—it was a dream come true to see those guys. But at the same time, not to belabour the point, it's like, okay, I wish they'd do this and then Robbie Blunt would come on and Jezz would come on and maybe Bob Mayo would come on. And Richie obviously would come on, and then they'd do some of *Shaken 'n' Stirred*.

It was a strange and very subtle nagging feeling, but I remember thinking that. So that just meant for me that somewhere in my mind, I knew I was going to return to *Shaken 'n' Stirred*. Like I say, I started out as a Beatles fan, and when you're a Beatles fan, you embrace a band that changed dramatically, especially once they got going around *Help!* right through to *Abbey Road*. They reinvented themselves every single album, and even fifteen, sixteen years after they'd broken up, I was still astonished at that. They were the ultimate progressive rock band to me. They never cared what the audience thought.

So as much as *Shaken 'n' Stirred* didn't speak to me. I respected it. I respected what I was hearing. And I grew to respect The Honeydrippers *Volume One*, which was kind of a novelty project. But I started to see Robert more and more as a guy that, again, thinking about Live Aid and the aftermath of that, as a guy who was a progressive artist. And Live Aid was an anomaly that I didn't really like, so I returned to *Shaken 'n' Stirred* probably right after *Now and Zen* came out, which I did not like. And it wasn't just because he was sampling and seemed to be tripping on the burgeoning hip-hop thing. It struck me as a poor version. And I won't call it a sell-out. I'm not going to litigate this record, but it just felt like a cash-in. Even though it seems modern, it's called *Now and Zen* and so reaches for the present but looks to the past.

If you look at the *Shaken 'n' Stirred* record cover, I loved it. I thought it was a very interesting cover and the fact that he wasn't on it, the statement was that this is something that you have to work to get into. I'm not handing you the personality of Robert Plant. And he's there on the back cover of course, but it's out of focus and obscure. It doesn't have the same kind of uber-cool former heavy frontman of Zeppelin vibe to it. But the cover, which I think he was part of conceptually, really drew me in. And then when *Now and Zen* came out, I had this very much in my mind. Now he was back to having the big, long hair and he's front and centre and it's like oh, you're no longer selling yourself as a progressive artist. You're selling yourself as a heritage artist, even though I didn't know the words back then. No matter what was on that record, the good stuff reminded me as not as good as *Shaken 'n' Stirred*. And the stuff I didn't like struck me as pandering or nostalgia for nostalgia's sake.

And then he went off and did *Manic Nirvana* and I saw these tours. And the other thing about *Shaken 'n' Stirred*, if you saw the tour, yeah, he might do the odd Elvis song, but he stuck to his guns, in terms of I'm a new artist, I'm not going to do Led Zeppelin songs. Now, maybe this is related to the Live Aid story, but I really respected that, that we weren't gonna get versions of "Black Dog" or whatever song you want to pull. It was about being Robert Plant. When I went to the Gardens show for *Now and Zen*, he brought out "Black Country Woman" and he had two or three others; he may have even opened the show with "In the Evening." And remember, again, on one level, it's neat to see these songs, but on another level, it was, oh, well, that guy I loved who had left Led Zeppelin… John Bonham had passed, and he was determined to reinvent himself. Now he was trading on something that I thought was a little beneath him. I don't know if that's a contrarian point of view.

So again, it was the *Now and Zen* era when and I went back to *Shaken 'n' Stirred* and I was much more evolved. I had gotten into Talk Talk and Midge Ure and Joe Jackson and a whole bunch of other British…I almost would say, post-new wave artists, a lot of artists that altered what I thought a record could do and sound like. And then you go back to *Shaken 'n' Stirred* and all of a sudden you marvel at it and admire it and you say this is pretty impressive production. All of a sudden, the whole record had a new sound to me, and I was ready for it; I was excited by it. So, this again, would be '88, '89, and that's where I've stayed with *Shaken 'n' Stirred*. It looms large in my music-loving life, and not because of nostalgia. I don't think about being nineteen or twenty or twenty-one when I put this record on. I think about how the eighties in my mind was—at the risk of sounding dramatic—the last great era for production.

Many of the artists that I loved, contrary to the popular notion that they were kind of lost in the eighties, were making great records. I bring up Paul McCartney because he was like this too. When he brought out *Press to Play* a year after *Shaken 'n' Stirred*, he got just slayed for that album. "It was him chasing" and blah, blah, blah. And I posit that it wasn't him chasing; he was doing what he did, like Robert did with *Shaken 'n' Stirred*, which is embracing the side of his artistry that was always restless, always interested in moving forward.

You think about that leap from Led Zeppelin *IV* to *Houses of the Holy* and yeah, Jimmy's obviously a huge part of that and John Paul and John. But to me sonically the type of songs and the humour that runs through some of *Houses of the Holy* with "D'yer Mak'er" and "The Crunge" was such a huge evolution. And that's how I felt with *Press to Play*, Paul McCartney's '86 album, and that's what I think of *Shaken 'n' Stirred*. It was for me the last time he was a rock artist, a progressive rock artist. I love his whole catalogue now, because everything gets better, I find, as I get older. It's one of the few things I enjoy about aging is you open up. So all of a sudden choices artists you love make that you didn't really connect to, you get it, you understand. Hopefully your references expand.

I started to recognise that the whole approach to this record was entirely different than the previous ones. And a lot of that had to do with a few factors. And I say all of this with admiration, but one was Richie Hayward. So the first two records, my understanding—and I remember chatting with Jason Bonham about this, and I've since read interviews with Phil Collins, and I've interviewed Paul Martinez, as well, for a book I want to write on Phil Collins—those first two records, *Pictures* and *Principle*, were done with Jason or with drum machines, always with the intent that either Barriemore or Cozy or Phil would replace those parts. And I know with Phil with *Pictures at Eleven*, he did all that work on that record. So six, I think, of the eight tracks, he did in three days. He was sent tapes, listened to the tapes, listened to whatever Jason was doing and came up with his own parts. With *Principle of Moments*, he had five days I think, same kind of modus though, listening to pretty developed demos, and then just putting his imprimatur on these songs. And of course, I loved it. And certainly, Phil was at his zenith then.

But as far as putting an album together, Robert didn't have a full-time band, although obviously Robbie had been there and Jezz and Paul had been there from the beginning. When you bring in a drummer, right from the start, that's going to change the record, especially someone as gifted as Richie Hayward was, this guy from Iowa who was again, capable of so many different styles and feels and grooves, not just with Little Feat, which was actually, as I realised in my thirties, quite a progressive band. I thought they were some southern hick band, but they were not. And I recommend people explore the Little Feat catalogue at least until Lowell George passed on.

Anyway, I'm all over the place, so forgive me. But that is one of the things that I love about *Shaken 'n' Stirred*, is that it's a band album, with a drummer right out of the gate who is there to develop the material with the other guys. And there is a sense I feel when I listen to that record of the bass player and the drummer connecting in a way that was absent from the first two. Doesn't mean it wasn't fabulous, but there's something completely unique in *Shaken 'n' Stirred* in how the rhythm section operates. I'll get to that later because there are certain songs where you really, really hear that.

Okay, so they got Richie, he's there from the beginning and the songwriting credits have changed. I think this is really important. I remember reading interviews or promo stuff that Robert did, junkets and things, that Jezz Woodroffe had a greater role on this record from a compositional point of view than the past two. And if you scan the credits, you can see that he had two credits on the first album, three on *Principle* and for this album he's got seven writing credits. And I don't think that's just Robert becoming more liberal with how he bestowed credits, because I had heard from Paul Martinez that he was pretty egalitarian that way. He wasn't cheap with offering up credits. But obviously, all you have to do is listen to that record and you hear Jezz's huge influence.

So, you've got this band and at the same time you've got Robert, who's, in my mind, still pushing forward. But again, this is in retrospect, I'd heard that maybe he'd finally left his wife at this point. He was a single guy. He was restless professionally, but he was restless personally and grappling. And plus, as every era seems to be, again I think of people like McCartney and Plant, the eighties was an inhospitable time for them. I think they were looked on as heritage acts before we really knew what heritage acts were. And I think it affects those guys. I remember reading interviews and Eric Clapton was doing the same thing. He brought in Phil Collins to produce a couple of records that people hate, that I think are the best of his career. But I think that was affecting Robert Plant right back to the *Principle of Moments* interviews. He didn't want to be written off as an old fart at thirty-four, was one of his quotes.

He was going through that as well. You're an artist, Martin, an accomplished writer and a lot of where you go is with these classic rock artists, for lack of a better term, though I loathe that expression, or for that matter heritage acts. You're also a very accomplished artist, painter, and I've done my share of writing docs and things like that; it's very, very hard to be accepted outside of what you're known for if you ever want to go to new places. That's something I learned acutely as I got older and now respect *Shaken 'n' Stirred* for.

Anyway, he struck me in retrospect as a guy in tumult—artistic tumult, personal tumult—and that fed through this record. The irony of that, of course, is that in many ways this is his most poppy record, for lack of a better word, his happiest or most up record. Toni Halliday, which is another key factor in my I love for this record, just completely altered the mood of *Shaken 'n' Stirred* and gave him a sound that was completely fresh to me and new. I hate using those kinds of cheap descriptors, but if you scan the credits, Toni gets a lead credit. Like, he doesn't bury her as a guest. She's up there with Jezz and Paul and Robbie; I think he gives her "additional vocals" credit. So she's almost a de facto part of the band, though she doesn't stay and doesn't tour.

And when I read that, especially when I went back to the album, I went, oh, this is profound. In one's little, freaky, geeky music world, when you return to things, you look for ways to understand what an artist is doing. And that hit me in a way that didn't hit me when I was nineteen. I took that as a statement. This person is an integral part of what this record is going to sound like.

And as soon as the record started, she's there cooing, "Cheat, cheat, don't do it now" and bringing in elements and a sonic angle or whatever you want to call it to a record that Robert hadn't explored meaningfully before. And she was an accomplished singer; contralto, I think she is. It gave it a place to go, *Shaken 'n' Stirred*, but it also infused it with a levity and a dreaminess and a euphoria that hadn't appeared before. It had somewhat appeared on Zeppelin songs, but on his first two records, there was a... not a crunch to it, because especially *Principle of Moments* goes all over the place, but there were moods on this record that he hadn't explored before. And a lot of that was Toni.

And a lot of that was Jezz. Jezz got into early sampling. I was reading an interview with him recently from about '86, where he talks about for "Too Loud,"

a sample. He was getting into early sampling, and he sampled the Nelson Riddle Orchestra, I think, for that, which has these strange orchestral stabs. And then of course, it made sense when I read that—oh, that's what I'm hearing when I put on these Beyerdynamic Amiron headphones, which make this record sound beautiful. You listen to "Too Loud" and there's so much going on, but one of the things that was going on was this early sampling. That didn't exist with *Principle*. Clearly, he was evolving and I know for that record, Robert was exploring Simmons drums and getting Phil and Barriemore to play Simmons drums, which in part makes that a progressive-sounding record.

But here he went whole hog. Again, in the Jezz Woodroffe interview I read—it was some keyboard publication—he talks about how Richie was a pretty nuts-and-bolts kind of player, acoustic kit kind of player. And Jezz was saying, "Well, for this album, go buy a Linndrum," which is an early drum machine. I think it's a Linndrum on Genesis "Mama" and it was a staple of the early to mid-eighties. This is with the idea that you're going to have to expand your palate.

And what Richie does on this record, if you're a drummer—which you and I both are, Martin—this record is one of the greatest records I've ever heard, at least in the rock idiom, with respect to how he seamlessly on one track… I think it's "Hip to Hoo" but also "Kallalou Kallalou," a lot of those songs, Richie Hayward seamlessly plays an acoustic kit, plays Simmons drums and plays percussion. Now some of this may have been overdubbed. But the way the Simmons drum and the acoustic drums layer into each other, again, Phil Collins is one of the few other people who can do this, and Neil Peart from Rush as well. But I think this is one of the most beautiful presentations of acoustic and electronic percussion ever laid on a record. Again, it just shifts the flavour and the mood and the energy of that record, constantly, through a song. It's really quite something, where he chooses, or where Robert or Tim or Benji or the band in their arrangement chose to switch up, sometimes in mid-verse, what he's going to do.

Again, just on that level, this record is so fascinating to me, but that's just one tiny element. So, to recap, you've got Richie coming on and being part of the writing process, and you've got Jezz exploring and given much more breadth to work artistically. He's much more there as a writer, and he's into all these early and very progressive keyboard voicings and things like that. And that's all just extremely exciting, especially when you return to it.

And I never bought into maybe some people out there saying—because you hear this a lot, "Oh, the eighties is about reverb, it's about gated drums or about crappy keyboard sounds." I've always resisted that. It just sounds like these guys knew what they were doing. Tim Palmer, Benji Lefevre and Robert, they just knew how to record. Whether it was in the mixing or the tracking, they knew how to create the stereo picture. Maybe it was mic placement, choice of instrument. Some of what makes this record sound so live, it seems close-mic'ed, meaning the mic is very close to the instruments of the amplifiers. Or it sounds like it's been plugged in direct, right into the mixing board, or whatever the case is. And again, I think about The Beatles and "Revolution." How they got that guitar sound is they just went straight into the desk. I think Jimmy did this as well. It's revolutionary. How do you make a recording sound like you're at a concert, where it's just so visceral and dragging you in? And that's what I thought Tim and Benji and Robert did with *Shaken 'n' Stirred*.

So back to Toni Halliday. The interesting thing to me about Toni now in retrospect is that I'm pretty sure the last time Robert had used or sung with a woman was "The Battle of Evermore" with Sandy Denny. So that to me, again as a fan, says a lot in terms of how far afield Robert had gone and how exciting that was. Because the last time was 1971 with Sandy on this Celtic and kind of brooding Tolkien tune with mandolins. And what's the refrain she sings? "Dance in the dark of night" and "Sing to the morning light," which is so different from what Toni was doing, which again is, "Oh, cheat, cheat, cheat, don't do it now." Like, just an entirely different approach to these kinds of textures.

And if you think about it, as I encourage everyone to listen to *Shaken 'n' Stirred* with a new and broader mind, there's only 14 years that separate Led Zeppelin *IV* from *Shaken 'n' Stirred*. If you explore the Foo Fighters catalogue, and you go from their first record to 14 years later, and you put those two records on, not much different. And yeah, I love Taylor Hawkins, so no disrespect to Taylor. They're different bands, obviously, but it just reminds me of what music was like back then—which sounds like the old man thing, but it's just a fact to me (laughs). The progression and the career that Robert had in those 14 years, I can put on Led Zeppelin *IV* and then I can put on *Shaken 'n' Stirred* and marvel at this journey. Because when I listen to Led Zeppelin *IV*, I still think it's one of the most extraordinary records. And that's incredibly intoxicating for me to hear an artist progress like that. And where I key into that is Sandy versus Toni and what Robert's doing. So that's that.

Back then mainstream artists, heritage artists, for the most part, seemed to be driven by progression, that they had to do it. They're obliged to do it. I don't really hear that now. And there's a lot of reasons why you don't hear that. It's the fall of the A&R guy. It's the fall of great management. It's shifting tastes. I was interviewing a guy named Jim Leverton the other day. Jim Leverton played with Steve Marriott. He was in Fat Mattress with Noel Redding and also Caravan. He said, "You remember, Ralph." I didn't really because even at my age, I missed out a lot. But he said, "Music used to be important. And that was the most important thing, not its popularity." Which is kind of a rose-coloured view, perhaps, because obviously commerce was always a big part of the music industry.

So when I think about *Shaken 'n' Stirred*, here was a guy who wasn't interested in anything other than moving forward; there's a restlessness. Some of the songs, specifically songs like "Too Loud," may not be to your taste. But I think a lot of music listeners if they're not doing so, they should explore the idea of having two seemingly contrarian ideas of not liking something but respecting something. And *Shaken 'n' Stirred* is a classic album although you don't have to love every choice he made. And "Too Loud" kind of puts a fine point on it. It's a pretty static song musically, and he brings in this guy Victor... it's a strange philosophical device. Especially when you're nineteen, you're not necessarily thinking it's kind of "The Crunge" part two, which is kind of a piss take, perhaps, on James Brown. I didn't know what "Where's that confounded bridge?" meant. Of course, later, I knew that there's no bridge on "The Crunge" (laughs). And that that was a joke. It was funny. And "Too Loud" struck me later as funny. It's just a funny piece; it's levity in the same way that "The Crunge" or "Hot Dog" or "D'yer Mak'er" or "Boogie with Stu" or any of those things that ran through Robert was funny.

So in that sense, I thought, okay, I can square that. It's not out of left field. It's just something that Robert does, as opposed to, "What is this weird dance music? This new wave crap?" It's like no, it's not that; it's something else. And "Too Loud" reminded me of "Who Dunnit" in that sense from *Abacab*, which people hated. "Oh, why did they not put on 'You Might Recall' or even 'Paperlate?'" Why did they put this awful crappy pseudo-punky thing on here?"

And again, maybe because I came to Genesis late, I thought it was great. It was like, oh, this is totally different. Let's go here for three minutes and fifteen seconds kind of thing. That's what I evolved into with "Too Loud." So I do go on, in my enthusiasm, but Toni was a key part of Robert's vision. And in many ways, *Shaken 'n' Stirred* almost feels like a Europop record, which again, you can hear somewhat in *The Principle of Moments* and not so much in *Pictures at Eleven*, but songs like "Wreckless Love" and "Stranger Here… Than Over There." And maybe part of that was how Barriemore approached the rhythm on those songs. But they were very forward-thinking songs versus say "Other Arms" or "Messin' with the Mekon." "Horizontal Departure" is a pretty straightforward tune. And I don't mean that in a pejorative sense, because *Principle of Moments*, I share your enthusiasm for it. They're just great songs. But he certainly was going off; he was moving somewhere with those two Barriemore Barlow tunes.

Anyway, so that sums up why I love the record. When I sit and listen to it, one of the things that mesmerises me about it—and I encourage people to try and hear it through perhaps this kind of thinking—is it's a record of duality. It's a deceptive record, where it appears to be one thing, but it's actually another. And as I said, it's a record born out of tension. But you can't really hear that tension. You can occasionally feel it. Robert obviously was enamoured with and had built his life on the blues. *Shaken 'n' Stirred* is not a blues record (laughs). You'd be hard-pressed to find any blues. Maybe with "Sixes and Sevens" there's something, but it's fairly absent. It's European. That's another thing I love about it. It largely feels like it's born in England and Europe, the dance clubs of Europe or Ibiza or somewhere exotic; it sounds exotic in places to me. At the same time, it sounds really progressive, like English progressive rock.

And yet lyrically it's one of his most accessible records, although it's got some of his most poignant and direct lyrics. And me being a lyric guy, you don't often think about Robert in the same way you might think of, oh gosh, John Lennon and Roger Waters or Peter Gabriel. You listen to Robert for his voice and for how he sings a line, but not necessarily for lyrics, although there are exceptions. But it's mostly how he sings those lines and how perfect, like The Beatles, how he could structure a line and marry it to a melody in this indelible way, where you thought, wow, that guy is a great singer.

But you didn't necessarily listen to Robert in the same way you might listen to Roger Waters, where it's like reading a book, where it hits you intellectually. And I thought this album has some tracks that crossed over into that, "Sixes and Sevens" and "Little by Little" being two of them.

And yet the album itself sounds really quite... some might say disposable. It's layered and pop and there's all these walls of artifice, one could say, and buried beneath all that is the lyrics (laughs). I don't see it that way. I see it as this duality. And I see that duality in, I guess, the cover. It's abstract-looking. Especially for a heathen like me who doesn't know a whole lot about art. I know a bit more now, but at the time, I thought, what is this?! What does this even mean? It was abstract yet at the same time, I was drawn into it in a way that I didn't understand as a nineteen-year-old. It was curious to me. That's the odd thing. Great art, even great abstract art, appears on one level to be saying, I'm the artist and I'll do what I want, and you can like it or not like it. But on another level, it's saying I dare you to explore this. And that's what that cover did for me. Because he's not there on the cover. He's not saying, I'm a former frontman, I'm a rock god, I'm this, I'm that. It's just saying, here's pretty colours and strange images and circles and lines and slabs of... I don't know, Martin, you would be able to describe it better because you're an actual artist. But again, it had this strange duality of being abstract, yet asking me to come in.

And that's this record—it's immediate, while at the same time, just sometimes out of reach, which seems kind of nebulous, and I don't necessarily think everyone's gonna understand what I'm talking about. But still to this day, that's how I feel. I'm in it and yet I'm out, which is really exciting.

Why do we listen to music? I can tell you why I listen. I listen to music to be challenged, but to feel something, not just nostalgia, not just, oh, I used to be eighteen. Now I'm in my fifties. But now I'm going to be eighteen for forty-seven minutes. Before we started recording, I mentioned I started teaching myself German. I did that not just to learn a language, but to push my mind to tune the radio to a new frequency. And that's what that record is, and remains 38-odd years later, is a new set of stations, a new frequency. It appears to be a pop album in many ways, but there's actually way more to it.

Again, I go back to Richie's drums, which have the sense of being both straightforward and part of a new wave kind of sonic menu while at the same time being incredibly complicated. And again, Phil is one of the few drummers that I know who can make something... you listen to "Turn It on Again," which I think is in 13/8 time. And it's not that hard to play once you master it. But it's a complicated drum part compositionally and it took a musician, a really clever guy, to come up with that. And that's what I hear with Richie. It's accessible, but at the same time it's like, wow, there's so much going on. So *Shaken 'n' Stirred*, to borrow from *Principle of Moments*, is not a horizontal departure or a lateral move, but it's vertical; it's a vertical departure.

Just again, to touch a bit on *Now and Zen*, when I listen to *Now and Zen*, I do want to mention, interestingly enough, the only song that really moved me on *Now and Zen*… I bought the vinyl but also the cassette of *Now and Zen* back then because when that came out in '88, the cassette gave you "Walking Towards Paradise" as a bonus track, and then I think the CD did as well. That song, which was relegated to a B-side of "Heaven Knows," that was my first exposure. I knew the single, the 45. You flipped it over and like many music fans you loved the B-sides that didn't appear on the albums. It was a cover, but that to me was an extension of *Shaken 'n' Stirred*. I felt that excitement again when I heard that song. The rest of the record, as I said, was either looking too far in the past or just doing… of course, this is back then. *Now and Zen* now is a great record to me but it's no *Shaken 'n' Stirred*. Even though popularity-wise, it seems like people think, oh, now he's found himself again. He's figured out a way to balance his past and his future again. That record did not do that for me. It was like ugh, you've ceased to be that progressive artist.

Shaken 'n' Stirred is a guy who's aware of his past but doesn't trade on it. And I think that's a key point for someone who admires artists for developing new things. If you're going to enter the past, do it in a way that it just kind of slides into you through your fingernails or something as a listener, and doesn't hit you. And now for the last 20 years or so, Robert has really slid into this idea, in the best sense of I'm going to do whatever I want. I'm not competing anymore in the marketplace. *Shaken 'n' Stirred* was a record where he was still competing in the marketplace. Obviously, the music industry was totally different then but now he just puts out records. You love them, you don't love them, you're frustrated that they're sometimes angular or impenetrable, but it's a guy doing what he wants. I love that and I admire that. And if I had the money to do that, I would be putting out books of poetry and all the rest of it.

Another thing I love about this album, which to me was largely absent… and again, this is my prog roots; I love concept albums like *Lamb Lies Down on Broadway* and *Quadrophenia*. Now, this may be a stretch to some people, but this came to me, I suppose later on, five or six years later. And people may roll their eyes, but I see *Shaken 'n' Stirred* as a concept album. But first of all, before I get into that, the other thing I love about this record is he didn't bury the lead in the sense that he was going in a new direction. He tells you right out of the bloody gate that this record is going to be up-tempo, that it's going to involve textures and sounds and arrangements that are definitely pushing the envelope, unabashedly drawing on new wave and technology.

But side two again, it's about this duality. Side two settles into a heavier, arguably more direct thing with "Easily Lead" on there and "Sixes and Sevens" and "Little by Little." It's something we're more comfortable with. Now he could have top-loaded that record with side two where everyone put it down and went, oh yeah, this is what I love, "Little by Little." But he doesn't do that. And back then obviously, most people put on side one first. And the other thing he did is he put "Little by Little" on side two. He didn't start with that song. I love that; I love the boldness of that. I love that you had to work to get to the familiar, which is a unique and admirable trait.

Compare that to *Principle of Moments*, where he starts off that record with "Other Arms," which is very familiar-sounding. That's the nice warm blanket of Robert that we wrap ourselves in. Then there's a break on "Other Arms," where Phil does some really kind of fancy footwork with his Ludwig Speed King, which again conjures that Zeppelin-esque thing. I don't know whether he's doing triplets on that bass drum, like single-footed triplets on that bass drum, but I first heard that and I thought, oh, that's familiar. With *Shaken 'n' Stirred*, all those kinds of concessions are off the table. It's like, this is what I am. This is what I'm doing. This is how I want to invite you in.

Now back to *Shaken 'n' Stirred* as a concept album. Again, in retrospect, I started to feel this way probably in the early nineties. I was reminded, again, not with a sense of nostalgia, but it reminded me of what my life was like on the weekends. And so go with me on this, Martin. You put this record on, and it's immediately brash and upbeat. This may sound silly, but you can't help but be physically moving around listening to "Hip to Hoo," while at the same time the rhythm is jagged. It doesn't let you settle in; it leaves you kind of askew. I couldn't help but be invigorated at the same time, even though I couldn't clap to it or whatever.

And that's how I often felt when I would start my day as a kid and as a guy in his late teens, early twenties, is that you're raring to go. Life isn't that simple, but you want to embrace it. And so I imagine that record being the story of a guy, because, after all, it is male music. It may not be now, but to me back then, I didn't know save for one friend of mine in college, this woman Franca, any woman who cared about Robert Plant. And even when she was into Robert Plant, it was not in the same way that I was. Anyway, I don't want to get too far afield. So that's how you start your day. Maybe it's Saturday and you're feeling up. But you're uncomfortable in your own skin. But you're looking forward to the evening, because the evening is going to be finally a good evening where you're going to have fun, maybe meet someone, all the rest of it.

And you follow that side one—again, this is in very general terms, in terms of moods—but by the time you get to "Too Loud," you're actually at whatever bar or club and you're probably talking too loud. And you probably had too many drinks, but you're still really up. So side one always struck me as that optimism of the day, on the weekend, going right through to the end of side one. You're now at the bar, and you're determined to have a good time but things are starting to revert back to how your life actually is, which is rarely as exciting as you want it to be.

And then you turn the record over. You get into "Little by Little," which is a very introspective tune about… that song could be about the collapse of his marriage. He could have been conjuring the loss of his son Karac. It could be about trying to shake Zeppelin, which I'll get to. It could be about a lot of things but it's introspective. It's the refrain of "I can breathe again." It's thoughtful, is what I'm saying. Which is if you were me in the mid-eighties going out, you always hit this wall where if the night wasn't going the way you wanted, maybe you went outside and hung out with your friends who smoked and we kind of commiserated about that.

And that side two, by the time you get to "Sixes and Sevens," you've devolved into life will never work out for me. Not to put too fine a point on it, to borrow from perhaps Buddha, "Life is suffering. Life is misery." And maybe, "Easily Lead" is an interesting placement. I think some of us probably when they went on these bar crawls had one-night stands that were never satisfying. Or were in the most ephemeral way. And no matter what, you couldn't escape the fact that "Sixes and Sevens" was going to return you to how you felt just as you started your day, that life was hard.

So that to me is the arc of that record: confusion and melancholy giving way to elation and optimism, given then to dance club partyness and really not trying to be someone else, into introspection, and then finally realisation that it takes a whole lot more than a night out to shed all of your vulnerabilities and insecurities. That's what I get from that record, which might strike people as weird. It's a concept album, but not of a strict narrative. It's a concept album of shifting, swinging moods, youth frustration, optimism fading into recognition that life isn't so easy to change.

Finally, I just want to talk a bit about why you should listen to this fabulous album from a song point of view. So you've heard "Hip to Hoo," and again, it's not only got Toni Halliday front and centre and it's got Richie exploring these percussion textures, but what sets this record apart too is the bass playing. You don't even have to be a player; I'm not a bass player, but I love the bass. I can listen to Joe Tex or The Faces or I can listen to any myriad of bands. I don't play the bass, but that's one of the elements I key into. And *Shaken 'n' Stirred* remains absolutely revelatory in terms of bass playing. It's beautiful. I can't think of enough superlatives. The Germans would say it was wunderbar.

And I mentioned earlier that I interviewed Paul, who didn't really remember too much about this record. But I said, "How did you get that bass sound? You must have done something different beyond the addition of Tim and Jezz." And he said, "Well, I changed my pickups in my Fender bass; I used EMGs, because they were brighter and more direct."

And just hearing that piece of information, it was like, oh! As any musician knows, or an adjunct to a musician, whenever you change your equipment in any field, here you're the same guy but you're producing a different sound. It boosts your ego, or your confidence, rather. And just tenfold. Even when I play the drums. If I had bought a new snare—or not too long ago, bought a timbale—suddenly you're the same guy, but you're playing it and a new sound is coming. All of a sudden, you're doing different stuff. And when Paul told me he had changed the sound of his bass, it clicked for me. That's in part why it sounds so fantastic, is he knows he sounds fantastic. He's trying something else.

And on that song, you also get the real sense of Paul and Richie locking into each other. They do some neat ensemble playing on that, just the way that song is structured, And the other thing about it is how this record was mixed, the stereo picture of where everything is. It's not only so vivid and wide, but it's very clever. And again, with "Hip to Hoo," Robbie Blunt does these stabbing rhythm parts. And if you're sitting there, especially with headphones on, or you've got a good set of speakers, the guitar sits in a great place. When you're listening to it, it's in this weird place where you go, "What is that?!"

It's just such an inspiring but meticulously thought-out stereo picture.

I know a lot of people love mono or narrow stereo. I'm a guy who loves exploring what stereo means. And this again is an audiophile's dream, this record. Luckily, when it made it to CD, it's been pretty sympathetic and hasn't been too butchered. But that original vinyl grows with whatever system you get. The better your system, the more extraordinary... when you improve your stereo, some records reveal their limitations. *Shaken 'n' Stirred,* like the second Midge Ure album, *Answers to Nothing,* it challenges your stereo to be better. It just gets better and better and more enveloping. So kudos to that production team. And that's why that record doesn't sound dated, because bloody great-sounding music shall never date in my mind.

The other thing about "Hip to Hoo" specifically that I loved, which, again, I urge people not to dismiss this record, is it tells you that Robbie Blunt has evolved. He was such a huge part of those first two records, with a lot of slide guitar and a lot of just heavy guitar. Listen to "Slow Dancer" or listen to "Worse Than Detroit;" this now was a different guy. And I'd heard even back then that Robert and Robbie fought over Jezz, and Robert wanted him to use a Roland guitar synthesizer, pushing Robbie like they pushed Richie. Robert, Jezz and Paul seemed to be the only guys completely comfortable with, "Okay, new tools, new sounds."

You hear musicians complain about this. "Oh, I had to use this" or "They made me do this." But they uncover sounds that you've never heard before. And Robbie's guitar solo on "Hip to Hoo," even when I was a grumpy nineteen-year-old, I thought, "What is that sound he's got on his lead?!" This kind of weird, snaky tone; I couldn't even figure out what that was. It wasn't distortion. It wasn't reverb. And maybe that is a Roland. I don't really know; I'm not schooled in being able to pick out a Roland guitar synthesizer. I thought it was a synthesizer, but it was unlike anything he had done before, that sound. And again, it's the first song. It's Robert saying, "You know what? Everything you think of me, you're not going to get." And how could that not be exciting? And I'm going to put this as the first track on the record. So that excited me.

"Kallalou Kallalou," for me that song is about Richie. Again, it's this guy who's an Iowa guy who is in this southern-sounding band from California. It's not that they weren't, as I said, extremely progressive. But here you get a sense that this guy can do what Phil did but not actually play like Phil, but explore like Phil did. But he sounds like Stewart Copeland, he sounds like Omar Hakim and he sounds like himself. And this is another track that I just think, man, say what you want about Robert—and this has borne itself out—he always has had great drummers. And with John Bonham's passing, that's what he took away. If I'm going to make music, I gotta chase John Bonham. I'll never find John Bonham again, but I'm going to find players that are intensely lyrical, musical, innovative, fearless, and who just can get inside a song. And that was Richie. I love Michael Lee and I loved a lot of the players since. But certainly as I got older, this record made me go back and buy some Little Feat albums to hear that guy outside of this context.

I won't go through every song, but "Trouble Your Money," I encourage people to look at those lyrics: "So when I wake up, every night it's the same/Just lying there staring and confused yet again." Again, maybe Robert has… "All My Love" is a pretty explicit lyric. But to me "Trouble Your Money" was revelatory in terms of his writing as being completely heart on your sleeve. And completely mirroring not just what it is to be a twenty-year-old, but to be a fifty-five-year-old. Because that's all you do as you get older. There's this grand myth that as you get older, and unless you've been very lucky and I wouldn't even say you're wealthy, but you've got let's just say fewer issues, you never ever lose the sense of lying there and staring confused. That's a timeless lyric to me from the pen of a Robert not really known for this. He's known for every inch of my love and mining J.R.R. Tolkien and stuff like that. Here he's as good as anybody. And that's what this record is. You've also heard it in "Ten Years Gone" from *Physical Graffiti*, I think, which is extensively about one of his first great loves. But it's a uniquely confessional record, and you wouldn't think about a Robert Plant record as confessional. That's another reason why I love it. And of course, even if you don't care about that stuff, "Trouble Your Money" has an unbelievable drum part where Richie brings timbales and he sounds like Stewart Copeland. It sounds a bit like the song "Regatta de Blanc," how he uses the rim and all the rest of it. Fantastic.

"Little by Little," I want to mention this. It's a commercial tune. Obviously, it was his biggest hit from this this album. But my God, listen to the bass playing. The bass playing is astounding. It's buoyant, yet it's loping and it's sinewy and it's melodic. And the choices and the places Paul goes, to me it's a defining moment in terms of arrangement and playing on this record. It's a great song. fabulous song, and the bass playing is unlike anything I've heard from Robert. And it reminds me of—and I don't do this as a disservice or out of laziness—but I had "Ramble On" on the other day, and the bass playing on that is so busy without ever being intrusive. It treads the line of being groovy and then busy and groovy and then busy. And this song just takes that to another level.

Just try and follow that bass line. When I was in university, I took a jazz class. I don't remember most of it, but one of the first things Professor Hartwig said was, "If you want to listen to music, you listen to the song. And then what you do is you do your best to figure out what instruments are on that song. And however many instruments are on that song, you listen to the song that many times and each time you put it on, you hone in on one instrument, or one harmony." And that forever changed my life and how I listened to music. And that's what I do; even if a song wasn't really reaching me, I'd say okay, I can hear a distorted guitar or I can hear a harmony part. I'm just gonna listen to that. And then at the end of that process, you put it all together and I guarantee you it changes how you listen to music. And "Little by Little," again, great song but the bass part is the best part.

Robert sings, "Little by little, my heart grieves/Little by little, I call your name/Little by little, my tears fall/Everything changes." Isn't that true? (laughs). I don't know; it's not this bromide. It's profound. Again, I don't necessarily attach Robert to profundity. I attach Gabriel and Dylan and Roger Waters and Springsteen to profundity. Lennon. So to encounter that kind of simple profundity, like "All You Need Is Love," I find that inspiring. But this is a darker statement, although he ends that with, "The air clears/Little by little, I can breathe again." So again, I talked a bit about being young, and how you have no choice even in your darkest moments. Lord willing, little by little you move forward and the air clears.

And the other thing about *Shaken 'n' Stirred*—I'm sorry, I'm just touching on everything because I love this album so much—is there's a Greg Lake album called *Manoeuvres* that came out in '83. It died a death, Chrysalis didn't support it, people didn't like it, it wasn't ELP, it was crap, kind of thing. And I was seventeen and I bought that record and it was revelatory for me because I'd never heard Greg sing so well as I did on that record. And on *Shaken 'n' Stirred* he embraces and uses everything that made him great. But he's just a much more mature singer with respect to his ability to convey emotion and shifts in emotion and shifts in mood. To me he's peaking as a performer, as a singer.

"Easily Lead," again, great vocal, probably in my mind the heaviest tune. Great lead guitar part, with Robbie popping back in to say, "I'm still that guy." But again, that's part of that side two, which I think is the more conventional side, considerably more conventional. And again, I don't use that as a pejorative. It's just another side of Robert's peerless artistry.

And finally there's "Sixes and Sevens," and I don't know if people know this. You know how I was talking about this disillusionment of a day? Well, sixes and sevens I believe is English slang for out of sorts, not knowing, confusion. I looked it up once. Knowing that in that Englishman kind of way, he's borrowing from something that I would have to work at as a Canadian, to understand what that means, again, I love that kind of stuff. And that's been in his approach. He doesn't necessarily explicitly tell you what the title means, always.

As well, this song might have the most beautifully recorded buzz roll I think I've ever heard. In the mid part of the song, Richie just lays out this roll, which lasts about three-quarters of a second. I talk about the bass part in "Little by Little" not just being about playing and arrangement, but how it was recorded, what instrument was being used. That moment in "Sixes and Sevens," the way Richie turns the snare drum into something that is liquefied to me, it's absolutely... the jaw drops. And if you don't listen carefully, it goes right by you, which is a shame, because that's a player. That is a bloody player!

And again, it's ostensibly a new wave record, a pop record, but with "Sixes and Sevens," Robert leaves you with the closest thing I think you get to the blues, though it's not blues in my mind. "So here I am making changes/Alterations to my house cards/I don't hold new arrangements/Am I at home? Am I at home? Am I all right?" He leaves you not only with a state of musical heaviness, but emotional heaviness—and a plea.

It's like a plea for support, and maybe supporting his head and maybe those around him, doesn't matter. It's something that is universal. You always need a hand, you always need a hug. You always need to not be alone, unless you want to be. For a record that to some was called disposable or slick or artificial, he plenty well lays it out. And again, it's that duality. It's light and it's heavy. It's slick but it's authentic. It's a myriad of colours. You can't escape the fact that there's a lot of greys and blacks that you may not see on the album cover. But it's all over the record if you listen to it, even though it's work.

But "Sixes and Sevens" is blues only by virtue of you can feel it. Even it balks at convention. It's not "I'm Gonna Crawl" and it's not "Tea for One" and it's not "Since I've Been Loving You." It's something else; Robbie isn't doing a long, extended slide solo. There's weird sounds. It sounds like Jezz playing some sort of Fairlight or a Jupiter. I don't know; I'm not a keyboard guy. But he's choosing to convey this moment of imbalance and melancholia in a way that turns his back on what he used to do.

So anyway, to sum up (laughs), I don't know if I can sum this record up. Because to me, there's so much to *Shaken 'n' Stirred*. It's a beautifully-produced, melodic album with a singer at the height of his game and with a lyricist baring his heart in a way that I hadn't heard him do before, through a whole album. It's an album that swings ferociously through emotions. It's ballsy, because yeah, he's got Toni Halliday and he lets his keyboard player full-on embrace technology, but it's never in a way that feels cloying or feels like a cash-in to me.

Again, the ultimate cash-in was he chucked this album. I don't remember how much he did on the *Now and Zen* tour of this record beyond "Little by Little." I think he also played "Pink and Black." But it became one of those records like Wings' *Back to the Egg* or Pink Floyd's *The Final Cut* or Richard and Linda Thompson's *First Light*. There's always records in people's catalogues that are consigned to the dustbin when really they never should have been. If you were born in 1950 and you were twenty when you bought Led Zeppelin *III*, *Shaken 'n' Stirred* may seem alien to you. But I landed with Robert on *Pictures at Eleven*. I landed through the lens of *Duke* and *Wind and Wuthering*. And I landed with Yes on *90125*. I'm arriving with no baggage. And I always challenge people, especially older guys I meet at music shows or through the work I do, and they have an aura of "I like the old stuff." And I pity that because we've all got to change.

"Everything changes," as Robert says. You can either go, "I'm not going to change. I just want what I want" or you can go, "No, I'll take this journey." Actually I'll end with that thought. I don't understand people who cherry-pick records, because it's never been my thing. I either love a writer or I don't. And when you're a Beatles fan, that's what you learn. Immediately. You love the artist. And no, you're not going to love every song, because that's nigh on impossible. Although there isn't a Beatles song I don't love. But for the most part I don't get it. And obviously being a Genesis fan and weathering the abuse thrown at the latter albums, or being a fan of

The Who post-Moon, weathering these ridiculous arguments of it's not the same anymore. That's the point. That's the point! You listen to *It's Hard* or *Face Dances* and lyrically, Pete goes to places that are completely connected with what he was always doing, completely exploring these things from a different point of view. There's been death, there's been change. You listen to *Shaken 'n' Stirred* the same way. A lot happened from 1977 when his son died to 1984 when he was putting this record together for an '85 release. So much changed. And if you love the guy as an artist, wow, is that not a huge amount of psychic energy to transmute into art? That is a gift to us. And that's what *Shaken 'n' Stirred* is to me. It's a bloody gift.

ESPARANZA
A1 90863
CRC
CR
SIDE TWO
℗ 1988
Atlantic Records
ROBERT PLANT
NOW AND ZEN
1. HELEN OF TROY (5:03)
2. BILLY'S REVENGE (3:33)
3. SHIP OF FOOLS (4:59)
4. WHY (4:12)
5. WHITE, CLEAN AND NEAT (5:28)
All songs written by Plant - Johnstone except "Why"
written by Plant - Crash. All songs published by Talktime
/Virgin Music, ASCAP except "Why" published by Talktime/
Virgin Music, ASCAP/Blue Maxx Music, BMI.
ST-ES-876702

RT PLANT
NOW AND ZEN
ロバート・プラント
ナウ・アンド・ゼン

ROBERT PLANT
NON-STOP GO TOUR '88
ON SALE SATURDAY
PLUS SPECIAL GUEST
CHEAP TRICK
FRI., JULY 29 · 8:00 PM
RESERVED SEATS $20.00/$18.50
TICKETS ON SALE SATURDAY, JUNE 25 AT
THE MADISON SQUARE GARDEN BOX OFFICE.
TICKETMASTER AND TICKETMASTER CHARGE
(201) 507-8900 · (212) 307-7171 · (516) 888-9000
PRODUCED BY JOHN SCHER
MADISON SQUARE GARDEN INFORMATION: (212) 563-8300
madison square garden
A Gulf+Western Company

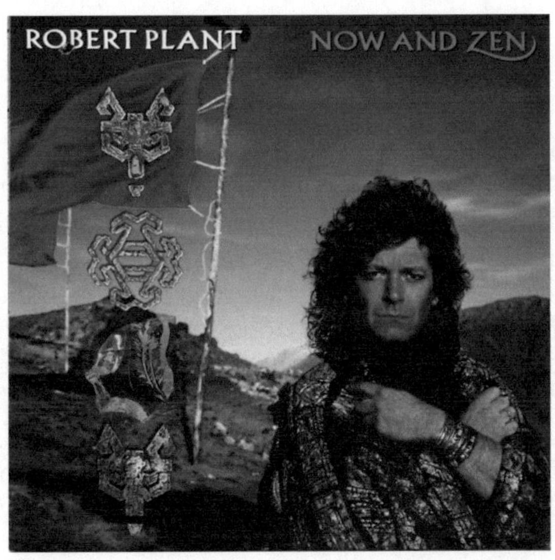

Now and Zen

"I have to tread very carefully here, and yet again, I shall brandish and I shall skirmish. The great thing about the game that we play, is that it has broken into shards and crystals, really. So what was the classification so many years ago of what you could actually hang your hat on as mainstream rock, has kind of gravitated and spiralled into all sorts of small filigrees. And I think that's probably a good thing. Once upon a time rock had turned into a really turgid soup of reinventing itself over and over again by repetition. So I don't think it makes any difference one way or another. I think a song is a song, and first of all comes a song, second of all comes the way it's promoted. And mainstream rock acts, I think everybody just bundles along, and there's a lot of other things to think about these days. Representation by video may be a fantastic thing. But where you place it and what happens to it and how it gets streamed and all that thing is in the lap of the gods, and maybe artists in the end just take a backseat and let it roll."

Robert Plant

Credits

February 29, 1988
Es Paranza/Atlantic 90863
Produced by Tim Palmer, Robert Plant and Phil Johnstone
Engineered by Rob Bozas, Martin Russell, Dave Barrett, Michael Gregovich, Tim Burrell and Jonathan Dee
Recorded at Swanyard Studios and Marcus Studios, London, UK
Personnel: Robert Plant – vocals, Doug Boyle – guitars, Phil Johnstone – keyboards, Phil Scragg – bass, Chris Blackwell – drums and percussion
Key additional personnel: Jimmy Page – guitar solo on "Heaven Knows" and "Tall Cool One," Marie Pierre, Kirsty MacColl, Toni Halliday – backing vocals

Side 1
1. "Heaven Knows" (Johnstone, Barrett) 4:02
2. "Dance on My Own" (Plant, Johnstone, Crash) 4:31
3. "Tall Cool One" (Plant, Johnstone) 4:40
4. "The Way I Feel" (Plant, Johnstone, Boyle)

Side 2
1. "Helen of Troy" (Plant, Johnstone) 5:03
2. "Billy's Revenge" (Plant, Johnstone) 3:33
3. "Ship of Fools" (Plant, Johnstone) 4:59
4. "Why" (Plant, Crash) 4:12
5. "White, Clean and Neat" (Plant, Johnstone) 5:28

A *Now and Zen* Timeline

November – December 1987. Robert Plant and his band record tracks slated for Plant's fourth solo album.

November 30, 1987 – April 17, 1988. Robert and his band embark on the UK leg of his Non Stop Go Tour, in support of the forthcoming (and eventually arriving mid-tour) *Now and Zen* album. UK progressive rockers It Bites support Robert during the latter stages; that band's Francis Dunnery will be one of a few guitarists on 1993's *Fate of Nations* album.

January 18, 1988. "Heaven Knows" is issued as an advance single from Robert's forthcoming fourth album. It is backed with the CD edition bonus track, "Walking Towards Paradise." "Heaven Knows" reaches the top spot on the *Billboard* Album Rock Tracks chart and No.33 on the UK charts.

February 29, 1988. Es Paranza issues a fourth Robert Plant album, entitled *Now and Zen*. Initial LP and CD copies of the album came with a small red flag in tribute to Robert's beloved Wolverhampton Wanderers football club.

April 1988. Issued as the second single from *Now and Zen* is "Tall Cool One," backed with "White, Clean and Neat." It reaches top spot on the *Billboard* Mainstream Rock chart and No.25 on the main grid but stalls at No.87 in the UK.

April 19, 1988. *Now and Zen* is certified gold in the US, followed by a platinum designation on May 9th. The album reaches No.10 in the UK, No.4 in Canada and No.6 in the US en route to eventual triple-platinum status, far and away Robert's biggest commercial success as a solo artist.

May 5 – December 31, 1988. Robert takes his Non Stop Go tour to North America, beginning with a series of Canadian dates.

May 14, 1988. A party is thrown for the 40th anniversary of Atlantic Records. Robert and his band perform "Heaven Knows," "Ship of Fools" and "Tall Cool One" as one small part of the nearly 13-hour long concert.

May 30, 1988. Atlantic issues a Robert Plant video package called *Mumbo Jumbo*, which certifies gold in the video category.

June 19, 1988. Jimmy Page issues a solo album called *Outrider*. Robert co-writes a song with Jimmy called "The Only One" and he also sings on it; recall that Jimmy contributed two guitar solos on Robert's album from earlier in the year.

August 1988. "Ship of Fools" is issued as the last single from *Now and Zen*, backed with "Billy's Revenge" in the US and "Helen of Troy" in the UK. It stalls at No.84 on the *Billboard* Hot 200 and at No.76 in the UK, while reaching No.3 on the Mainstream Rock chart. Like "Little by Little," "Ship of Fools" features in an episode of hit cop show *Miami Vice*, in fact the series' two-hour finale.

Martin talks to Reed Little, Douglas Maher and Pontus Norshammar about *Now and Zen*.

Martin Popoff: How does Robert's experience with *Shaken 'n' Stirred* shape what he does with *Now and Zen*? Or does it?

Douglas Maher: Well, *Shaken 'n' Stirred*, all things considered, bombed; it was a complete bomb. Or let's just say it's not what the label wanted, and at the end of it, it's not what Plant wanted either. And in retrospect, you find that Robert Plant disparages his own work anyways, whereas you tend to find artists that have a personal favourite time of theirs and everything else. I know you know, Martin, because I've read a lot of your work and we've had a lot of conversations, that artists have a struggle within them to embrace what they did in the 1980s for some reason. And I always hear this, that they feel they should have been heavier, this sounds outdated, I should remix that album one day. But these are time capsules that capture that moment. And *Now and Zen* was a mammoth record. Huge. Triple-platinum. And I suspect it's even higher. A lot of labels, especially after you leave them, they're not big fans of going back and doing an audit. That's why you see a lot of albums that just sit at one particular certification level for like 30 years.

Anyway, the thing that I love about this period, Plant was into The Cure at this point. He was listening to R.E.M. and Hüsker Dü and Depeche Mode. The Fixx and Pat Benatar were influences on this record. It's like, what?! The Bangles, The DBs, Faith No More, the early Faith No More pre-Mike Patton. He bottled up all of these things that he was listening to and brought in a power-pop synth-rock sound that you never expected coming from Robert Plant.

I'll use this analogy a little bit when I'm describing this record. But this was Robert Plant being Robert Palmer. It had a lot of crossover, and they had albums out at the same time. *Heavy Nova* came out a few months later; that was more of a mid-summer release. But Plant liked a lot of artists that you would not expect. And I love using this reference point. I know that you can have an appreciation for this with your studies of where rock was at this point. This was Poison territory, Whitesnake territory, Bon Jovi territory. But I'll be damned if I didn't think that there wasn't somebody holding a copy of *Big Generator* or *Hold Your Fire*, whether it was somebody in that new band of his or an engineer or somebody.

Because they captured the sound of that time versus going through the blasting guitars, which Plant despised at that time. Plant openly hated the spandex movement. He had no respect for it. He thought they were all clones of each other and of Zeppelin. And I don't know if people in general recognise this fact. But Plant never sniped more at David Coverdale than he did between this time and *Fate of Nations*. In that window, it was a constant. Any time that you would see him do interviews on radio or MTV or on *Rockline*, he got a dig in on Coverdale.

Because the comparisons were just so blatant on what was happening, which, I don't know if that's fair. Because David Coverdale had been around forever at that point as well and he has a voice of his own. Yes, he was very Plant-influenced, and I understand Plant taking exception with it because Coverdale was getting way bigger success and notoriety at that point, especially with the 1987 *Whitesnake* record. That generation wasn't looking at it and going, "That guy's just ripping off Robert Plant" or whatever. No, they were like, "Oh, he's the new rock god. He's that frontman." And then you had Kingdom Come that came out and got crucified, and Robert Plant was right there, going after Lenny Wolf. So Plant was at a stage where he didn't like any of what was going on.

Martin: And Reed, what is your take on what Robert Plant is proposing in 1988?

Reed Little: First off, I've mentioned on some *Contrarians* shows that I was not a Led Zeppelin fan when I was a young man. I know it's weird with my age and my musical preferences, but I just didn't know anybody who listened to Zeppelin. By the eighties I was living in a small town in Montana that had no rock radio station. So we only got music from MTV. For me, Robert Plant as a solo artist is the first Robert Plant I ever heard, and that would have been "Big Log" and "In the Mood" with "I'm in the mood for a melody" and all that.

So I'm not bringing Zeppelin baggage with me, which is particularly interesting for this album. And I remember when this album came out in 1988, you could not escape it. It was everywhere. "Tall Cool One" was everywhere. It was on the radio. If you'd walk by the student dorms, kids were playing it in the dorms. You heard it coming out of people's cars. And I remember pundits like Kurt Loder on MTV talking about how this album was a return to form for Robert Plant, how people were comparing it to Zeppelin combined with some other bands, one being The Cars.

And I think all of that is total crap. Even though there is sampling of Led Zeppelin material in the song "Tall Cool One," this album has nothing to do with Led Zeppelin. In fact, to me it's a sad example of generic corporate rock. You recently did a show on *Sea of Tranquility*, talking about what makes music dated, and for me, exhibit No.1 on how technology dates music is *Now and Zen*. Even Robert Plant acknowledged that. I think his exact quote was that "Some of the songs got drowned in the technology of the time," which is absolutely true. But even without that, there's no Led Zeppelin in the songwriting on this. It just sounds like Robert Palmer in the 1980s, especially within what I think of as the *Miami Vice* years, which is '84 to '89. It had this sound that every artist used. Phil Collins, INXS, Peter, Gabriel, Toto, Asia… all of these guys used the exact same gated drum sound that Phil Collins and Hugh Padgham accidentally created on Phil's solo album. They used the same keyboard sounds, the same guitar sounds, the same styling of reverb on the vocals.

Now, the performances are great. The band is great. After three solo albums, Robert has ditched his previous backing band. He's got all brand-new musicians, and they produce an extremely and to me overly contemporary album that will always sound exactly like what it is. But if you told me this album came out in '84 or '86 instead of 1988, I would absolutely believe that because that whole time period is functionally interchangeable.

Martin: One thing he's not doing is participating in the hair metal space.

Reed: No, and obviously, I don't know what Mr. Plant thinks, but I would have to say that he simply embodies some general image of an aristocratic rock star to the point where I doubt it was too much of a conscious decision. He's been disdainful of heavy metal from all the way back in the seventies. He did not want Led Zeppelin thought of as a heavy metal band. He clearly never saw himself as a heavy metal singer. Despite the influence of Led Zeppelin on so many of the hair bands that were ascendant in 1988, I think it would have been fairly easy for him just to do his natural thing and avoid that. And the musicians on this album, they didn't come from other bands but they're all fantastic musicians. I can't say a bad word about the playing on the album. But what they created together is just… if you took off Robert Plant's vocal, you could put on Tina Turner or David Bowie and get the same album basically.

Pontus Norshammar: To understand what Robert's doing, I compare him to Paul McCartney in a sense. Paul McCartney came from this enormous band, The Beatles, and he could do anything after that. But the breakup of The Beatles and his rift with Lennon left him in a bit of a funk; he didn't know what to do. I think he was quite depressed. And he tried for many years different kinds of music to find his own feet, and then he finally achieved that with *Band on the Run*.

I think Robert Plant is the same. If we look at him, he has two traumas beginning in 1977. He loses his son and Led Zeppelin ends in the most tragic way that you can possibly end a band, with someone dying. The trauma from both events must have been dire, including the band situation, since Bonham was also his teenage friend. So I think he wanted to get away from it. He was the one who went through the out door.

So, after searching across the first three albums, we get to *Now and Zen*, and it's both strange and a very typical 1988 record. It's almost like a Bryan Adams album without the clout, without the heaviness. It's very radio-friendly, and built for these new mainstream rock charts or album charts. I've looked at those, Martin, just for fun, and those charts never rocked anyway. *Now and Zen* is actually very much a keyboard record. You have Page on "Tall Cool One" and he's not there. He's just doing a solo and it's a piano-based rocker. And you have female vocalists all over the record. You have very much an eighties production and it sold well. He was at No.10 in US and No.10 in the UK. You and Pete Pardo did a show once on albums that are front-loaded, and I must say this record is back-loaded for me. I think side two is better than side one.

Martin: What do you think of the album cover?

Reed: This is going to sound weird, but it reminds me of *Ace of Spades* by Motörhead, which in turn reminds me of *El Loco* by ZZ Top. It's part and parcel of the video shoot they did in Morocco. And you've got the flag there with the symbol of his favourite soccer team on it. It's actually pretty eye-catching. I don't have any problems with it. It features clearly the album's draw. You've got Robert Plant on it and I must say he's looking fabulous at forty.

Douglas: As the album cover went, Robert hated his picture on it. He wasn't a fan of it. He thought that it was too dark on the colouring on his face, and he wanted it to be more positive and uplifting. And he had originally smiled. He had gotten to the point where even with Zeppelin's history with Atlantic, there was always this war that was going on with these legacy artists.

Martin: Okay, past the wrapper, the first thing we hear is "Heaven Knows," this icy, austere, mysterious ballad. What are your thoughts on this one?

Reed: Okay, so first, I think it's weird that Plant starts with a song on which he doesn't have a songwriting credit, and then releases it as the first single. It's written by keyboard player and co-producer Phil Johnstone, and David Barratt, a composer for TV-type of guy. So immediately, with the opening of the song, that very first drum roll, we are setting this album in the *Miami Vice* years—it's just stuck there like a fly in amber. Now, there's nothing inherently wrong with that. Everybody in 1988 loved that. But you listen to it now and instantly you know the era it came out and it will always sound like that. You've got your gated drums, you've got keyboards as the most prominent instrument, again, very common in mainstream rock.

The pundits at the time called this a hard rock record. This is not a hard rock record. This is just a straight-up mainstream, album-oriented rock record. You've got choirs of backup singers, very common at the time. There is guitar but it's melodic and the keyboards are the most prominent instrument, and not unusual in a song written by a keyboardist. What I find really fascinating is you get to the guitar solo, and it's got a wonderful guitar solo. And then it turns out that solo was played by Jimmy Page. It's the least Jimmy Page-sounding guitar solo I can think of. It sounds exactly like Dan Huff or Steve Lukather or any of the other hot LA session players. Doesn't sound anything like Led Zeppelin.

But just the fact that Page played on it I think caused people—I don't know if they were just reading the liner notes instead of listening to the music—to say, oh, it's a return to Zeppelin form which it absolutely is not. It's got a weird lyric about a vacuous partner, probably part of Plant's LA experience where he met all of these body-obsessed people out in Hollywood? I think it's pretty slight. In fact, I think the lyrics on most of the album are pretty throwaway. It has the one famed couplet. "You were pumping iron while I was pumping irony," which is interesting. But it makes no sense whatsoever if you think about it for just two seconds. It's a perfectly serviceable song; it sounds fine. But it's no better than that.

Weirdly, it reached No.1 on the Album Rock chart—there are so many charts.

Douglas: So you have Johnstone and David Barratt, who was producing Mervish musicals in the UK at the time. Again, it's so weird how people find each other. Again, Plant heard that song. That's where "Heaven Knows" came from, a publishing house song that was presented to him, which blows my mind. So musically, Barratt and Johnstone, they work together on that, and that was one of those publishing house songs that was presented to Plant and he's like, "Gotta meet these guys." He couldn't get it out of his head. It was just one of those songs that he's like, "I've got to do something with this guy," especially Johnstone.

The video for "Heaven Knows" was filmed in Morocco. A whole bunch of money was spent there using the true locals. I remember watching a making-of-it mini-documentary. And it was in the mountains, where he had penned the lyrics to "Achilles Last Stand," where they shot the video, and it might have been about 40 or 50 miles away from where he wrote "Kashmir" as well, the same location. And the locals and what have you were actually schooling him on where he was filming and the complexity of the different tribes and things like that. That's what you see in the video. You had the modern Muslim Arabic movement, and you had this more archaic form, if you will, that had dated back hundreds and thousands of years and all throughout that region.

Anyway, with "Heaven Knows," when you first heard it, and you had been listening to "Little by Little" and "In the Mood" and "Big Log," and then you had The Honeydrippers mixed in, with "Rockin' at Midnight" and "Sea of Love." Plant was all over the place. So what winds up happening here is that eighties adult contemporary rock starts developing before your eyes, and "Heaven Knows" is a song that captures that mood perfectly. And Plant even said—which I think is just unbelievable to me when you write a song—that the lyrics don't mean anything. It was him riffing. And when you start digging deeper into it, you're like, it's just random thoughts put to a great tune, which is what he wanted to begin with. He just wanted the song. There's my proof, once again, showing that it doesn't matter what the song's about. So anyway, that's kind of how we arrive with "Heaven Knows." And that song is still a staple to this day, while it managed to do well in an era that was very, very difficult for artists that were starting to get boxed in, if you were REO Speedwagon or

Boston or what have you. Your airplay was diminishing on MTV and radio. Robert Plant was a guy who started appearing in 1969 and all of a sudden, he's hanging with the big guys on the charts and in regular rotation in 1988. So "Heaven Knows" is important. That song was able to hang with Ratt and Cinderella and all those guys who were going platinum, seemingly without breaking a sweat.

Pontus: And on the topic of Jimmy playing on "Heaven Knows," I don't know if he really wanted Jimmy Page on this record, or the record company, which was Atlantic, albeit with his own imprint said, "Oh, it's a good idea if you have him here." Because if you listen to those songs, Jimmy is very, very pushed to the side. On "Heaven Knows," he's on the right channel, far to the right channel, and on the other one, "Tall Cool One," he's on the left channel, the opposite, while on the next track, Doug Boyle is right, left and centre. He's more prominent. So there's a feeling I get that, "I have to do this because someone wants me to do this. But I'm not sure whether I want to do it."

Martin: With a little pull-back on the production, I could envision "Dance on My Own" on *The Principle of Moments* or *Pictures at Eleven*.

Douglas: Sure, and "Dance on My Own" is my favourite song on the record, easily. That song made it to No.13 on the *Billboard* AOR charts. It was really, really popular where I lived, in the Miami, the Fort Lauderdale market. It became a very accessible pop rock song that had this phaser guitar mixed with this fusion guitar that was kind of thrown in there to offset it from being a pure pop song. And again, Johnstone is just killing it on keyboards. The song is catchy as hell with that chorus. That became the first time I think that Plant found a way to cross over into that radio situation, in a positive and creative way. You had your Zeppelin fans who are still calling up, they still want to hear "Dazed and Confused" and "Stairway to Heaven" and everything else. And then you've got the man who's responsible for those songs doing this synth-pop/rock/dance music fusion mix of a song. It's a 1988 of-the-time-type song that you always caught yourself dancing to or humming or whistling to—and of course the song actually begins off with whistling. It had that earwig thing that went in there.

So underrated and under-discussed, especially for a song that charted so well. If it had a video, it absolutely would have been a way bigger hit, in my opinion. But the interesting thing is that Plant opted to leave it alone. Atlantic put it out in late June to make it a summer song. And it was rising into the Top 10 come mid-August. But with no video support, like there was for "Ship of Fools" and "Tall Cool One" and "Heaven Knows," it died. It's a real shame, in my opinion, because Atlantic knew he was touring into December at that point with no new video.

It's analogous to what happened to Rush. Without more videos back then being fed into what were two different video channels playing everywhere, you're slitting your own throat you are killing your own record. You are killing the visibility of it. MTV had literally hundreds of videos that were coming at them every week and every month that they could choose from. And Atlantic had such a relationship with MTV, successfully pushing bands like Winger and White Lion. And Robert Plant is this guy from 1969 who's having radio hits and is hanging on the radio charts with these new guys. It was just unbelievable. And "Walking Towards Paradise" and "The Way I Feel" were thrown out there in late fall with no videos either.

Martin: But not as official singles, right?

Douglas: Well, they were released as singles to radio and they did chart. They only stayed out there maybe five or six weeks. You can probably reference that to *Billboard* and *Album Network* and those things at that time. And I remember because I had seen this tour. Chris Blackwell had broken his arm. That's when Pat Torpey came in. This is just a year before Mr. Big. The tour started and they were one show in and the drummer broke his arm. Pat Torpey had been recommended to come in and he played the majority of the tour there. He had to learn the entire setlist in four days. I'll never forget that. That was remarkable to think that somebody could accomplish that.

Reed: Whistling is a strange way to open a rock track. But this time we get a lot more prominence with respect to guitars. Keyboard is still the primary instrument, and for most of this album, that's going to be true. I hear at least four distinct keyboard sounds in this song, and two individual lead guitar sounds. And for a song produced now, that's pretty weird. But in the eighties, that was just how production was done. Once again, we get really sparse, pointless lyrics. The narrator sees a beautiful woman who drives him crazy, but he's content dancing on his own. Is that a masturbation reference? Maybe, but if so, that's a pretty strange thing for the forty-year-old Robert Plant to be singing about, right?

Pontus: I consider "Dance on My Own" to be an eighties synth-pop proposal that just disappears. Don Henley pop, perhaps, although the guitars are more present. Those eighties Duran Duran clean guitars... if you've heard "A View to a Kill," you know what I mean. There was this clean sound back then that is quite forgettable.

Martin: Next we have smash hit "Tall Cool One." I'm feeling a Billy Idol vibe with this one, along with a vague blues structure, given the call-and-response and the vocal melody.

Reed: In structure, yes, but it's so non-blues in the delivery. I think that's just Robert's comfort zone in terms of writing and arrangement. But it doesn't sound anything like a blues. The lyric is not a blues. Let me get this out of the way—I hate this song. I do not understand why this song is so popular. This song is the pinnacle of commercial success for Robert Plant, and I absolutely hate that. But it charted higher than any other single Plant song ever put out on the mainstream Hot 100. So not the Rock chart; he was at the top of the Rock chart many times. But this song charted higher than any other song within the mainstream, on the Hot 100. Like I said it was everywhere in 1988. You just couldn't get away from it. And I guess it's catchy, is the best thing I can say about it. It's danceable. The little guitar stabs that kind of pass for riffing are very memorable.

The arrangement reminds me of a catchy Thomas Dolby or Devo tune. You've got alternating instruments going back and forth. The lyric is possibly the worst lyric that Robert Plant ever wrote. It's so juvenile. In the back third, you get those inserted pieces of Led Zeppelin songs which at this point, sounds desperate to me. Like, there's no reason for those to be in the song. But that's what everybody remembers about the song, that and the fingers-snapping. Finger-snapping sticks in people's heads. And it was the kind of thing you could not even make fun of in 1988, because all of the things that I find ridiculous are exactly what people love this song for. This song drove three-and-a-half million album sales for Robert Plant, making *Now and Zen* his best-selling album. I don't understand any of that. Figuring out mainstream music appeal is not my background. Good grief.

Douglas: "Tall Cool" one was the first rock song I could think of where they used samples from another song in it. Rush actually did it, with "Cygnus X-1," but other than that, I had never heard samples of other songs being used in a new song, being mixed in like a rap DJ would, scratching it in there. What a hit. What a monster hit. This song was so popular.

There was a show called *Club MTV*. It was like an *American Bandstand* rip-off. As time went on, it became more hip-hop-oriented and pop and dance and everything else. If you ever get the time—a friend of mine uploaded this a few years ago—go watch that on YouTube—"Tall Cool One" on *Club MTV*. Okay, you have six minutes of people dancing to "Tall Cool One," which is very repetitive. "Lighten up, baby, I'm in love with you" probably gets said 150 times. But it's so catchy.

And again, you have another crossover moment that is going on here. Plant does the unthinkable, which you never saw coming in a million years. The song gets so big that Coca-Cola launches a huge campaign around the song. I remember thinking, I'd never heard of Led Zeppelin doing commercials. Like, that wasn't necessary, for a band that sold over 100 million records. So seeing Robert Plant being tossed a Coca-Cola Classic by girls on the stage and things like that, you're like, is this really happening now?! But they were hijacking artists to do that. Robert Palmer did it with "Simply Irresistible," for Pepsi. Van Halen did it for Nissan with "You Really Got Me" and did it for Crystal Pepsi as well with "Right Now." So it was really fascinating to see that turn of events.

The interplay at the end just blows me away; it works so well. It samples "Black Dog," "Dazed and Confused," "Whole Lotta Love," "The Ocean" and "Custard Pie." And of course there's lyrical nods to "When the Levee Breaks," and "Black Dog," with that iconic "Hey, hey, mama." The first time you heard it, you knew it was gonna be a massive hit; you just knew it. It hit No.25 on the Hot 100 and was a No.1 AOR hit. Radio programmers were flipping over this song. There was Jimmy Page as guest star, plus the catchiness of "Lighten up, baby, I'm in love with you" was something that Plant and Johnstone worked hard on.

The video was groundbreaking; they threw the kitchen sink at it and it worked. Plant was playing the part of this modern-day Elvis Presley. I don't think Robert ever left that love of fifties music behind. He somehow found a way to put rockabilly into these songs in the 1980s and make it seem modern and cool and fresh. Why? Because he's Robert Plant. He can do that. It was like Elvis Presley meets Freddie Mercury on "Crazy Little Thing Called Love" meets Robert Palmer meets "Radio Gaga" on the video.

As a trivia note, The Fabulous Wailers were a Northwest band who did a lot of instrumental fifties-type stuff, like "Wipe Out," that kind of thing. Well, they had a hit song called "Tall Cool One." So again, there's Robert and the 1950s and you find it in every record. He just wants to be that cool hip cat.

Pontus: When it comes to "Tall Cool One," the thing is, my introduction to Robert Plant solo was the Knebworth live album from 1990. So it was a celebration of Silver Clef Foundation. It has everyone on it, including Tears for Fears, Genesis and Pink Floyd. Robert Plant was on it and they played "Tall Cool One," "Hurting Kind" and "Liars Dance" and they played "Wearing and Tearing" with Jimmy Page. That was my introduction. And of course those tracks rock better. But if you look at "Tall Cool One," you also have the problem with the samples in the end, which, to me, just shows what we are missing, really. It appears that was an answer to Beastie Boys, who had just sampled some Led Zeppelin without asking. That's quite ironic. How many times were they accused of a different kind of sampling? Roll over Willie Dixon and tell Jake Holmes the news, right?

Martin: Next is "The Way I Feel." Here's another one where Phil Johnstone is playing like Jezz Woordroffe. With more of an analogue drum track, I could imagine this being on the first album.

Douglas: As I alluded to, "The Way I Feel" was a late radio single, and no video, sadly. This is my own Rush bias, but if you've read the lyrics, it looks a lot like "Twilight Zone." It's like a follow-up to the journey he was on back at "Big Log." There's a fantastic drum intro by Chris Blackwell. I don't know, the song evokes the jazzy pop VH1-like fusion that was going on at that time.

Reed: I consider this one pretty generic. I feel bad kind of dismissing these songs as generic because they're so professionally appointed, so well-performed. But there's no identity to them. That said, I do love the guitar solos. One thing, by the time we get to the end of *Manic Nirvana*, the next album, I have learned to love Doug Boyle as a guitar player. And he turns in two fantastic solos here, with these great staccato, arpeggiated lines. But they're in the service of a generic song, and they've got a generic tone.

And I also like the chorus. There's a fabulous melody and Plant's voice is amazing, as it is on the entire album. I didn't mention that on the first three songs because you can just kind of take that as a given. He's such a great singer, even when he's singing pure tripe. But there's some substance here. Plant's now forty, he's hitting middle age, and the lyrics are looking back and forward. When he talks about partying and maybe taking it "a touch too far," that's looking back. And then he talks about the stranger riding in the car with him and not recognising the man in the mirror. That's looking forward. And those are the types of lyrics you only get from a middle-aged guy, right? You're at that midpoint of your life and looking in both directions. And then add to that the fact that he's driving the whole time, and you've got this added sense of motion and time passing.

Pontus: I hear "The Way I Feel" and think, the eighties were remarkable for these types of songs. There's the clear, U2 guitars, with more focus on Boyle here. The guitar solo is good. That was what I meant when you listen to "Tall Cool One," where you realise there's more guitar on the tracks that don't feature Jimmy Page. Doug Boyle does a great job on this record as does Phil Johnstone. As for this bassist, Phil Scragg, I can't say much because the bass isn't prominent. But Johnstone is the musical director and did that for many years. And if we look at the next one, *Manic Nirvana*, in my opinion, it's a better album and it's basically the same people.

Martin: Over to side two of the original vinyl, and we've got a busier track, "Helen of Troy," which to me sounds herky-jerky, a good fit for *Shaken 'n' Stirred*.

Douglas: Although it smooths out for the chorus, which to me sounds right out of the Alex Lifeson school of chord progressions, with a sprinkle of blues in there. Something tells me that the band was really in tune with their contemporaries, and Plant was right there with them, being inspired by the same things, not so much British synth-pop, but more like British styles of playing and British production techniques.

The title refers to the Greek goddess, the most beautiful woman on the planet to Zeus and Leda. Here's the interesting thing. So Zeus and Leda, if you go back into Greek mythology, Leda was a Spartan queen. If you take off the "a," you get Led. And her representation, any time you look at Renaissance art, you see her and a swan—Swan Song. So Plant is always referencing his past. In fact Johnstone had told him, at that point, to stop trying to run from his past and embrace his accomplishments, while creating something for the future. There's no shame in providing connections to the past.

Reed: I'd say "Helen of Troy" is the hardest-rocking track on the album so far. We have a genuine guitar riff at the beginning, which is exciting. And then the keyboards come in and we're back in *Miami Vice* territory. We have slide guitar, which provides some sonic interest, mixing things up a little bit. Once again, I love Plant's voice and his vocal melody, but the lyrics are weak. So great singing, great performances, but it's a throwaway song. It's only "Tall Cool One" that irritates me, and everything else is fine. But it doesn't stick with me.

Pontus: The first half of the album is keyboard-heavy but on the second half, the guitars pull ahead. They're especially lively on "Helen of Troy," as is the drum performance, which is actually somewhat proggy, and even a bit like Richie Hayward on the last album. So yeah, lively rhythm and good guitar work. It's the first major rocker, in a way. Much of the album is programmed drums, but here Blackwell lays down a very good beat. But since it gets drenched in all these keyboards, you tend to think there might be some programming as well.

Martin: Crudely speaking, it sounds like to me like the album's about half-and-half, programmed versus a kit. "But "Billy's Revenge" is the real thing, snappy, tasteful, groovy.

Douglas: Yes, Honeydrippers-gone-rock, driving riff—our doo-wop-loving Plant returns with somewhat of an ode to Elvis. Actually, it's a song about two characters that are in a hot love chase named Billy and Jenny. It's like, instead of Tony Banks ghost-writing these songs, Robert called on Brian Setzer from The Stray Cats. There was a zany 1916 short movie called *Billy's Revenge* as well, a silent film, a black-and-white short. And I always wondered if Plant borrowed from that. Because the song itself is zany. The story between the two characters is zany.

Reed: That intro, I know it's swing jazz, but it always struck me as a pseudo-African kind of rhythm, with a choir warming up like they're getting ready to raise the curtain on a performance of *The Lion King*. And then we go into rockabilly, which is totally out of left field, completely unexpected. And that makes it, for me, the most interesting track on the album. It's got minimal keyboards and the rhythm section is swinging like they're The Stray Cats. It's not really my cup of tea, but because it's so different, I love it. And I feel like Plant put a lot more effort into this lyric. It's a story about these lovers who are really into each other, and then they kind of fall out of love and she cheats on him and he's gonna get revenge and they're still very passionate, just not about each other. I guess that's a pretty universal theme. I appreciate all of those ingredients, from the oddball music through to the story.

Pontus: It's a 1950s rocker that actually works fairly well. It's quite tongue-in-cheek. As well, Doug Boyle sounds more like Jimmy Page on that track than Jimmy does on his two cameos.

Martin: Next we have "Ship of Fools," which, to my mind, given the chord changes, sounds like a new version of a Led Zeppelin ballad, epic, dramatic, maybe even a little self-important.

Pontus: Yes, and major track, of course, and a beautiful ballad. And it's really well-balanced—you can hear that they actually provide space and breadth. Crystalline, clean guitars, eighties trappings with respect to keyboard sounds. It has the Phil Collins electronic drum bit but also, plainly, an acoustic kit. Live it was far heavier, and longer, and Robert really vamps on it. Live, they took it to another level. This is one I would like to hear from one of his recent bands or configurations, as more of a folk or American arrangement. I would like to hear it in that context, because it's a well-written song.

Douglas: "Ship of Fools," massive hit, No.3 AOR chart, No.84 on the Hot 100. For him, at that age and what have you, to be on the Hot 100 is very impressive, especially given how it was so pop-filled. The title takes us back to book six of Plato's *Republic.* You can see where Plant is going with these themes; there's always a connection into these deeper thoughts. But unfortunately that allusion doesn't transfer over to the actual lyrics. It's about the journey of life and the uncertainty of change. It's love and loneliness and feeling crazy and lost in the seas of life. In the end he returns to his loving ground instead of being on the turbulent ship and rough seas, the chaos of life.

Reed: "Ship of Fools" is easily my favourite song on this album. It was released as the third single. On the Hot 100—not the Mainstream Rock Tracks chart, but on the Hot 100—it only hit No.84, conclusively proving that rock fans in 1988 had terrible taste. Because this song is so much better than "Tall Cool One." It has Plant's best singing on the album and he sings great on most of the album. We get three full verses and a chorus. Now Plant always uses a lot of repetition, so there's still a lot of repetitive things in the song. But it feels like a full song where even when repetitive, he pulls it off with conviction. I love it unconditionally.

We hear the first appearance of what sounds to me like a piezo electric guitar being played rather than an acoustic, which was something that really started to appear in studios in the eighties. It has this very particular sound that doesn't sound like an acoustic even though it's used for acoustic guitar parts. And it's probably the least *Miami Vice*-sounding track on the album, which is ironic because it's the only song to actually appear in an episode of *Miami Vice*.

Martin: I don't know why, but I love "Why!" It's the most shamelessly new wave thing on the album, or the closest thing to actual synth-pop.

Douglas: I see it as kind of the brother to "Dance on My Own" on this record, but heavier. Still, it's a keyboard song, but soaring and siren-like, due to the guest vocals provided by the late Kirsty MacColl. With my paper goods business on eBay, I have so much Kirsty MacColl. I'm always shocked that there isn't a bigger move on her stuff, knowing the legendary status she has, partly from her sudden death, tragic that it was. To this day, I don't understand how somebody gets away with killing her and only has to pay a $2,000 fine. It's another track that found connection with dance clubs in America at the time. I'm sure up there in Canada, you had no idea that "Why" was being played in dance clubs in America. It's unbelievable. The entire record has a tremendous commercial potential. Anyway, "Why" presents a fun side of Plant that sadly vanished over later decades, as he became more political and folk-driven.

Reed: Now, immediately after we hear my favourite song—"Ship of Fools," with original elements and a great electro/acoustic sound—with the very next song we jump right back into that eighties corporate rock thing. "Why" sounds like Bryan Adams meets Debbie Gibson, especially with the female voice on the chorus. Ironically, it has one of the more muscular guitar arrangements on the album, which enhances the Bryan Adams-ness of it. Bryan, for all his vagaries, he actually produced pretty good guitar music back in the eighties.

The lyrics are 80% repetition, and in the 20% that's not repeated, there's not a lot of substance. You've got a lot of Robert singing, "Oh, she wants it bad" and all these other things. Honestly, I just think of those as a vocal tic of Plant's. If you stuck a microphone in front of Plant, all that oohing and aahing would just automatically pop out of his mouth. And this is probably a little off the beaten track, but the song reminds me of rock songs you would hear in Japanese anime shows of the 1980s.

Pontus: I consider "Why" to be the equivalent of Ultravox on a bad hair day.

Martin: Nice (laughs). What do you think his goal is as a personality at this juncture? Is he looking on admiringly upon what Peter Gabriel has accomplished? Or Sting?

Reed: I would be inclined to think it's exactly the opposite. Because he already had garnered respectability from his first two albums, if not the third. People loved those albums. They fawned over them. What they didn't do was move a lot of units. I think he was looking more at David Bowie, who, after years of being a critical darling, Bowie released *Let's Dance* and suddenly he's a megastar. And Plant was maybe thinking, why am I not getting back into these big paycheques? I'm Robert Plant. And so, after the oddball *Shaken 'n' Stirred*, he corrected and put out an album designed to hit all of the commercial beats—and he was clearly successful with that.

Martin: Moving on, "White, Clean and Neat" is both strange and ambitious. I think it adds to a narrative that there's enough interesting music on here to drag the album toward a more respectable place than just the eighties pop world.

Douglas: Yes, sure. "White, Clean and Neat" is basically Plant addressing, in his opinion, the white-washing of music from America as it transferred over to Britain. You hear the samples of like the radio DJ or TV announcer. I'm not sure whether those were actual clips or if that was just studio-produced from that time. But he's mentioning people like Pat Boone, Debbie Reynolds and Eddie Fisher, her husband, and how black music and black radio wasn't getting across the pond over there. So you got Tommy Steele and Frankie Laine, who of course were nothing like Elvis Presley. But it wasn't until Bill Haley and the Delta Blues and what was happening in Nashville, that Nashville sound, when that came to Plant, that changed who he was as a kid and as a teenager, and he never went back.

That was a real statement song. Plant had this, if you will, awareness. He knew that people had often and chronically said that Led Zeppelin owed its career to just nothing but black artists, black blues. And there's 100% truth in that, not that it's a bad thing or wrong thing. Led Zeppelin made unbelievable and legendary rock albums and songs. And I think Zeppelin wound up finding its own sound much later on, without the dependence on early blues. But you definitely hear that on the first two albums.

But he's aware of that criticism. It's almost like a white guilt thing that's taking place in 1988, with Robert Plant becoming woke before that's even a thing thirty years later. He's saying, look, I recognise that there was something else going on in music, and we were being spoon-fed and that everything was white, neat and clean. American life was *The Donna Reed Show*. So this was an oblique nod and an expression of respect for where a lot of these artists were pulling their influences from.

Reed: So this is a very strange song. We're back opening with finger-snapping. I cannot think of any other rock artists that recorded as many finger-snaps as Robert Plant. It's like the Sharks and Jets opening this song. And in fact, this entire song has an almost Hollywood musical kind of feel to it, which is why I bring up the Sharks and Jets. In keeping with the theme, we go past the fifties rockabilly. This is more like forties swing music. It's like the Andrews Sisters, right? Plant is singing about 1954, and that's a little bit before the accepted birth of rock 'n' roll as a popular art form. So we're still pre-rock in his influences. And he's singing about his childhood. He says he's five years old on August 13, 1954, which is true, given his accepted birthday of August 20th. So he's a week before turning six, so this sounds like a specific memory versus something linked to his birthday.

As for the white-washing, this is the *Ozzie and Harriet* version of an America. But it's interesting, the whole "clean, white sheets" bit comes right after he's been singing about his mother soothing away his father's aches and pains at the end of a hard day's labour. Then he says, "touch the boy inside the man." Taken together, is this about your parents' sexual relationship? If it is, that's weird in any context, but for a rock record, that's like doubly weird.

That's an interesting possible sub-narrative here, but there's another one behind the obvious comment on the appropriation of black rock 'n' roll. He might be making a comment about the fashion at the time, the clean, white, below-the-knee skirts. You've got Debbie Reynolds and then Johnny Ray and Pat Boone. Of course rock 'n' roll, from 1954, actually, right up until the sixties, was American. No matter how much the British claim it after the British Invasion, America invented it and then popularised it. But his point was that on both sides of the pond, it was being white-washed.

Also in a general sense, you can see this song being about growing up in England and looking to the USA for entertainment. I've read a book about this, that post-war Britain was so bleak that the US looked like heaven. But it's interesting in that he's saying that the white, clean and neat version was artificial or contrived or engineered, or worse, culturally appropriating. As for the music, as I say, the structure is very old-school or traditional, but the arrangement is drenched in tropes from the mid-eighties. Still, there's some inventive, noisy Doug Boyle guitar in it that's interesting.

Martin: There's a CD bonus track called "Walking Towards Paradise," which I never had until the *Nine Lives* box. 1988 was two years before the forced end of vinyl and I actually bought both this and *Manic Nirvana* on vinyl, without question.

Douglas: Yeah, whereas I was a cassette guy who went into CDs permanently in '88. It was a stupid marketing ploy. That song sounds like it could have been on *Heavy Nova* by Robert Palmer. Again, it was another song he didn't write. He went to another hitmaker. Jerry Lynn Williams wrote it. It was so odd to me that Atlantic was pushing publishing house writers on Robert Plant at this time. He wrote a bunch of hits for Clapton and Bonnie Raitt and Stevie Ray Vaughan.

But just like Phil Collins, Williams got cleaned out in a divorce and he died dead broke. That song went nowhere. It was complete filler. It's surprising that they would go to the extent to spend the money to get that track and do that to it. And it's also surprising that since he was aiming more pop, that they didn't go with a Diane Warren song or something of that nature. They go with a guy who is doing more of a Clapton or Bonnie Raitt thing. Bonnie's *Nine Lives* album from 1986 had a Jerry Lynn Williams song on it and so did *Nick of Time* from 1989.

Reed: With "Walking Towards Paradise," we finish like we started, stuck in those amber *Miami Vice* tones. And it's so interesting that after my disdain for this album, I actually really like this song. I don't know why, because the lyric is forgettable, albeit it's not one of Robert's own. There's more that piezo acoustic sound. I don't even know how to describe this, but there's a weird low-frequency resonance in the guitar, like a low pass filter, something that makes it sound very different sonically than the guitars in the other songs. Although the structure of the song is very much the same, it's still very keyboard-heavy, but there's just enough difference to it that it leaves me feeling positive about the album listening experience. The rest of the songs, I feel like I'm just kind of flipping through them, except for the swing track, "Billy's Revenge," and "Ship of Fools."

Martin: Actually, as a closing comment, we've compared Robert in this era to a lot of different artists, but I want to mention two more: Iggy Pop, circa *Blah-Blah-Blah*, and way in another world, U2 during the "messianic" years of *War* and *The Unforgettable Fire*.

Pontus: He wants to be on the radio. He wants to be an AOR musician. He doesn't want to be the ex-Led Zeppelin singer. He doesn't want to replicate those things. He wants to make an eighties album that is pleasant, that is good, that can really go far with the masses. Or rather, I'm not sure it's exactly where he intended to go, but he went that way, perhaps getting there with compromises. But I think he wanted a hit and the way to get a hit was to sound this way in 1988. In that sense, sure, we're quite close to Iggy Pop at this time.

Martin: I imagine the label did not want another *Shaken 'n' Stirred*.

Pontus: No, and that's why Jimmy Page is here. They wanted him to add some credentials and they wanted material that could get him on the radio. The singles were "Tall Cool One," "Heaven Knows" and "Ship of Fools." He wants to play it safe and all of these do that along with covering three different bases. But if you listen to the tracks live, they are heavier, they're more lively, they're not so compressed and conformed.

But yes, Atlantic is telling him that we want you to have a hit and they got a hit. Whether he was satisfied or not, I don't know. I think he was satisfied that he didn't have to sculpt music that sounded like Led Zeppelin. Did you know that the Kingdom Come self-titled was released on the same day as *Now and Zen*? I bought that album on the strength of "Living Out of Touch," which I heard on radio before I heard "Get It On." But it's interesting that he tries very hard to get away from Led Zeppelin and now he had to sit and defend himself with this band releasing that guitar-driven almost clone band music on the same day. So he's juggling listening to Whitesnake and Kingdom Come and a few other hair metal bands, maybe Badlands, doing this Led Zeppelin-style music while he's sounding like Bryan Adams or Robbie Robertson or Sting or even Billy Idol. He doesn't want to do Bon Jovi. He doesn't want to rock, really. He wants to be as middle-of-the-road as possible. That's my take on it. He wanted to be a radio star that could attract as broad an audience as possible. And he had a good name to use as a solid foundation for that.

Douglas: Right, and then there's Heart, which is a weird one. Because Heart is doing the same thing as a lot of these bands. To address your comparisons, Martin, he's closer to that specific Iggy Pop album than U2, obviously. But this publishing house songs idea... a lot of the reason that Heart doesn't like performing a lot of their eighties hits is because they didn't write them. Those songs were someone else's that were given to them. As far as his personality goes in this *Now and Zen* period, I'd say up to this point he's been kind of laid-back and this distant stranger. Like you're slowly getting to know him. Now he's flirtatious. He's like a pop idol or a rock god, people are throwing themselves at him—again.

One of my favourite Robert Plant quotes from this time was him saying, "Well, the album's huge. So I guess people like me again. Or so that's what the label tells me." You bring in an A&R team and you have all of these reps who are going, "God, we're gonna do so well with this." They all say the same shit. All of them; "Oh, this is a hit and this is a hit and this is a hit." Plant was at the point where he's like, "I think you think that. And while that's a decent song, these are better. So we're gonna go with these."

It doesn't necessarily mean that Plant picked. And in fact a lot of artists don't get that opportunity. The label picks. The label comes in and says, "You can pick the first single. Whatever you want to rep, we'll work with you on it. But we think we know best, what should be the singles." Plant was like, "Well, I'm not going to do any more videos. I'm not going to promote this thing anymore, if we don't do it in the order that I want to do."

So interestingly enough, having this relationship with Ahmet Ertegun, previously it was like the "Don't call me Bob" version of Robert Plant. It was more like an episode of Plant knows best on this, and it was frustrating for Atlantic. So this was the record that the label got its way and said, "This is the direction this should be going in." That's why when he shopped "Heaven Knows" and seemed amenable to being over-commercialised, they're like, "We're going to show you just how big Robert Plant can become again, in 1988, if you let us." He did let them and it worked. With *Now and Zen*, he was having a moment.

And then flash forward, when you go into the Page Plant thing from '94 and onward, he was never the same. With *Walking into Clarksdale*, once that whole thing happened, Robert Plant as you knew him in the eighties through *Manic Nirvana* and *Fate of Nations*, that guy disappeared. He's no longer there. All of a sudden he was a folk artist. He was your guy who was going to embrace Middle Eastern sounds, African sounds, tribal sounds, Americana, all the way. And don't get me wrong; there's a huge audience for that. And the Alison Krauss stuff is really polished and well done. It really is. And they played theatres and what have you. He's found what he wants to do in his life. But I really believe that has consumed him. It has nothing to do with not wanting to go back and do Zeppelin; that's just not who he is anymore. No need for it. And he can pass up billions of dollars, literally billions of dollars, to reform Led Zeppelin and tour, and just be comfortable in his own skin because that's who he identifies with now. Not this guy from the eighties. "Ship of Fools," absolutely could have been a Sting song. That Robert Plant person doesn't exist with us anymore.

ROBERT PLANT
Manic Nirvana
Vancouver Sept.
Edmonton Sept. 22
Calgary Sept. 23
Saskatoon Sept. 25
Winnipeg Sept.
Toronto Oct.
Montreal Oct. 4
Ottawa Oct. 6
IT'S COMING FOR YOU
MOLSON CANADIAN Rocks

7 91336-4
ROBERT PLANT
Manic Nirvana
SIDE ONE
HURTING KIND
(I'VE GOT MY EYES ON YOU)
BIG LOVE
SSS&Q
I CRIED
SHE SAID
NIRVANA
ESPARANZA RECORDS DISTRIBUTED BY ATLANTIC RECORDING CORPORATION, 75 ROCKEFELLER PLAZA, NEW YORK, NEW YORK 10019. A Warner Communications Company ℗ © 1990 Atlantic Recording Corporation for the United States and WEA International Inc. for the world outside of the United States. © 1990 Robert Plant. All Rights Reserved. Printed in U.S.A. Warning: Unauthorized reproduction of this recording is prohibited by Federal law and subject to criminal prosecution.
0 7567-91336-4 9
ROBERT PLANT
Manic Nirvana
SIDE TWO
TIE DYE ON THE HIGHWAY
YOUR MA SAID YOU CRIED
IN YOUR SLEEP LAST NIGHT
ANNIVERSARY
LIARS DANCE
WATCHING YOU
ESPARANZA

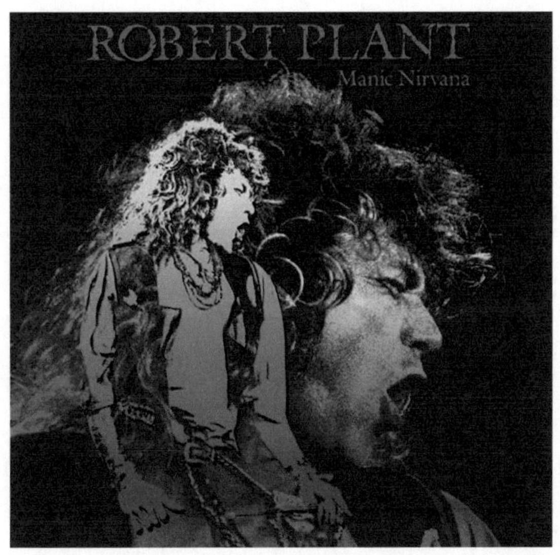

Manic Nirvana

"There is no process, really. I carry a book around with me everywhere I go, and a very good pen or a very sharp graphite pencil. And I have a sharp tongue to go with it, and I guess my senses are still pretty fine/strident. And so I listen and hear and catch every kind of unexposed kind of repartee that you get around you and all the kind of folly, and you write it all down. And it's not so much about where the guitar solo comes; it's about where it doesn't come. And where you get these pieces of music that are like, almost a trance section of music, where it gives me a great opportunity to write melody atop of that. So it's a good place to be. The difference is, that the whole approach is more frivolous now. It's a lot more easy-going, a lot more fun. And with contemporary recording techniques, you can mess about very quickly; you can develop structures and also very quickly you can dump 'em. And I'm inspired by so many other things, so many other music and artists. Really, it's about material and the consequences of life. As long as I've got something to talk about that fits against a pretty chord progression, I shall write songs."
Robert Plant

Credits

March 19, 1990
Es Paranza/Atlantic 91336
Produced by Robert Plant and Phil Johnstone; co-produced by Mark Stent
Engineered by Mark Stent
Recorded at Olympic Studios
Personnel: Robert Plant – vocals, Doug Boyle – master guitars, Phil Johnstone – keyboards, some guitars, Charlie Jones – bass, Chris Blackwell – drums, some guitars

1. "Hurting Kind (I've Got My Eyes on You)" (Plant, Johnstone, Jones, Boyle, Blackwell) 4:04
2. "Big Love" (Plant, Johnstone, Blackwell) 4:24
3. "S S S & Q" (Plant, Johnstone, Jones, Boyle, Blackwell) 4:38
4. "I Cried" (Plant, Johnstone) 4:59
5. "She Said" (Plant, Johnstone, Jones, Boyle, Blackwell) 5:10
6. "Nirvana" (Plant, Jones, Boyle) 4:36
7. "Tie Dye on the Highway" (Plant, Blackwell) 5:15
8. "Your Ma Said You Cried in Your Sleep Last Night" (Stephen Schlaks, Mel Glazer) 4:36
9. "Anniversary" (Plant, Johnstone) 5:02
10. "Liars Dance" (Plant, Boyle) 2:40
11. "Watching You" (Plant, Johnstone) 4:19

A *Manic Nirvana* Timeline

March 19, 1990. Robert Plant issues a fifth studio album, called *Manic Nirvana*. It reaches No.15 in the UK and No.13 on the *Billboard* Hot 100, ending the year at No.71.

April 16, 1990. "Hurting Kind (I've Got My Eyes on You)" is issued as a single from *Manic Nirvana*, reaching No.1 on the *Billboard* mainstream Rock chart, No.46 on the Hot 100 and No.45 in the UK. The CD single version includes three non-LP tracks, "Oompah (Watery Bint)," "One Love" and a rendition of The Remains' 1966 garage rocker "Don't Look Back."

May 1 - 30, 1990. Robert and his band tour in support of *Manic Nirvana*, taking the campaign first to mainland Europe.

May 18, 1990. *Manic Nirvana* goes gold.

May 31 – June 7, 1990. Robert promotes *Manic Nirvana* in the UK.

June 1990. "Your Ma Said You Cried in Your Sleep Last Night" is issued as the final single from *Manic Nirvana*, reaching No.8 on the Mainstream Rock chart and a lowly No.90 in the UK.

July 5 – November 26, 1990. The *Manic Nirvana* tour shifts over to North America.

December 12, 1990 – January 20, 1991. After a one-off in Greece, Robert conducts a second UK leg in support of *Manic Nirvana*.

December 17, 1990. *Pictures at Eleven* reaches RIAA platinum status in the US.

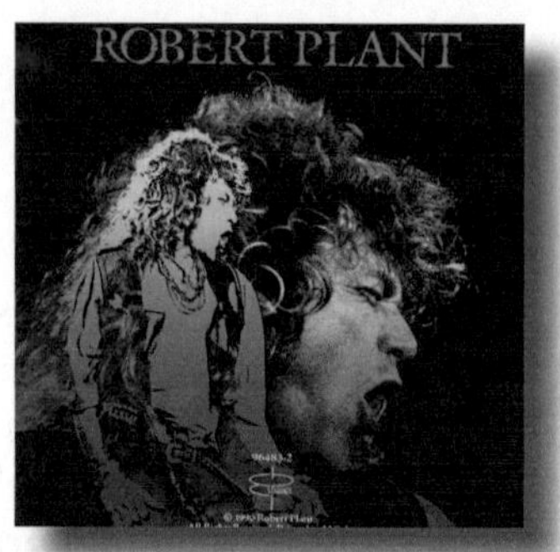

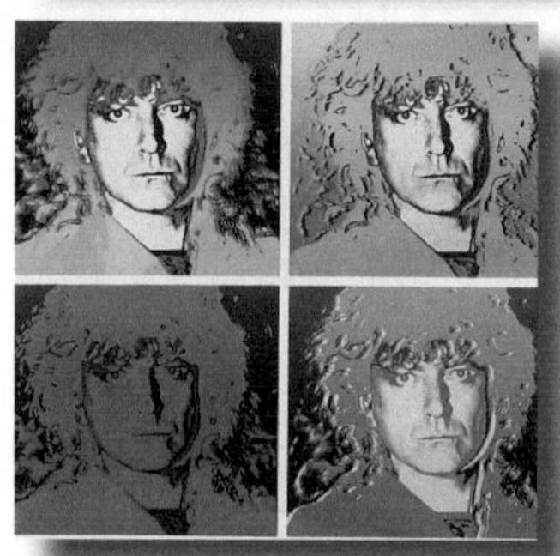

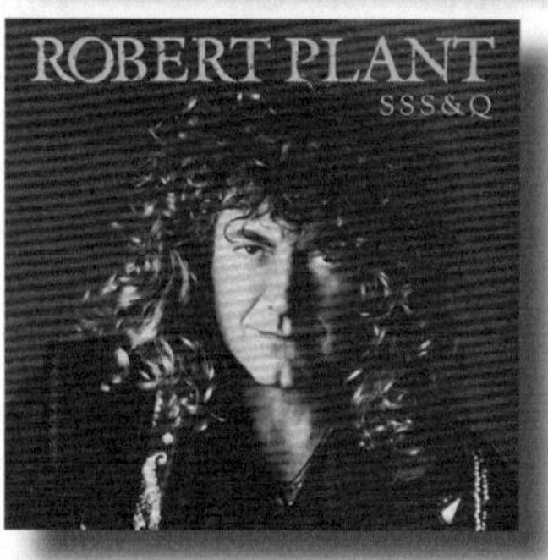

Martin talks to Joe Becht, Todd Evans, Reed Little and Pontus Norshammar about *Manic Nirvana.*

Martin Popoff: Okay, moving on to *Manic Nirvana*, Joe, perhaps set the stage for this one, going back a couple albums.

Joe Becht: Sure, well, as I purchased all of these albums, there was always this dark cloud about when is Robert getting back together with Led Zeppelin, along with rumours, little hints, temptations. Led Zeppelin at Live Aid had been such a letdown for me. So I always had a jaded opinion listening to these records, not so much the first two—I thought they were extremely good—but beginning with *Shaken 'n' Stirred.* I've always wondered how much Robert shapes the music on the solo albums and how much the band steers the direction, or style. Is he playing what the band wants or is the band playing what he wants? And on that one, Robbie Blunt is a great guitarist, but he was subsumed to some extent. It sounds to me like what Rush did in the eighties. I just I hear a lot of *Miami Vice*-type synthesizers and strange and annoying ear worms in the songs.

I was already not happy with The Honeydrippers and Jimmy Page and The Firm was missing the mark and now we get this. "Hip to Hoo" I found scatterbrained, "Kallalou Kallalou" has the female backup vocals, "Trouble Your Money" sounds to me like reggae done too fast. "Too Loud" is the one where Robert talks about being inspired by the Talking Heads. I don't hear it. David Byrne is a genius, to me, and this isn't genius. Again, I'm hearing Rush, along with The Human League or Soft Cell. The album also has a Police vibe, which carries over into *Now and Zen*, to some extent, maybe through the austerity of the production, or the guitar sound, which everybody was into at that time, especially Rush. The Police definitely had a sound, which worked great for The Police but it didn't work great for these other bands

I found the mid-eighties to be a maligned, fallow period, for me. The New Wave of British Heavy Metal is over, replaced by hair metal, which by the time of *Manic Nirvana* is getting well out of hand. The eighties music scene was a let-down for me in general and *Now and Zen* didn't help. Even though, oddly, you listen to Jimmy Page during this period, with *Outrider*, and he's still playing that dark, analogue Jimmy Page guitar music, which you got somewhat on the reed two Firm albums as well.

I never saw Zeppelin live and I've never seen Robert solo live, although I saw Page Plant twice. I saw Jimmy on the *Outrider* tour with Jason playing drums and he played some Zeppelin songs. But he's playing the UIC Pavilion, which was like the number three venue in Chicago, right around the Aragon Ballroom, and I don't even know if it was sold-out. I'm like, this is Jimmy Page! And I don't even know if he had 5000 fans there. You could get Zeppelin back together and they're selling out multiple nights at the Chicago stadium. Anyway, yeah, I was wanting heavier things, more riff-based rock than what Robert was delivering. The death of Cliff Burton hit me hard; that created a void in me and for some reason a real dismissal of any of my heroes like Robert Plant using too many synthesizers or programmed drums.

As for Robert's headspace, I've read so many interviews with him and the theme was always to sound young and fresh and stay away from the legacy of Led Zeppelin. I don't know if it was resentment or bad memories because of the death of his son and other tragic events, like losing Bonzo. I remember one interview where he was asked, "Why don't you just keep on going? And maybe use Jason Bonham." He goes, "Well, Jason's not John." He was steadfast that because there is no John Bonham, there would never be a Led Zeppelin and he stuck to that. So now up into *Manic Nirvana*, he's five records into the theme of trying to stay relevant.

We all got excited because Jimmy Page played on *Now and Zen* and of course, "Tall Cool One" had the sampling of the Led Zeppelin songs. So all of us lost it. We're like, okay, it's happening, it's got to happen, they're playing together. So again, there's that cloud over my Robert Plant experience—when are they going to get back together? But that being said, I ended up really liking *Manic Nirvana* and it still holds up for me. It takes what he did on *Now and Zen* and it goes a little bit better. I think it's one of those good transitional albums into the nineties, released in March of '90. There's some big drums and everything else and man, I just really like it. There was a little too much album-oriented rock on *Now and Zen* but that's somewhat put to the side on *Manic Nirvana*.

Martin: Nice recap. Okay, Reed, what does Robert change up for what is essentially a very hopeful album, given the smash hit he managed with *Now and Zen*?

Reed Little: Strangely, he hardly changes. One of his co-producers is gone, but it's the same band. He's still Robert Plant and is still producing, along with Phil Johnstone. And I think it's interesting that based on using almost exactly the same elements, he winds up with an album that sounds considerably different, to my ears anyway. We're still using that eighties gated drum sound, but now the keyboards are mixed way back and they've pushed Doug Boyle's guitar to the front. So this is a very heavy guitar album, which I love. It's the way people describe *Now and Zen*, in my mind—almost everything they say actually applies to *Manic Nirvana*. *Manic Nirvana* is very much more Zeppelin-esque than *Now and Zen* ever was. It's way more hard rock. It's got so much more guitar. And again, I think that's interesting because it's the same people but yet producing a different result. And maybe it's just because it's two years later.

Todd Evans: At the time, I was disappointed that there was no more Phil Collins or somebody sounding like Phil Collins. I was disappointed that the drums were mostly programmed. For *Now and Zen*, I felt like he still had kind of sophisticated songs that I felt sad didn't go with the feel of the first three albums. So *Manic Nirvana*, I didn't give it a chance, because I didn't like "Hurting Kind," for starters. Now I consider myself to be completely wrong about my first impression of this record. But as a follow-up to *Now and Zen*, I think it's more adventurous than that album.

Pontus Norshammar: I think this is a far better album than *Now and Zen*. It's heavier, he's gotten back to being slightly psychedelic and addressing the Eastern-flavoured stuff that he truly likes. I think he's in a better place. The record is very easy to listen to, it's quick, it's fun, it's the same musicians, but it's feels like Doug Boyle is far more present. It's a rocking album with a positive vibe, but also a throwback to the late sixties hippie days. You have samples of Wavy Gravy at Woodstock and there's talk about nirvana as a religious thing amidst psychedelic touches. Something must have happened to him that he really felt like, oh, I'm gonna do a rock record. If you look at the sleeve, you have the psychedelic colours and he looks like an old hippie. I actually love it.

Martin: Does anybody else want to comment on the album cover?

Reed: I love it. Robert is a forty-two-year-old hippie at this point and he's looking the part, with that tie-dye colour scheme. It looks like something you would see on a blacklight poster in Haight Ashbury. But he looks great, with Robert doing one of his big Robert Plant-esque screams. I think it really draws you in. Comparatively, *Now and Zen* is serene, Zen-like, even though there's nothing particularly Zen-related on the album. Whereas manic means energy. But then again, *Manic Nirvana* doesn't make any sense, again, Robert borrowing a Buddhist concept with the idea of nirvana. But I love that picture. I think it's eye-catching and it sets a mood for the album.

Todd: That's a logical album cover. While it's a very good image, I also like the layout and the design of it, the font and everything, the colours. To me there's a similarity to the album before it, like, "Here's Led Zeppelin Robert Plant." Here's the hippie guy in a scarf. It's a selling point, maybe with a touch of laziness to it, conceptually. But sure, slapping his face on the cover is probably a pretty good marketing decision.

Martin: There's something both dated and annoying about that title. It's like Zodiac Mindwarp, this idea of sticking flashy words together that don't belong. You see this in grunge too.

Todd: Yes, I agree. The only thing I can say positive about that is that there is a song called "Nirvana" and the record does sound manic to me.

Joe: With that cover, he's teasing us. He's like, I'm back. And maybe Zeppelin is coming back (laughs). He looks like Led Zeppelin's Robert Plant. That's *my* Robert Plant. No mullet or anything. Kicks ass. As for the title, I agree as well. It's a precursor of what's about to come in the nineties with grunge. And ironically, with the Seattle scene you get a throwback to—and resurgence for—Led Zeppelin, especially with Soundgarden.

Martin: Into the album and we get "Hurting Kind (I've Got My Eyes on You)," unnecessarily complicated title and all. It's a "We mean business" statement, right?

Reed: Yes, for sure. So right off the bat, I love that he opens with a punchy rocker. We get space rock guitar at the beginning, which is a throwback to hippie times, and then immediately into that muscular riff. The message is that this album promises to be more hard-rocking than *Now and Zen,* which opens with "Heaven Knows." That put me off as a hard rock fan, whereas this one, I'm like, oh yeah, let's hear what this has to say.

Which is weird, because I'd say this song is engineered to be the second "Tall Cool One," although it's better than "Tall Cool One" in my opinion. Now clearly, commercially, that was not the case. This song made it to No.46 on the Hot 100, so it was nowhere near as successful. But 1990 was not 1988, so maybe tastes had changed. I don't think Plant's lyric is anything to write home about, but his vocal performance is still wonderful. And he changes it up by having many parts he sings where it's just voice and drums. There's no guitar or keyboards, so there's nothing to distract you from the voice. And then they kick back in with the chorus. But yeah, Plant is showcased on this track and I think that really works.

Todd: "Hurting Kind (I've Got My Eyes on You)" was incredibly huge when it came out down here in the south. It was on the radio all the time. I think it's got great riffs. One of the things about this album is that the guitar riffs are loud, hooky and effective. The song makes a big first impression, signalling that the album is going to be a noisier, more electronic album, with noticeable electronic drum fills. The chorus is super-catchy. At the end where the background vocals repeat, "All right, I've got my eyes on you," during the last minute especially, they sound like Sisters of Mercy to me, almost Goth-sounding, which I think is a style of music Robert Plant could actually pull off (laughs). I'm not a person who objects to drum programming or electronic drums or that kind of technology, although having said that, it's not always the best thing for heavy rock, or when you're simultaneously pushing a heavy rock message.

Pontus: "Hurting Kind" is a catchy, in-your-face rock 'n' roll opener, great riff, great performance from everybody. I really like it. It captures a vibe and was a great single. He feels more at home here. He feels more pleased with himself, I guess. As Reed says, it's the follow-up to "Tall Cool One" but with more guitars. It feels more present; it's not calculated in the same way. He's rocking out. I feel like he's thinking he can stand by this song.

Martin: Do you think he's keeping an eye on the success of Whitesnake?

Pontus: I think so. And also the difference between 1987, when he recorded *Now and Zen*, and 1989, when he records *Manic Nirvana*, was that even the hair metal scene was getting grittier. There was Whitesnake, Badlands, Guns N' Roses, Skid Row, Blue Murder, and Black Crowes was right around the corner. Another band I think he was influenced by was Living Colour. This album can be funky but heavy at the same time, somewhat like Red Hot Chili Peppers, but more like Living Colour with the guitar thing—the guitar is more prominent. But I think he also wanted go back and add a psychedelic vibe to certain things, which was also in vogue at the time. Woodstock had had its 20th anniversary and you could feel that certain bands went that way. It's too early for grunge, so he's not really there. He's channelling something that he was a part of. He often talks fondly about Moby Grape and those sixties bands.

Martin: It gets even louder and noisier on the second song, "Big Love," underscoring the idea that "Hurting Kind" is no anomaly.

Reed: Exactly, and listen to that drum groove and tell me that it doesn't sound more like John Bonham than anything that came off of *Now and Zen*. Now it's still that eighties gated drum sound but it's got those giant thuds. He's really pounding them hard and it sounds like a John Bonham groove, an actual Zeppelin groove. Maybe Plant had been trying to avoid it for so long that he finally relents and he just puts it on like a comfortable pair of shoes. The strangest thing about this song to me, though, is how much it reminds me of Aerosmith more than Led Zeppelin. The concept of "Big Love" is almost a callback to like "Big Ten Inch" off of *Toys in the Attic*, but rhythmically, we're closer to "Love in an Elevator."

Martin: And "Rag Doll" as well, with the added electronic percussion accents.

Reed: Right. Aerosmith completed a huge comeback with *Permanent Vacation*, and *Pump*, with "Love in an Elevator," came out in 1989, six months before *Manic Nirvana* and it was a massive hit. I have to think, just looking at it from the outside, if I were Robert Plant, I'm thinking, okay, *Now and Zen* did well and people said it was hard rock, and they wanted more Zeppelin. So I'm going to give them a Zeppelin-esque track and bring in some elements from this other hugely popular band. All of that would seem tailor-made to create a hit, although, as it turns out, "Big Love" wasn't even issued as a single. And of course, *Manic Nirvana* in total only certified gold, so about one-seventh of the sales of *Now and Zen*. You had a lot of people jump on the Robert Plant bandwagon, probably because they loved that one song, and then they jumped back off. *Manic Nirvana* sold functionally about the same as each of his first three solo albums. So he's back selling to his core audience.

Todd: "Big Love" starts with these loud drum fills right at the beginning which, if they aren't programmed, they may as well be, because they sound so processed and drenched in reverb. Whether it's to emulate the gated Phill Collins sound or not, I don't care for it. Another thing I don't like about the song is that it's got this kind of Mutt Lange-like background vocal shouting. It just sounds like a bunch of people shouting the words "big love" and it doesn't necessarily fit the song. I find it obnoxious.

Martin: Well, along those lines, Todd, lyrically, it seems to be about him flying to go see his girlfriend, but he has sex with the flight attendant in the washroom, right?

Todd: Yeah, that's my impression of it too. And he's not subtle in describing it. It would have been better off if he were a little more subtle. It's not offensive, but it's just like, oh my gosh, really? It's a little eye-rolling. But on the positive, there are some background vocals in the song that *aren't* the shouting that are actually pretty cool and save it. But yeah, not a fan.

Pontus: "Big Love" should have been a single. It's rocky with a great chorus and harmonies. It has meaty organ and heavy guitars. And the rhythm reminds me of "Rosanna" by Toto, or Little Feat. He had worked with Richie Hayward, the Little Feat drummer, earlier. It's a band playing and most of the band credited. "Hurting Kind" is written by all of them, and "Big Love" is Plant, Johnstone and Blackwell. So, both are written from a drummer's perspective. And in "Big Love," he namechecks Jimmy Page, in the ad-libbing in the end. He says that he visited this motel, and he got the same room Jimmy Page once stayed in and then something about having remodelled it after the '75 tour. So, he offers a bit of a send-up of Jimmy.

Martin: This "dance metal" theme persists with "S S S & Q."

Joe: Yes, which stands for "soak, shake, splash and quake." Again, he's singing about a woman. I really like it. Doug Boyle kicks butt on this one; he starts with a Stevie Ray Vaughan sound and then it goes into a great chorus, and then Doug does a big, bold lead. Like "Big Love," it's got a huge—and yes, danceable—drum groove and sound. And actually both songs borrow from the blues but then it's such a modern sound, you barely notice.

Reed: So we have another song that starts with muscular guitar that I absolutely love. This time the main influence is Jimi Hendrix, rather than Led Zeppelin. Doug Boyle, fantastic player, wears his influences on his sleeves, Jimmy Page being one of them, but he was obviously big into Hendrix too. There's a lot of Hendrix-isms on this album and on this song. It also represents another big move away from the *Now and Zen* sound. The choir of female backup singers is mostly gone, but we get a little backup singing occasionally. But what we get is Plant doubling and tripling his own voice on the choruses, which provides a very different vocal sound. Frankly, I like it, because it further underscores or accents Robert's wonderful, distinctive voice. And again, he is the primary selling point of his albums, so having more of him on them is a good thing.

Todd: "S S S & Q," like "Hurting Kind," is built on catchy riffs. I think it's a better song than "Big Love." It still has a drum sound that I feel is not very refined. It's got those little vintage action TV show samples in it that sound like *Batman* or something—pretty cool. He was really into samples then. After hearing "Tall Cool One," you expect to hear some samples on this record, so that doesn't really bother me. It's got some digital orchestra hits, which are very eighties, when we're now into the nineties. But it's just barely the nineties, so I forgive him for that. It's a song that delivers more of what you expect, lots of zesty sounds and action points, the stuff that everybody talked about with that album, but really in-your-face. All of that stuff is pushed to the front of the album. It makes me want to forgive "Big Love" for being like it is, because I think it's done with purpose, to grab your attention. And it does; I'll have to give them credit for that.

Pontus: "S S S & Q" is where I really hear a Living Colour influence. It's funk rock with thick guitars, great riff; it's a grower. Prince might have been an influence as well; he was big at the time. And this one is also a full band composition.

Martin: We get a total change of pace with "I Cried," which is almost jarring, next to the uptown funk of what comes before.

Reed: Yes, "I Cried" is much more of a retro song, even lyrically, where he's talking about his youth again. We're back in Zeppelin territory, we've got an acoustic opening, and it sounds to me like the piezo electric sound, lots of space, lots of reverb. The lyric is apparently an ode to a poster on his wall, or a beautiful woman that he saw in a movie and fell in love with when he was a kid and knew he would never have so he cries. He name-checks Stella Stevens, who was a beautiful starlet—she actually just died in 2023. She was ten years older than Robert Plant, so that made her about the right age to have a poster of her. But again, notice, even though it's a good lyric and I love this song, isn't that strange subject matter for a 42-year-old man to be singing about, how much he loved this poster of a beautiful woman when he was a kid?

But I feel like a theme across both this album and *Now and Zen* is nostalgia. Post-age 40 Robert Plant was in a very nostalgic mood and he's constantly doing these retro feels. He's throwing in more Zeppelin, he's going back to Hendrix and Elvis and Moby Grape and all of these other things that influenced him when he was young. So, that's old man music, right? When you're in your twenties, you wouldn't write about, gee, I knew I was never going to get this woman and I cried. That's an old man's lyric.

Pontus: "I Cried" sounds to me like a British folk ballad. It's got these nice vocal harmonies built from acoustic to electric and then back again. It's a beautiful, beautiful song. This is what was missing on *Now and Zen*, this idea of letting a song breathe a bit. I think "I Cried" still stands up well today.

Joe: I appreciate the almost West Coast psych acoustic guitar sound of this one. It's about lost—or, really, unattainable—love, which always tugs at my heartstrings. It has a great guitar progression and then at 2:50 the beat picks up and gets heavier. I'm all in on this song for sure.

Todd: I think "I Cried" is the first great song on the album. It's got a hooky chorus that kind of rocks and the whole track rhythmically is just really compelling. I feel like I missed this one back in 1990 and I was glad to reacquaint myself with it.

Martin: Here comes one that I never heard for years, because I bought the vinyl.

Todd: Yes, "She Said" is cassette- and CD-only. 1990 is kind of the end of the line for vinyl in the States. I'm not sure what it was like in Canada; I assume it's pretty similar. But basically people were starting to make CD-length albums, so the record companies were editing them to fit on a on a single record. One of the last examples of that is Queen *Innuendo*, which is '91, which is really the very end of when they stopped pressing vinyl in any large numbers. But I don't think they should have left this song off. It's got a really cool synth opening and the synth string padding during the part where he sings, "I don't know why" and really all throughout, the track is really pretty sound. And it's not overbearing; it's not something that somebody who doesn't like synths is going to object to and I think it's rhythmically innovative throughout. "She Said" is my number two track on the album.

Pontus: "She Said" seems to be influenced by Prince; cool, funky Prince riff on that one, pretty heavy, and then it goes into this mid-tempo funky thing. And I think there's a James Brown sample in there. I feel like this cool, modern rock Prince and Living Colour vibe continues on "Nirvana" as well, with similar edgy guitars and thick drums.

Joe: "She Said" is very cool, with this chunky guitar sound, and the keyboard that leads into that bridge section where they say "Whatever you do," I like that a lot.

Reed: "She Said" is the first song we get that opens with a synthesizer sound, which I'm a little bit trepidatious about. But luckily the hard rock guitars kick in and all is forgiven. We have finger-snapping again. Does anybody ever record as much finger-snapping as Robert Plant on rock albums? I don't think so. And we have more Prince-like guitar stabs. Doug Boyle was obviously a big Prince fan because there's a lot of Prince on this album.

Martin: INXS as well, right?

Reed: Well, I think of INXS, despite being Australian, as having that very typical eighties guitar sound. But yes, my mind went to Prince but you could just as easily go to INXS with that sound.

Martin: How about The Fixx, Duran Duran, maybe. Alex Lifeson?

Reed: I wouldn't say Duran Duran. I don't know that I would go to The Fixx, but parts of this song… and the reason I bring up Prince is because there's a part of this song at about the two-minute mark that reminds me exactly of Prince's song "Kiss." You again have a lot of repetition in the lyric; it's Plant so we can't get away from the repetition. But the repetition is spread out through a much bigger overall composition. So it doesn't sound like the guy's just repeating "I don't know why" over and over again, even though he in fact repeats "I don't know why" multiple times during the song. All told, it's pretty successful for me.

Martin: And the uptown, upscale urban rock party continues with the ersatz title track. Again there's Prince, but also Dan Reed Network, even Billy Idol at the time.

Reed: Yes, we're back in Prince territory with "Nirvana." Energetic guitar opening; I really think Doug Boyle is a fantastic player and they give him much more of a spotlight on this album. Plant's singing is back in his vocal style from Led Zeppelin. We get another fairly basic lyric about sex, despite the title. And it's another song, the second on this album, where we get Plant singing without a lot of instrumentation behind him. Although this time it's drums and bass instead of just drums. But still Plant is featuring himself so much more on this album instead of having the technology drown him out. It has a fantastic guitar solo. Towards the end of the song it has some sampled voiceover bits. I almost always find those annoying. They take me out of the experience of listening to the music.

Todd: "Nirvana" features a similar rhythm guitar approach to "She Said" and there's a really cool guitar solo. It's like "Tall Cool One" to me in that it's somewhat irritating; it gets on my nerves a little. But it's not a complete failure, because it's interesting enough. And like you say, the guitars seem to be inspired by INXS and The Fixx. As for

Doug Boyle, he's an important personality in this era of the band. I love Robbie Blunt, and I remember reading an interview when *Now and Zen* came out where Robert Plant said, "My old guitar player, all he ever wanted to do was play the blues." And I think he was annoyed about that. He wanted to have a guitarist that was edgier and more in tune with some of the alternative music that was out at the time. That's the impression I got, anyway. But I like the guitar on these two albums, although it's not what I wanted at the time. But typically, I like that kind of guitar.

Martin: Things heat up for "Tie Dye on the Highway," although those are clearly programmed drums powering what is otherwise the heaviest song on the album.

Joe: "Tie Die on the Highway" might be my favourite, because it's got a great riff and it kick ass. You had an episode of your podcast, *History in Five Songs with Martin Popoff*, on "Kashmir"-sounding songs, and I think there's a little bit of that in here. He does the harmonica and I'm a sucker for harmonica, especially when Robert Plant plays it, like in "Nobody's Fault but Mine," which blows me away. And I think Doug Boyle's solo here is as good as any by Jimmy Page.

It's funny, "Nirvana" and "Tie Dye on the Highway," even though they're the hippiest-sounding titles and I'm generally turned off by a lot of the hippie movement, these are two kick-ass songs as far as I'm concerned. One thing though, it starts out with the Woodstock dialogue from Wavy Gravy, "What we have in mind is breakfast in bed for 400,000." I'm not a huge Woodstock guy, so I'm turned off by that (laughs). But I see that title as, hey, let's go back in time and take what was great about rock 'n' roll and bring it into the nineties. So I thought it was a great tune. This is what I needed from Robert. This is what I needed to revitalise my love for hard rock.

Reed: That Woodstock quote, that would be pretty obvious to a man in his 40s, I guess, but for me as a kid, I was like, who is this and why is it at the start of this song? The actual song is quite good; we're back in Zeppelin territory. It sounds like it could have been on *In Through the Out Door* maybe. Great guitar lines. You've got a harmonica, the first time that harmonica is played on the album. It's got a folk influence, but unlike Zeppelin, which embraces the folk, here the folk is simply providing a chord progression, a background, and it's all presented still very hard rock. And the lyric, once again

Plant is looking back at a point in his life and enjoying himself singing about hippies.

Martin: Again, I'm hearing an Aerosmith influence, particularly a Joe Perry influence.

Reed: Yeah, and isn't that circular, because obviously there's so much Zeppelin influence on Aerosmith to begin with. And now by the time we get to 1990 and Zeppelin has been gone for ten years, Aerosmith had their career resurgence in the late eighties and is now one of the biggest bands in America again, and Plant is absorbing some of those Aerosmith influences back into his music.

Martin: I'm just amazed that with songs like this, *Manic Nirvana* didn't sell better. It sounds like a hit album. It's got all sorts of bells and whistles. But maybe some of them can be categorised as cheap laughs.

Todd: Yeah. Well, "Tie Die on the Highway" is a perfect example. It's almost too obvious. Let's see what kinds of classic rock things can I talk about? Well, I can talk about tie dye and the highway—let's put that together. The chorus is cool, kind of trippy. But again, it's got that Alex Lifeson *Hold Your Fire* guitar sound, which clashes with the whole organic theme of "Tie Die on the Highway." But the harmonica and the spoken word, I think, is used to good effect. I don't normally like harmonica, but I like it in this song. And I always like spoken word. I'm a big Supertramp fan (laughs).

I remember the song really well though, because my girlfriend at the time was a big Grateful Dead fan. And so any reference to anything hippie she latched onto. And she liked Robert Plant and of course she liked "Tie Die on the Highway." and so I heard it a lot. She also liked "Farm on the Freeway" by Jethro Tull, and I always put those songs together in my head because of that. But yeah, I feel like it's too obvious. It's like, "Hi, I'm Robert Plant from Led Zeppelin. Here's a song about hippies." But I think it works.

Pontus: I really love "Tie Dye on the Highway," the Wavy Gravy Woodstock clip, the heavy blues riffing, the psych harmonies in the chorus—the song has a cozy, nostalgic, psych feel. And you can also hear samples from Stills and Crosby. You can hear Crosby saying, "Tell them who we are" and Stills says something like "Three days."

And Wavy Gravy also says, "We must be in Heaven, man." Obviously Robert wasn't at Woodstock because they were somewhere else. But I think he wanted to go back and revisit those sorts of psychedelic influences.

So, this album represents both before and after Led Zeppelin. There's a blank thing in the middle that he doesn't want to go to. I never met the guy—I shouldn't over-analyze him—but I get the same feeling as you did that, as long as it's not Led Zeppelin I can go back to Woodstock because I wasn't there. And he felt Woodstock was a great thing. It was a great thing to be around in the sixties. But I don't want to touch on this big band I was part of. I'd rather be with Moby Grape.

Martin: It's almost like he's posed a challenge to himself to combine his own late sixties influences with late eighties modern rock in a way.

Pontus: Yeah, because this is also an interesting thing. The whole record is modern, but it has this nostalgic feel. It has a retro feel and yet it's steeped in this modern sound, this nineties sound. I've always said that 1990 has a special sound, because you feel people moving away from the major echo and reverb sound that was the late eighties into something more robust. But it still has these big drums. If you listen to Nirvana's *Nevermind*, it's a punk record. It is what it is. But it's still of the eighties with those big drums. I think that in the nineties you went back to basics in a way that you couldn't in the eighties. He's doing what he wants to do here. He wants to go back.

Martin: You each seem to have tracks that bother you on this album. I'll go with "Your Ma Said You Cried in Your Sleep Last Night."

Reed: Yes, I understand that. This is a really strange track. We get Plant singing like Elvis, so we're back in 1950s territory. It's a cover song. Now I know it's not actually Elvis, but a man named Kenny Dino and the song came out in 1961 and got to No.24 in the charts. I'm sure Plant loved it when he was a kid; he would have been 13 in 1961. So it's the perfect age to fall in love with this style of music. I haven't listened to the original, so I don't know if Kenny Dino sounds like Elvis but Plant absolutely delivers this material like Elvis Presley. We have the insertion of actual Led Zeppelin again and once again, I find it completely unnecessary and out of place. This time it's a little piece from "Black Dog." Although I'm going to give Robert Plant a little credit that I don't give him on *Now and Zen* because that album just rubs me the wrong way. I just like this album so much more. But I feel like rather than simply inserting Led Zeppelin for no point, he's actually illustrating, hey, this type of music is where I got the feel for things like "Black Dog."

Todd: For most of my life I have absolutely hated this song, but I've turned around on it. I get why he wanted to do it so bad. I wish he had cut this song off the vinyl instead of "She Said," but it's fine. He sampled the bass drum sound right off the original Kenny Dino 45 and puts something in the liner notes about the scratchy sound and why he did it. I don't know, as a sixty-year-old guy, I like it more now. It's grown on me.

Joe: He does like a rockabilly sound but it's electro-rockabilly and I think it works. But after *Now and Zen*, we're in the CD era and maybe the album is too long and we don't need this. Although "Anniversary" is near the end and that's a great song. In fact, the songs on *Manic Nirvana* are generally a little longer, such that in the old days, depending on the tracks, he could have gotten away with an eight-song album. But with this song near the end, I felt some fatigue setting in, even though it's saved by Doug Boyle.

Pontus: "Your Ma Said You Cried in Your Sleep Last Night" is interesting because that is a fifties song, albeit from 1961, which he steeps in modern technology. And he liked it enough to make it the second single. Kenny Dino was a one-hit wonder who used to sing demos for Elvis. "Good Luck Charm," for instance, he used to do. So, we all know that Plant is a huge Elvis fan. He could tackle this fifties thing, although his arrangement is early nineties, with electronic drums that pretty much take over.

Martin: "Anniversary" kinda washes away "Your Ma Said You Cried in Your Sleep Last Night" on a foamy sea of synths.

Todd: Absolutely, yeah. "Anniversary" is my favourite track on the album and comes close to being my favourite Robert Plant song ever. I really love those just out-of-this-world synth washes. They sound like some of the stuff on The Cure's *Disintegration*, really lush. And it's an exceptionally good vocal from him. I like the military snare and it's well integrated into the recording, which is pristine. It's a welcome change from the cluttered programmed sound of the rockier tracks. Killer guitar solo, really cool false ending, synth bass… this song just knocks me out.

Pontus: It's an epic ballad, very keyboard-driven, expansive, panoramic feel to it, but still, it's a lesser song for me. This one kind of disappeared for me on the album.

Reed: I must say over the years, in the eighties, I was one of those heavy metal guys who said, ugh, to hell with synthesizers, that's not real music. I have grown to love synthesizers. And this song, the fact is that with synthesizers, you instantly get that one particular eighties feel, even though this is 1990. So this is dated a little bit but it sets a mood.

Once again, for like the fifth time on the album, the theme is nostalgia, reminiscence, wistfulness. Plant is singing about an anniversary. Now it's a very nonspecific anniversary. There's a reference to love, another reference to death, but it could be any sad anniversary. But regardless, the music maintains this nostalgic mood, which heightens the effect of the lyric and makes it poignant. It's kind of sad, even if you don't really know what he's singing about. And there's no guitar on this song until we get to the guitar solo, which really stands out. Now that was a studio-type trick, right? Delaying the guitar. But it's very effective. The ending of the song takes a strange turn. We've gone through this melancholy, melodic, ballad-type of song, but at the end we get industrial sounds, chimes, laughter and what I can only describe as an orgasmic sound from a woman's voice and Plant screaming. So you get a literal release at the end of a very cathartic-sounding song. But that makes me feel a little strange at the end of it (laughs).

Martin: And just generally speaking, what are your thoughts on Robert as a lyricist?

Pontus: He's very much about love interests, and he balances looking back but tries to speak in a modern way. I never felt he was a great lyricist. I don't see him as bringing a major message to the world, really. But I must say also, English is not my native language, so I might miss out on some things.

Martin: And how about a report card on his singing?

Pontus: He's in good voice throughout these two albums. He can still scream. He can still go high and really present a good balance and be in control of his voice. The major drop for him was in '74 or '75 when he had his operation. When you listen to *Physical Graffiti*, he drops a few steps there. But I think he controls and steers his voice better in the eighties. But yes, he needed some surgery, after which he couldn't get as high as on *Houses of the Holy*. They actually rearranged "Over the Hills and Far Away" and gave it a new melody so he could do it live so it didn't put a strain on his voice.

Martin: Interesting. Okay, more surprises are in store: "Liars Dance" is just voice and acoustic guitar, over and out in 2:34.

Todd: Yes, it's an acoustic moment on a very noisy and electric album. It sounds the most like Led Zeppelin than anything else on the album. It's perfectly pleasant and probably exactly the right length.

Reed: And I'd say that's really an acoustic guitar, rather than piezo electric guitar. Obviously, this is territory that Page and Plant mined in Zeppelin, and yet I don't think this song sounds particularly Zeppelin-esque. I think it's more reminiscent of Plant's earlier solo work, like "Big Log." It's pretty short. It's written by Doug Boyle and Robert Plant and it's a fantastic two-person song. I absolutely adore this song. Plant really sells the lyric, Boyle plays amazingly. It's a fantastic interlude on this otherwise pretty solidly hard rock album.

Pontus: It's more of a British folk boom song rather than Led Zeppelin-like, more akin to Davey Graham. Joni Mitchell, Bert Jansch and John Renbourn kind of thing, almost an acoustic blues. It's great to see him do this. It comes after this huge, orchestrated song and it works very well. He played it live at that concert I saw, and I think it was a throwback for him. This is where he wants to go and in fact ends up on the later records.

Martin: Closing with "Watching You" really drives home the point that all the rock star lasciviousness and playfulness has pretty much melted away for the last three songs running. Previously there was only "I Cried," and even that is comparatively cheery.

Todd: For sure, and you're right, "Liars Dance" acts as a bridge to "Watching You," which is a great closer. Even though it's got that Phil Collins gated drum influence on it and the jangly guitars and it's high energy, it's really quite serious. It's also got bass pedals towards the end. I think it's just intense and a really effective closer.

Reed: So again, to me, I hear a song that acknowledges Plant's roots in Zeppelin. I think the success of *Now and Zen* really drove home to Robert that people wanted more Zeppelin from him. But it still sounds like modern Robert Plant. Now, he does something very different with the mix of this song. Every instrument is at the same sonic level, including his vocal. Every other song, his vocal is pushed way up, with the guitar just behind and then everything else is down. On this song, everything is at a flat level, which makes it difficult to focus on any particular instrument. Instead you just get this sonic stew. It's how people sometimes describe prog rock, where you're supposed to just sit back and let the whole thing wash over you. You're not concentrating on the lyrics or the rhythm, just the totality. Also, there's a world music vibe here with the simple, tribal drumbeat. I don't know if it's Moroccan or flamenco—those two things are not unrelated—but it's something that is completely absent from the rest of the album, so when it appears here at the end, it really stands out. Also there's no guitar solo. All told, it's an unexpected way to end a hard rock album.

Joe: "Watching You" is a mystical fantasy and it works as an album-ender for me, with Robert really diving into his subconscious. But as I said, the album feels long to me by this point, even though this is a strong closer. I guess I'm all partied-out after "Nirvana" and "Tie Dye on the Highway," but the cool thing is that Robert has a lot more to say still, and deeper things to say.

Pontus: "Watching You" has an acoustic feel but it's dominated by tribal drums that make it big and almost bombastic. But it grows on you. There's some Asian, possibly Tibetan, spoken word stuff in the middle of it. It's a good ending to a record I like a lot. He's in a happy place here, revisiting his past and simultaneously going forward. He's discovered more about himself, which possibly wasn't accomplished to this extent on *Now and Zen*.

Martin: Excellent, and Reed, you've taken a look at the bonus tracks. What have you found?

Reed: Yes, well, I'll start by saying I hate this "Oompa (Watery Bint)" title so much. It's so Robert Plant, too. It's like he comes up with these stupid nonsensical titles that are, I'm sure, working titles in the studio where they just have to mark what song they're working on. They come up with something and then he never bothers to change it. I see that and I'm instantly annoyed.

All of these bonus tracks were on the European release of "Hurting Kind," and they really sound like bonus tracks. They're not of the same quality as the tracks on the main album. "Oompa (Watery Bint)," kind of rockabilly, is the most *Now and Zen*-esque song of the set to me. I don't know if it was a holdover from that album or if he was just still in that mode when he was writing it. Either one of those things are pretty plausible, given there's only a two-year gap between the two. It's fine. Again, wonderful solo. I have learned to love Doug Boyle's playing and he just plays beautifully on this song. And there's a voice at the end that sounds like it's talking over an old walkie talkie or staticky radio or something. I can't hear what it's saying. But again, those things always annoy me.

With "One Love," we're back to the fifties and sixties. We get an actual Bo Diddley beat, which I'm sure is in Plant's DNA, so I'm not surprised that it makes an appearance. But once again, it's Plant in 100% nostalgia mode. He's looking back to his youth. We also get slide guitar. I happen to love slide guitar when it's used sparingly. But yes, prominent slide guitar and some honky-tonk piano in the background on a very late fifties/early sixties-sounding song. "Don't Look Back" is a Billy Vera song, but again, the theme is nostalgia. All three of these songs and this whole album have me suspecting that Plant was spending a lot of time thinking about his teenage years. And again, 42 years old, that's when you start doing that thing, because half your water has already passed under the bridge.

Martin: All right, well, any closing remarks? What's the angle here with this *Manic Nirvana* album? Is the career template or the presentation template Sting or Peter Gabriel? Is it something less serious, like Billy Idol?

Todd: Well, I'd say it's a different approach versus Sting or Peter Gabriel. I think his first two albums are definitely that. With *Manic*

Nirvana, I think he's trying to do something different that's on the cutting edge of all the technology available to him, which is a lot. And he also wants to let everybody know that he's okay with being the guy from Led Zeppelin, that he's okay with dressing like a hippie and using Zeppelin samples and referencing old lyrics and stuff like that. It's hard to put my finger on it. I'm one of those people who likes *Shaken 'n' Stirred* a lot, even though it's a weird, strange album. But then *Now and Zen* came out and it was better received, and I think he liked how that felt. People talked about *Now and Zen* before it came out because of the Led Zeppelin sample on "Tall Cool One," and that gave it a big push. And I think he was saying, that worked for me but I'm going to explore this new technology further, even if it angers some older fans. And I respect that.

Martin: Again, it's kind of surprising that *Now and Zen* goes triple-platinum and this one only goes gold, right?

Pontus: And it's also the year the Led Zeppelin box set came out, and so he's high-profile throughout the year with the album and with the box set and stuff. I don't know how he felt about that. But we can see that slowly he becomes... we get the Page Plant reunion just five years later. But yeah, at this point I think he wants to make a rock album that's a revisiting of his past but without touching Led Zeppelin, particularly, and maybe that wasn't enough for the marketplace.

Todd: Yeah, and I remember that this album went cut-out. It ended up in discount bins. I remember thinking at the time, given that I'd essentially dismissed it, that that made sense. But now I'm as surprised as you are.

Martin: And in retrospect, it seems like this was the last time he'd be trying to hang onto his youth.

Todd: Yeah, I agree. And it makes me wonder if he knew that going into it, that that's what he was going to do. It's a brash, in-your-face album, in terms of both sound and bravado. At the time, me and most of my friends who liked Robert Plant really felt like it was an annoying, noisy record.

Martin: Is it his *Achtung Baby*, do you think?

Todd: Kinda, although it doesn't have the cool factor that *Achtung Baby* had. I heard that and scratched my head and went, "What the hell is this?" and then it creeped into my brain and won me over. *Manic Nirvana* is more like, I'm gonna try all this stuff. I'm gonna hit you really hard with just one crazy thing after another and some of it's going to fail, but some of it you might like. *Achtung Baby* feels more reserved than that. It feels more calculated to win you over. Whereas this is just like, I'm gonna have some fun and try a whole bunch of stuff.

ROBERT PLANT FATE OF NATIONS

ALL RIGHTS RESERVED · UNAUTHORIZED COPYING, REPRODUCTION, HIRING, LENDING, PUBLIC PERFORMANCE AND BROADCASTING PROHIBITED
fontana
℗ 1993 Phonogram Ltd London
The copyright in this sound recording is owned by Phonogram Ltd. (London)
LC 0211
33
STEREO
514867-1
1
ROBERT PLANT — FATE OF NATIONS
1. CALLING TO YOU (Plant/Blackwell)
2. DOWN TO THE SEA (Plant/Jones)
3. COME INTO MY LIFE (Plant/Blackwell/Boyle/MacMichael)
4. I BELIEVE (Plant/Johnstone)
5. 29 PALMS (Plant/Johnstone/Jones/Blackwell/Woods)
6. MEMORY SONG (Hello, Hello)
(Plant/Johnstone/Jones/Blackwell/Woods)
Tracks 1, 2, 3 copyright control
Tracks 4, 5 & 6 copyright control/EMI Virgin Music Ltd.
Produced by Chris Hughes and Robert Plant.
Engineered by Michael Gregovich
Mixed by Tim Palmer
BIEM STEMRA

Supporting the first two albums, December 12, 1983, Hammersmith Odeon, London.
(Ilpo Musto / Alamy Stock Photo)

Shaken 'n' Stirred tour, August 10, 1985, Wembley Arena, London.
(Ilpo Musto / Alamy Stock Photo)

At the WEA Records offices, 1986.
(Ilpo Musto / Alamy Stock Photo)

February 4, 1988, Brown's Hotel, London.
(dpa picture alliance / Alamy Stock Photo)

Supporting *Fate of Nations* on December 23, 1993, Brixton Academy, London.
(Mel Longhurst / Performing Arts Images MLO / Alamy

January 28, 1994, at the National Auditorium, Mexico City, Mexico.
(RTAceves / MediaPunch Inc / Alamy Stock Photo)

Robert Plant, Jimmy Page and Neil Young on January 12, 1995 at the Rock & Roll Hall of Fame ceremonies, held at the Waldorf Astoria Hotel, New York City. Led Zeppelin was inducted at this time.
(Michael Brito / Alamy Stock Photo)

June 10, 2002 at the London Astoria.
(Ilpo Musto / Alamy Stock Photo)Stock Photo)

Robert and Jimmy, performing as Page Plant, January 24, 1995, at the Rock Over Germany festival.
(dpa picture alliance / Alamy Stock Photo)

With Alison Krauss at the 51st Annual Grammy Awards, held on February 8, 2009 at the Staples Center in Los Angeles, California. The duo's *Raising Sand* album won five awards, including Album of the Year.
(Tsuni / USA / Alamy Stock Photo)Stock Photo)

Dreamland tour, July 11, 2003, at the Mazdapalace, Milan, Italy.
(Fabio Diena / Alamy Stock Photo)Stock Photo)

Supporting *Mighty ReArranger*, August 26, 2005, at the Rock en Seine festival in Saint-Cloud near Paris, France.
(Bruno Klein / Abaca Press / Alamy Stock Photo)

Robert and his son Logan watching Wolverhampton Wanderers in 2006.
(David Bagnall / Alamy Stock Photo)

September 26, 2008 at the Austin City Limits Music Festival, Zilker Park, Austin, Texas.
(ZUMA Press, Inc. / Alamy Stock Photo)

In the press room at the 2008 CMT Music Awards, held at the Curb Event Center, Nashville, Tennessee.
(Tammie Arroyo / AFF / Alamy Stock Photo)

Robert performs with Band of Joy on September 2, 2010 at The Forum in Highgate, north London.
(Yui Mok / PA Images / Alamy Stock Photo)

Left: Plant's only concert in Germany in 2011 took place at the Zitadelle in Berlin-Spandau, on August 3. This was a make-up show for a postponed gig in October 2010.
(Britta Pedersen / dpa picture alliance archive / Alamy Stock Photo)

Robert and Band of Joy perform at the Big Chill Festival, August 7, 2011, at Eastnor Castle Deer Park in Herefordshire.
(PA Images / Alamy Stock Photo)

US President Barack Obama speaks with the surviving members of Led Zeppelin (left to right John Paul Jones, Robert Plant and Jimmy Page) during intermission at the Kennedy Center Honors, December 2, 2012 in Washington, DC.
(White House Photo / Alamy Stock Photo)

John Paul Jones, Robert Plant and Jimmy Page on September 20, 2012, gearing up for the release of their *Celebration Day* live DVD, which documents their historic reunion concert of 2007.
(WENN Rights Ltd / Alamy Stock Photo)

December 8, 2017 at the Royal Albert Hall in London.
(Simon Reed / WENN Rights Ltd / Alamy Stock Photo)

July 27, 2018 at the Milano Summer Festival, held at the Ippodromo San Siro, Milan, Italy.
(Roberto Finizio / Alamy Stock Photo)

June 13, 2019 with the Sensational Space Shifters in Stockholm, Sweden.
(Davide Sciaky / Alamy Stock Photo)

A round of applause is in order for a life well lived. Robert in the stands before a Premier League match between Wolverhampton and Liverpool, February 4, 2023.
(Mark Fletcher / MI News & Sport / Alamy Stock Photo)

Fate of Nations

"I think by the time I got to 1991, *Fate of Nations* was an album, a collection, where I was able to deal with various topics, and I wasn't creating little pastiches, which I had done on maybe *Manic Nirvana*. I've always… I was always moving across. My sensitivities were developing. And I think 1991 takes us to twenty-two years ago, something like that, twenty-three. How old would I be? Forty-two. So yeah, I guess it was just waking up. And also, if you go back in time, back to Zep, back to whatever it was, some of the songs are from all stages of my time as a writer. Some have carried far more importance than others, because the music gave me a place to land with something with more intent to put across. Because, what I was writing about when I was 20 is like what you were thinking about when you were twenty, and what we write about when we're in our forties is what we're thinking about when we're forty."

"You know what? My whole deal, like every artist, don't let an artist tell you that they're doing it for the public, because, if you play soccer, you play soccer for yourself. You become part of the team, you want to be a good player, and if you're a singer or a songwriter, you've got to have a certain amount of—and maintain—self-esteem and continue to develop, and that's what I tried to do with my life as a musician. And I am very lucky, because it flows well for me."

Robert Plant

Credits

May 25, 1993
Es Paranza/Atlantic 92264
Produced by Chris Hughes and Robert Plant
Engineered by Michael Gregovich
Recorded at RAK Studios, London, UK, Sawmill Studios, Fowey, UK and Monmow Valley Studio, Monmouth, UK
Personnel: Robert Plant – vocals, Kevin Scott MacMichael – guitars, Phil Johnstone – harmonium, acoustic piano, organ, electric piano, electric orchestra, backing vocals, Charlie Jones – bass, Chris Hughes – drums
Key additional personnel: Francis Dunnery – guitars on "Come into My Life" and "Promised Land," Richard Thompson – guitars on "Come into My Life," Oliver J. Woods – guitars on "Down to the Sea" and "Memory Song (Hello Hello)," Doug Boyle – guitars on "I Believe" and "Network News," Pete Thompson – drums on "Calling to You," "Come into My Life," "Promised Land," "The Greatest Gift" and "Great Spirit," Michael Lee – drums on "Memory Song (Hello Hello)," Chris Blackwell – drums on "Promised Land"

1. "Calling to You" (Plant, Blackwell) 5:48
2. "Down to the Sea" (Plant, Jones) 4:00
3. "Come into My Life" (Blackwell, Boyle, MacMichael) 6:32
4. "I Believe" (Plant, Johnstone) 4:32
5. "29 Palms" (Plant, Blackwell, Jones, Boyle, Johnstone) 4:51
6. "Memory Song (Hello Hello)" (Plant, Johnstone, Jones, Blackwell, Woods) 5:22
7. "If I Were a Carpenter" (Tim Hardin) 3:45
8. "Promised Land" (Plant, Johnstone) 4:59
9. "The Greatest Gift" (Plant, Blackwell, Jones, MacMichael, Johnstone) 6:51
10. "Great Spirit" (Plant, Johnstone, MacMichael) 5:27
11. "Network News" (Plant, Blackwell) 6:40

A *Fate of Nations* Timeline

1991. Shirley Wilson (sister of Robert's ex-wife Maureen) gives birth to Robert's son (and fourth child), Jesse Lee.

January 1991. At the conclusion of the *Manic Nirvana* tour, Robert decides he wants to revisit and embrace select parts of his past.

April 1993. Issued as an advance single from the forthcoming sixth album is "29 Palms," backed with "21 Years," from *The Inner Flame: A Tribute to Rainer Ptacek*. Rainer was an Eastern European guitar prodigy who died of a brain tumour at the age of forty-six. Robert guested on two tracks on the album. This song features just Rainer and Robert. "29 Palms" became one of Robert's most successful singles in the UK, reaching No.21. On the *Billboard* Album Rock Track chart, it got to No.4. The CD single version adds "Whole Lotta Love (You Need Love)," also created with Rainer Ptacek.

May 1 – July 16, 1993. Robert Plant and his band conduct an extensive European campaign in support of *Fate of Nations*.

May 25, 1993. Es Paranza issues, in North America, a sixth Robert Plant album, entitled *Fate of Nations*. The album is issued on Fontana in the rest of the world. It reaches No.34 on the main *Billboard* chart and No.6 in the UK.

June 1993. "I Believe" is issued as a single, followed in August by "Calling to You."

September 10, 1993. Robert Plant appears on *David Letterman*, performing "I Believe" and "29 Palms."

September 15 – December 1, 1993. Robert and the guys play North America in support of *Fate of Nations*.

December 1993. "If I Were a Carpenter" is issued as the final single from *Fate of Nations*. It reaches No.63 on the UK charts. The B-sides are live versions of "Ship of Fools" and "Tall Cool One" recorded at Montreux.

December 6 – 23, 1993. The *Fate of Nations* tour moves back to Europe.

December 7, 1993. Achieving gold status in the US, *Fate of Nation* becomes Plant's last (strictly) solo album to certify.

December 14, 1993. Reprise issues *Wayne's World 2: Music from the Motion Picture.* Opening the 13-track album is Robert on a cover of "Louie Louie."

January 15 – 28, 1994. Robert plays South America and Mexico.

August 9, 10, 1994. Robert plays Marrakesh, Morocco.

October 14, 1994. Robert Plant and Jimmy Page issue a live album called *No Quarter.*

April 11, 1996. "Page Plant" album *No Quarter* is certified gold.

April 21, 1998. Robert Plant and Jimmy Page issue a studio album called *Walking into Clarksdale,* which is certified gold in the US two weeks later. Bassist in the four-man band is Charlie Jones, from *Manic Nirvana* and *Fate of Nations.*

July 6, 1999. Birdman Records issues *More Oar: A Tribute to Skip Spence.* Opening track is Robert doing a rendition of "Little Hands" from the Moby Grape founder's lone solo album *Oar.* Spence had been terminally ill with lung cancer at the time of recording and died on April 16, 1999. Plant covers Moby Grape's "Skip's Song" on 2002's *Dreamland.*

July 23, 1999 – December 2, 2000. Robert and his new covers band embark on the Priory of Brion Tour, playing sporadically but regularly throughout Europe across these many months, mostly small venues. The band consisted of Robert along with bassist Paul Wetton, keyboardist Paul Timothy, drummer Andy Edwards (Frost, IQ) and original Band of Joy guitarist Kevyn Gammond.

April 22, 2001. Robert and his new band, Strange Sensation tour without an album, beginning with a Scandinavian campaign before moving over to America and then back to Europe for the summer festival season.

June 19, 2001. Afro Celt Sound System issue a third album, entitled *Volume 3: Further in Time.* Robert Plant is guest vocalist on a track called "Life Begins Again." It's a duet with Welsh folksinger Julie Murphy, who would also tour as a support act to Plant.

July 30, 2001. Cast issue their fourth and final album, *Beetroot.* It's the last stop for guitarist Liam "Skin" Tyson before he joins up with Robert Plant as part of his backing band, Strange Sensation.

September 7, 2001. Now and Zen is certified triple-platinum in the US.

ITB AND MCP PRESENT
ROBERT PLANT
PLUS SPECIAL GUESTS
NEC ARENA BIRMINGHAM
WEDNESDAY 14th JULY
96·4 BRMB
TICKETS: £14.00 AVAILABLE FROM B/O TEL: 021 780 4133
(SUBJECT TO £1.40 PER TICKET BOOKING FEE).
PERSONAL APPLICATION TO NEC (NO BOOKING FEE),
ODEON CINEMA, TICKET SHOP,
MIKE LLOYD MUSIC HANLEY,
ICC/NIA & BRMB/WAY AHEAD BIRMINGHAM,
NEWCASTLE AND WOLVERHAMPTON, WAY AHEAD/MERCIA FM SHOP
AND POSTER PLACE COVENTRY, WAY AHEAD NOTTINGHAM & DERBY.
(ALL SUBJECT TO BOOKING FEE).
BRIXTON ACADEMY
FRIDAY 16th JULY
CAPITAL 95·8 FM LONDON
TICKETS: £15.00 AVAILABLE FROM B/O TEL: 071 326 1022
STARGREEN 071 734 8932, TICKETMASTER 071 379 4444,
FIRST CALL 071 240 7200, ALBEMARLE 071 580 3141
(SUBJECT TO BOOKING FEE).

…そして "詩" は永遠
の輝きを取り戻す…
ロバート
プラント
アイ
ビリーヴ
アルバム『フェイト・オブ・
ネイションズ』からの第2弾
シングル!!
歌詞付
PHCR-8037
¥1,500 税込(¥1,456 税抜)
95.9.24まで

Martin talks to Todd Evans, Rick LaBonte and Douglas Maher about *Fate of Nations*.

Martin Popoff: After absorbing *Manic Nirvana*, what were your initial impressions of *Fate of Nations*?

Douglas Maher: Well, to set the scene, I feel like *Manic Nirvana* was essentially a stepping stone that failed him commercially in comparison to what *Now and Zen* did. The singles weren't anything to write home about, compared to "Calling to You," which had punch right out of the box. You feel like, okay, I'm going for a ride here. But *Manic Nirvana* fell short in a lot of ways that were unexpected. The anticipation for it didn't play out. It wasn't as successful as *Now and Zen* with MTV. Zeppelin fans thought it was too commercial, too poppy and they could see Robert Plant wasn't really into becoming a modern-day pop star, and they didn't embrace it. And Plant had gotten into this whole thing with sequencers and samples of different sound bites and things, with *Manic Nirvana* especially, which is a record that I think collapsed in on itself from lack of good material. "I Cried" was another one they threw out to radio and it just didn't have the staying power; it didn't stick. *Now and Zen* is known for three or four songs, but that's one of those records that honestly could have spawned off five or six hits if it had been pursued properly.

But everybody knew that Robert Plant was capable of making better music than what he was giving us with *Manic Nirvana*. *Manic Nirvana* was empty calories. It's almost like this schizophrenic Robert Plant moment that nobody talks about, this belaboured experiment to modernise his roots. Musically it's forgettable and both musically and lyrically it's just not a record that carries a lot of water or a lot of weight. And I don't think that anything from it has been played live by him in decades. It feels like one of those albums that he might look at and say, "Well, if I could do this over, I would; I would re-do it this way." It's hitting the panic button. There's a musical crisis with that record. *Manic Nirvana* was not accepted at radio either. Program directors, PDs, were kind of banging their heads. There were two or three tracks that were getting maybe heavy phones for a few weeks and then you could see the drop-off in sales. There's an identity issue going on with that record. Everything seems to be addressing, in my opinion, the good old days, but he wants to frame it in this modern context. It's just a mess.

So, with *Fate of Nations*, we get a bridge album. We start to see Robert Plant transform and move away from what is popular and what is going on in music at that time. What I remember from that era is that you had *Get a Grip*. You had *The Spaghetti Incident?* and *In Utero*, you had *Vs.*, you had *Siamese Dream* and from Rush, *Counterparts*. You had Radiohead, Sarah McLachlan, Crash Test Dummies and from U2, *Zooropa*. You go down the list. There was Tool, Lenny Kravitz, Primus, Depeche Mode Collective Soul, Anthrax. I was like trying in my head to think what was dominating at that time and it's not clearly one style, but it's also definitely not Robert Plant.

Fate of Nations was Robert Plant trying to get back to 1973 in a lot of ways, because you saw organically what was happening in the music scene. People were taking on a lot of different things. People like to pigeonhole this as the grunge era, but grunge really wasn't that long. Grunge was maybe three or four years, and then it went into nu-metal, rap-rock, where you started to see Limp Bizkit and Korn and things like that. So where do you put a guy who's now in decade number four? Where does that guy fit?

I think what happens is that on the musical side he puts all that aside and goes back to purely what he wants to do. But on the lyrical side, the planet's melting, the Gulf War had just wrapped up, technology was starting to be introduced into society that was giving us more information. Previous to this, Plant being the guy who was always off in the country at his castle or whatever, he didn't need to concern himself with geopolitics and all of those things. Now information was becoming more readily available. I'm not saying he was on the Internet in '93 or anything, even though it was available, but cable news was exploding—and especially in real time. And so I think he grasped onto those things. As you put it, his new persona is that of a wise old man. He has these decades and decades of gained wisdom that he's about to bring upon us. But you still find the 1950s rockabilly Robert Plant and the hopelessly romantic Robert Plant still is in there.

Todd Evans: When I heard the real drums on "Calling for You," I felt a lot better about it (laughs). He started making these gestures on *Now and Zen*, but I think he's becoming increasingly confident about being okay with people thinking of him as that Led Zeppelin guy. And I don't know whether that's anywhere near accurate, because I can't climb into his head. Also there's more of that Middle Eastern influence, which you hear immediately on "Calling to You," plus additional "Kashmir" influence in terms of orchestration.

Martin: Yes, and I feel he's also untethered from any sort of style. The eighties is over and he didn't participate in hair metal. Grunge is over and he didn't participate in that either. He's floating in a sea of possibility with respect to the art of album-making. He doesn't hook himself up to anything sitting out there in pop or music culture.

Todd: Yeah, I remember the place that I worked at when I was living in Athens, Georgia. I worked in a photo lab and there was a lady that worked there who was from the UK. And she was much older than me—in her 50s, maybe 60s—and she was just over the moon about this album. I was more like, I'm gonna step lightly—maybe I'll buy that Robert Plant album, maybe I won't. And she was just like, "Oh, you gotta hear it." So that's what I always think of when I when I think of this album is Pauline, my UK friend being very excited about it. But it is Zeppelin-esque, so maybe there's your link to the seventies, which to me is now an era, like you say, untethered by style.

This is a transitional album. On *Manic Nirvana* he covers "Your Ma Said You Cried in Your Sleep Last Night" and that's kind of an image from the sixties, as is the title and album cover. He's now going to continue to reflect on his own musical tastes from way back and, as overlap, dip his toe into Americana.

Rick LaBonte: I agree, *Fate of Nations* is Robert definitely coming to terms with his past. It almost starts as a joke, when Beastie Boys sample Led Zeppelin without permission and then Robert samples himself on "Tall Cool One." And then he invites Jimmy Page to do a couple of guitar solos. Live, you'd get Zeppelin songs but they'd be deep cuts, like "Black Country Woman," "In the Evening" and "Trampled Under Foot." But every album he'd venture more into that Zeppelin territory with no conditions. By *Manic Nirvana*, he throws in a "Black Dog" lyric and "Tie Dye on the Highway" is the first time you really felt like he was doing a full-on Zeppelin-type song since "Slow Dancer," in my opinion.

When you get to *Fate of Nations*, he's just fully onboard embracing it. We're past snippets or brief flashes. He's saying I'm that guy that was singing those classics. His hair might even be longer than it was around the time of *Presence*. He looked like a sheep dog sometimes when he turned his head, because you couldn't see his face. He was such a long-hair, and he really embraced the hippie movement. He retained the best of his band from *Manic Nirvana*. Phil Johnstone joined him, Doug Boyle is on two tracks, but he added a young kid on guitar, Kevin MacMichael, from Cutting Crew, one of us, a Canadian (laughs). People forget this, but Robert himself also plays a little acoustic guitar on *Fate of Nations*, on "Promised Land." Other than that, the only instrument he's ever played on one of his albums is harmonica. And then, lo and behold, he brings in Michael Lee on drums, who plays like John Bonham. He's only on two tracks on the album, but Robert would take Michael Lee on tour, and then he would be the drummer for Page Plant from that day forward. But yes, all those songs are done in different places with different musicians.

Martin: To what extent does this album cover work for you?

Todd: I like it but I don't love it. I like the typeface and the layout of it, and the photo with the brother and sister and teddy bear, I think it's just okay. The significance is obvious, I suppose, and actually pretty ahead of its time, prescient, given climate change. And the booklet is even more political. It's not exactly what we previously thought of as Robert Plant's preoccupations, but it's not a misstep. I think it works.

Rick: What I like is that for the song titles on the back and all through the booklet, he used the same kind of *Lord of the Rings* font they used on Zeppelin *IV*, on the inside sleeve. But I like that he's political here. The album cover shows the kids looking at the world melting, but the theme of the day back then was more about oil and conflicts in the Middle East.

Martin: The booklet is basically a pictorial version of "Network News."

Rick: Oh yeah, big time! And I'm twenty-three years old, dude, and I'm getting involved in environmental issues. I'm the chairperson of the environment today for Local 444; I'm a community environmental organiser. And at that point I'm like, I can't believe my hero is talking my language. Because I was worried about climate change. I was worried about the Gulf War. But showing those little kids, it's like, that's who's ultimately getting exploited by George

Bush and the geopolitics of oil and that's also who we're supposed to save the world for. That's such a good message. He's saying, we need to pass it on. My ancestors were born so my kids could have a planet too, and so on. I think that's so fantastic that he would do that. And of course he's a father and now a grandpa and he's realising he has a voice that people listen to, so he's going to offer a point of view. Plus everybody knows he's one of the original flower child hippies, so it's consistent for him to talk about this. Not to mention the fact that he owns a lot of green space; he loves nature.

Martin: Okay, first track "Calling to You" certainly makes a statement. In fact, I feel like when people forget what's on this album, "Calling to You" is always remembered and serves as a microcosm for the whole thing. In other words, people equate the album with "Calling to You."

Todd: Yeah, that's a good way of putting it. My first impression of it was hearing the real drums, although it's got this bright, heavily processed guitar sound at the beginning, which I always think of as the Alex Lifeson *Hold Your Fire* sound. A lot of people who are very traditional in their rock tastes don't like those kinds of sounds, but I think it's kind of cool. Anyway, the song quickly becomes very traditional with the heaviness and Middle Eastern influence and the synth arrangement that sounds like "Kashmir." It's not that long a song, but I feel like maybe it could have been pared back because it gets repetitive after a while. That's kind of my take on it.

Rick: "Calling to You" is an awesome, Zeppelin-like track, guest violin, incredible video. In fact Page Plant would do this one live. It's almost like Robert's sending a smoke signal message to his fans from all eras, "calling to you, calling to you," asking us to tap into the good spiritual vibes he's putting out. It makes me think about channelling and positive thinking—it's really powerful.

Douglas: "Calling to You" is a beast of a rock song, mystic and haunting. Being on the radio against all of those new grunge bands, it held its own, which is a very difficult thing for somebody who's been around four decades to pull off. Nobody really wanted to hear from the guys from the sixties or seventies anymore, other than like Van Halen, Rush, Aerosmith. I thought it was interesting that he went with Chris Hughes the Tears for Fears guy to produce this album.

Roland Orzabal is a perfectionist. Everybody who knows the story of Tears for Fears, another band that I adore and love, knows that. But I thought he did a really good job with this record. Everything in the sound picture really captured where Plant and this sprawling cast of characters was taking this.

Martin: Nice. I feel like we're even more in that space with "Down to the Sea."

Todd: Sure, yeah: "Life is a big tambourine; the more that you shake it, the better it seems." That stood out even before I ever read the lyrics. It's cool and relatable; everybody knows what he means by that but what a novel way to say it. "Down to the Sea" is more contemporary-sounding than the first track but that Middle Eastern influence is still there.

Rick: "Down to the Sea" is a co-write with his bassist Charlie Jones, which is rare. Interesting that Led Zeppelin has a song called "Down by the Seaside." Really good song in terms of vocal performance. This is a sneak preview of the world music we're going to see more of soon, particularly with the exotic percussion here.

Douglas: With "Down to the Sea," we're more in an Indian music space. Plant continues on a spiritual exploration about age and wisdom and the water taking him home. I like to think of this as Jon Anderson from Yes gone solo, but with a far better band that's backing him. I think Jon Anderson has suffered a great deal in his life from surrounding himself with a lot of players who were nothing really to write home about, kind of copyists and plagiarists, if you will, from the prog scene, where it all starts sounding the same after a while. But this is a Jon Anderson song lyrically, and musically too, just with a far better band.

Martin: And it's interesting that there's a world music percussion vibe to the next one, "Come into My Life,' but it stops there; this one is not Middle Eastern of melody.

Rick: Yes, that's right. "Come into My Life" is framed on acoustic and it's another one where as a vocalist, you really want to take notes. For example, there's this really nice "Come on, come on, come on, baby" section which reminds me of "D'yer Mak'er." It's the same phrasing, just in a different key.

Todd: "Come into My Life," I feel has a flaw. It's got this great, vigorously strummed acoustic rhythm guitar pattern during the chorus but overall I think it's just too long. There's one part where he says, "When you get there, I wanna be there," which is kind of a boring line and he repeats it three or four times. Midway through it, I'm bored. But I do like all of the guitar sounds. That's one of the two tracks that Francis Dunnery plays on and I'm a fan of Francis Dunnery. I like his playing and I can tell it's him. So that's the good part of it.

Martin: Playing aside, it's just cool that Francis is on it, right? That guy's a legend.

Todd: Yes, he is (laughs). And at the time it came out, I didn't know who he was; I discovered him like two or three years later.

Douglas: With "Come into My Life," Plant is starting to recognise his own mortality and he's on a spiritual awakening, a search for hope, mercy and understanding. It's the start of what will be typical nineties/2000s fare for him.

Martin: Yes, and what will come… as a metaphor, I like to think of him as the only rock star I know who now says to the photographers, "Try make me look older."

Douglas: 100% (laughs). Let's not get into Carl Jung here, but yeah, we know what's going on. But what you're saying is 100%. You can go back and look at any live footage—or anything behind the scenes for that matter. I've done this for decades with Plant, watching the transformation back, including the folksy and the Ritchie Blackmore-styled Renaissance clothing. At this point it's a combination that's mostly various forms of retro, and yet he's addressing these modern subjects in *Fate of Nations* such as global warming and war and all of these things really for the first time. But I get your point, increasingly he's proud of the lines on his face.

Martin: Next is "I Believe," with a heartbreaking lyric about his son Karac dying so young.

Douglas: As far as I'm concerned, this is the second best song Plant's ever written, after "In the Mood." The only reason I put "In the Mood" above this is because I think sonically and musically it's a better flowing song and Phil Collins on that song is just perfect; everything is locked-in on "In the Mood." I'm sure somebody would tell me to go read this Zeppelin lyric or what have you, but I don't know if there's anything from his solo material that has been more connecting with the listener than "In the Mood."

This song being about Karac, it becomes the sequel to "All My Love." Martin, I can't be more honest about this. There's a magic to that song and there's a magic to that video that captures the essence of a parent losing their child. And you can hear the moaning still, like you heard in "All My Love." You can hear the longing and the loss that is there. And as a parent of two kids myself, that song affects me deeply every time I hear it and affected me when I was much younger as a teenager, listening to that song, because I was about nineteen when that came out, and I'd lost my father at age eleven. And I thought to myself—and absolutely, this is pre-Internet—I'm like, this is about his son. There's just no doubt about it.

And the night he performed it on *The Tonight Show*, right when Jay Leno had taken over, it was so awful. And then when I saw it live I wasn't satisfied either. This is the problem that I have with Robert Plant solo, is when I go see a band, I want to see the songs at least resemble what's on the record. He has this tendency to speed everything up or rewrite the arrangements so that they're often acoustical or whatnot. It's usually very basic, no frills. He never really has a big stage production or anything. He doesn't give honour to songs that deserve it. And I was really surprised when I did see this tour at just how disappointing it was that he wasn't singing the notes, he wasn't harmonising, there were guitar parts missing. It was a real disappointment that Plant has the tendency to do that. I've seen him six times. I walk out most of the time and I'm like, yeah, it was a good show, but does it blow me away? No, because it doesn't sound really like anything that I'm used to.

Even "Tall Cool One;" that song hasn't been performed how it's supposed to be ever. It's always so fast and it's always got distortion and we gotta have multiple players just sounding like they're playing on Led Zeppelin *I* or *II*, doing all this feedback and distorted crap all the time. It's just not necessary. That's where the appreciation for bands like Yes and Genesis and Rush comes from with me, and Steven Wilson and Porcupine Tree or Dream Theater. These bands take such time and care and effort to sound like, hey, here's the song you know. Van Halen was the same way. This is what y'all love and this is what you're all gonna get. If it's David Lee Roth, you're not getting the voice though. But yeah, I remember him playing "I Believe" on *The Tonight Show* and the song just did not transfer well to television at all.

Todd: I kind of feel like when we get to "I Believe," that's when the album starts getting really good. From hereon to the end, it's really strong. And when the album came out, I used to think it was front-loaded. But now that I've gotten older and spent some more time with it, if anything, it's back-loaded. But "I Believe" was my favourite track back when it came out. There's some chord changes that are really beautiful. And there's some really pretty guitar work that's kind of a repeated pattern. It's almost a new wave approach, and then the chords change around it, which I always think is a cool thing to do. "I Believe" puts the album back on track. The lyrics, of course, are really touching and the background vocals are nice. There's a couple of guitar solos and both of them are kind of different-sounding and understated. But yeah, "Tears from your mother, from the pits of her soul/Look at your father, see his blood run cold," that's just some powerful wordsmithing.

Rick: I agree that this is one of the greatest songs Robert's ever written. It's got a fairly conventional pop melody but of course the lyrics make you think. Musically, it's got this U2/The Edge guitar thing going on in the background and it's interesting, the type of chords that they play. It's another great vocal, and when he holds that falsetto note, man, the way he does it is pure ear candy. And in the lyrics, besides the tragic story and those emotions, he finds something constructive to say, basically saying despite what happens in life, try not to be so cold, put out some goodwill to your fellow man.

Martin: Next is "29 Palms," and the lush, timeless pop writing and attendant production values persist.

Douglas: Yes, and again, convincingly leaving the eighties technology of the last two records. This is not about 29 palm trees in California, even though in the video he drives around San Bernardino. It's about an affair with Alannah Myles, who he had been on tour with during *Manic Nirvana*. And he touches on that in the song where he references her velvet glove. We all know who had a massive hit called "Black Velvet." Plant played "29 Palms" on *David Letterman* and I saw him live the following night.

There was a separation that was going on with his wife and into a divorce right in that time period. It was a very touchy subject; it was taboo to talk about this stuff. I remember being in radio at that time and somebody saying that to me, that, "Hey, did you know that Robert Plant a year ago was sleeping with Alannah Myles?" And I was like, "Well, I thought he was married." Like, "Yeah, well, not anymore; that's ending." And then he wound up I think having an affair with his ex's sister. So the bad boy was still there.

But Robert Plant was always a very committed family man as far as that was concerned. Page had to talk him back into not retiring. He was going to become a school teacher when his son died. He was just going to leave music altogether. And Page convinced him to come back. And then I know that Plant had developed this in the early eighties, where you almost got this zero fucks attitude about whether he was going to be seen as popular or not. It became, "I am Robert Plant and this is what I'm going to do." Anyway, I own the "29 Palms" CD single, which had "21 Years" and "Dark Moon" on it, with another version of "Whole Lotta Love." Some of that could have gone on the album because I think there's some filler spots where something like "Dark Moon" might have assisted.

Rick: The guitars on "29 Palms" give me a "Big Log" vibe, although it's more up-tempo and rockin'. But yeah, to me, I picture Robbie Blunt playing this, given how lyrical it sounds. I like the call-and-response structure and it's dramatic and yet delicate, with macho hard rock Robert Plant and Robert Plant, the softie, all in one song (laughs). I love that contrast of personality. And although it's not something with bells and whistles, the production itself serves as ear candy.

Todd: Again, they give you these really creative repeated guitar patterns, kind of the simplistic, less is more approach where the guitarist is repeating something, but then when something changes, you really notice it. That's kind of a Police or an eighties Genesis thing. It's got a really nice country-flavoured guitar solo that's very brief. But to me, it sounds like Vince Gill, the guy who's in The Eagles now, who is a really good guitarist, but kind of simple and laid-back. I just think "29 Palms" is great melodically; it's extremely melodic and the chorus is memorable and it's one of my favourite Robert Plant songs, actually.

Martin: "Memory Song (Hello Hello)" is the less popular or punchy follow-up to "Calling to You," I suppose.

Rick: Sure, and like "Calling to You," it's a tip of the hat to Zeppelin. It's one of two featuring Michael Lee on drums, so yeah, the drums are big and bombastic and very John Bonham-like, from the playing through to the production. It sounds live off the floor, one take, with all this cool vocal ad-libbing and guitar licks at the end. It's like they're performing right in front of you.

Douglas: "Memory Song," dreams, memories, scratch lyrics, at least compared to some of the others on the album, Page-like solos. Very Zeppelin in an *In Through the Out Door* style, in my opinion. It's a lot of the oh-oh-ing, and, ugh, I hit my maximum with Robert and that a lot of times over the years.

Todd: I don't like the title of this one; I just find it messy and gimmicky. Also—and he does this a couple of times on this album—I don't think it has a chorus. It kind of goes A, B, A, B and then there's a C, which is a bridge, but it's kind of not a bridge to anywhere. And then it kind of goes A, B again. I like that; I like it when somebody does a song and it's not going to go where you expected. It's just going to do these two things. And then this third thing, the C part. The part in the middle where he sings, "You touch my soul" for the second time is really beautiful, and that's where we also get the "Hello, hello." It's just a gorgeous chord progression.

Martin: I love this album too, but the one unfortunate thing is that there's no band. It's just a huge pile of people scattered about the songs.

Todd: I don't care for that. I would rather he had a band. I'm gonna go back to my lazy and predictable love for the first three albums, because even though there's a couple drummers on the first two and then Richie Hayward on the third, it still felt like a band. Even though *Shaken 'n' Stirred* is a weird album, Richie plays more like Phil Collins than he did in Little Feat. It's still the same big drum sound with effects on it, but still clean. So when this album came out with the individual credits per song, which was helpful, I was less happy about it. Although one of the backing vocalists on the album is Máire Brennan, and she was in Clannad and her sister is Enya. And

I thought, well, that's a really interesting person to be on a Robert Plant album.

Martin: Talking about not being happy, I certainly wasn't thrilled seeing a cover of "If I Were a Carpenter" on the album. That just killed the creative vibe for me.

Todd: No, I didn't like that either. When I was a younger man, it was definitely all about oh, geez, a cover, great. Like, I waited three years for this album. Why is there a cover? And why is it *this*? But I think it's really good. It represents that preview of the Americana to come. And another thing that I really liked about it, it's got this very cool 1960s pop string arrangement, and this really echoey drum sound played by Chris Hughes from Adam and the Ants and Tears for Fears, who is also the producer, so he has a big role. He plays on eight out of 11 songs on the album. So it's an interesting sound, very traditional, something you would have heard on a Wrecking Crew recording from the 1960s, like one of the Davy Jones Monkees songs or something like that. I think it's classy; it sounds sophisticated. The lead vocal is kind of Zeppelin-esque. It's an interesting song for him to be singing like Led Zeppelin Robert Plant on, but it's a cool combination.

Rick: Yes, a Tim Hardin song, a pretty faithful acoustic arrangement. It's a "Going to California" moment. Robert would actually piggyback this song with "Going to California" and other acoustic songs when he played it live. It's a beautiful song, and he brings strings into it like he did with "Sea of Love." He delivers that song better than anybody I've ever heard, a testament to what a great singer he was.

Douglas: I do think there was a level of fear and insecurity in his lyrics and the imagery of this album. I don't know if I'm thinking too deep or what have you, but "If I Were a Carpenter," even though it's a cover, supports that premise for me. That's a song about somebody having issues with their own masculinity, and going through a divorce and a separation and all of these things. I think he feels like part of his own world has just crumbled in on him. And he needed to look at that from a musical perspective and say, this is what made me who I am and what was in my soul. He was reaching back into this kind of songbook to re-identify. He did it with his look and he did it with his flirtatious behaviour, which became much more grandiose at that time. He was embracing this idea of... I'm still popular four decades later. How about that? But yeah, Tim Hardin song, gorgeous video, stunning string arrangement. But why is Robert Plant singing about male insecurity? This is the guy who talked about having his lemon squeezed down his leg.

Martin: But it's complex. The rock star is still there.

Douglas: The rock star is still there but there's also the coming full circle, where you do feel like you are in '71, '72, '73, at times. I don't think Plant ever went back to the sixties with these kinds of records. I think he was trying to capture moments and feelings and vibes from those times but musically, I don't think so. I think it was more about the early seventies, and he was able to get himself and his band to that place or in that mindset fairly easily. *Now and Zen*, the original name of that album was *Summer of Love*. So the intention originally for *Now and Zen* was to have that be more of an open, flower power/ Summer of Love vibe. And that's when the label stepped in and that's where Phil Johnstone and the publishing house songs happen, and it worked. He'd learned his lesson, at least for that specific project and time period. and everything else. Do I think he's taken it to extensions that I don't think were necessary? Yeah.

Martin: I'll state for the record that the production on *Fate of Nations*, at least to these ears, is completely conservative. It's just like a sober, timeless late seventies kind of production, right?

Douglas: Totally agree. And it doesn't surprise me that Chris Hughes, being a perfectionist and working with Tears for Fears, could find that sound. He has the ability to tap into that. If you listen to any Tears for Fears record, sonically they're masterpieces. And that is something that I'm glad that Plant did with this and didn't make it overly grungy.

Martin: "Promised Land" sounds like one that if he would have added electronic drums, could have fit on *Manic Nirvana*. It's junky and funky and just kind of irritating.

Todd: Yeah, "Promised Land" I like because of the Hammond organ, but maybe that's the only reason. It's an okay track. It's a bit of a dip in the second half of the album.

Martin: I gotta say, Todd, I'm generally super-impressed with Robert's lyrics in the solo canon, more than in Led Zeppelin, but quite often, it's like he's playing the role of a blues lyricist or a trite love song or pop song lyricist and he kind of checks out, but with intention, or self-awareness.

Todd: Well, I feel like that's what makes him good, is that a lot of times I don't notice them and I have to deep-dive to really appreciate them, even the one I don't like. He's only got one that stands out that I don't like, and it's one a lot of people point out: "I was pumping iron while you were pumping irony." And so even when I don't like it, it can be amusing. But yeah, because he's not the best enunciator, it causes you to read the lyrics, and then you're pleasantly surprised at how poetic and intellectual he can be, or even usually is.

Rick: "Promised Land" is a throwback to when he brought out the harmonica for "When the Levee Breaks," where they cranked the delay on the harmonica to where it's so distorted that it's overlapping each other. He has about a quarter-second delay on it, so like one second and a quarter the note works out, playing overtop each other. So displacing that with the beat, it sounds cool. And it's a good song, but maybe not as important as the others. I also think he puts a little bit of tremolo on his voice like he did on "Hats off to (Roy) Harper." It's a jammer. They needed a jam, and hats off to that technical thing that he did on "When the Levee Breaks."

Douglas: I think the lyrics to "Promised Land" are fairly scratch, pretty stupid, "Baby, baby" bullshit. But I hear "Hey, Hey, What Can I Do" tangents, with some church organ mixed in. And by the time you get to the end of this record, you start thinking to yourself, how much closer are we to a Led Zeppelin reunion, right? He's borrowing so much now from his catalogue on each of these records, that regularly you're hearing three to five seconds of Zeppelin tunes popping up here, there and everywhere, even in the main riffs, which is both intentional and funny.

Martin: I get an austere *Now and Zen* vibe from "The Greatest Gift;" pretty ambitious ballad, with a bit of a soul influence.

Rick: Yes, wonderful, dramatic song with Plant as a vocalist at his best; I love everything about it. One of the things that makes this album awesome is the way that it's produced and mixed, so like the instrumentation and then the proper separation so that you can hear everything in the mix. I'm surprised this song never got the attention it deserved. He's given us rockers, but it's songs like this where you get to see his sense of vocal melody. It's so sugary, so sweet. This album has all the lushness and brightness that I think is lacking on *Dreamland*. All the frequencies are represented, and everything can be heard. But yes, this is one of those songs where you say, "You want to know how to mix an album? Listen to 'The Greatest Gift.'"

Todd: This is my favourite track on the album. It's a nice and dreamy kind of a groove with a gorgeous string arrangement by this guy named Lynton Naiff, who is from this obscure jazz rock band called Affinity and eventually ended up in Toe Fat. But the string arrangement is just spectacular, one of the best I've ever heard, and just pervasive throughout the song. He really makes this track special. And this is the other song Francis Dunnery is on, and his guitar work is very atmospheric. I like pretty much everything Francis does. He's a little out there psychologically but he's a great guitarist and a really creative composer with a big solo canon, and of course he was in It Bites. In fact, Genesis wanted him to join the band when Phil left and he turned it down. He would have been perfect, because not only is he a full-on guitarist and writer, but he's got a voice that sounds like both Peter Gabriel and Phil, who of course, weirdly turned out to sound quite similar.

Douglas: If there was ever an A&R person with a soul, they would have demanded a video for "The Greatest Gift" and pushed this song at VH1 and adult contemporary radio. It's got gorgeous melodies and the harmonies and string arrangements are top-notch. And the lyrics are gut-wrenching, a confession of the soul thing to a guardian angel, and then delivered in an R&B style. It could have been an absolute monster, if people were actually paying attention anymore after the third or fourth single. But it just had too much competition. Plus you started entering that era of music where you were getting pounded by hip-hop and rap and hard rock and you were leaving the hair metal stage behind. The powers that be in Robert's corner were caught meandering with radio. The identity crisis had arrived for Plant and he's got to make the decision. He's at that crossing point here. Where am I going to go?

Martin: I guess the answer is, given a vast generality about the rest of the catalogue, kind of lo-fi and quiet.

Douglas: 100%. It's a telescope into the future. You're literally sitting there in that song and going, "I see what's coming." But he took a long time, because you've got the Page Plant stuff, two significant albums and a lot of touring. It's nine years until the next solo album. That's a long time. And then to come back into commercial rock radio? Good luck. It's next to impossible, especially once you hit the 2000s. If you think you're going to be successful in any of these new formats, forget it. MTV was not going to play you. And rock radio at that point was treating legacy acts like, "Yeah, we might give you one track that we'll throw into rotation when the record comes out."

Martin: Kind of weird, but we're in that same smooth R&B space with "Great Spirit," and it's even got "great" in the title, also like the last one.

Rick: Yeah, and really putting you in that place is that wah-wah guitar at the beginning, a bit funky, not quite what they call chicken scratch, but rhythmic like that, plus those girl group backing vocals. It's a great arrangement, with lots to arrange. The first bit of lyric is "Who has chased the moonbeams?" and then later you get "The accident remains the same," which both remind me of Zeppelin. This is a style that he's never really done, but still, there are these touchstones that keep it anchored as a Robert Plant solo song.

Todd: "Great Spirit" has this funky laid-back groove with lush background vocals. There's a great bluesy guitar solo which, according to the credits, would be Kevin MacMichael from Cutting Crew. It reminds me of a Marillion song called "House."

Douglas: Thinking about "Great Spirit," you might agree with this or maybe not, but I've always though, okay, Lenny Kravitz gets hits with stuff like this. But Robert Plant in 1993? Yeah, not gonna happen. And the leading reason—and I think there's no greater truth to this—it's because it's Mercury Records. And Mercury Records in 1993 no longer gives a shit about rock music. They don't care about rock bands the way that they used to. They've made their fortunes on Def Leppard, Bon Jovi, Scorpions and Rush. You could go through all these other bands that Mercury had to get them through the eighties and really capitalise on monster records that probably paid for hundreds of penthouses, nationwide or worldwide. I was shocked that Robert went with Mercury, knowing how R&B-centric and pop-centric and hip-hop-centric they were getting. But yeah, they had gone away from being really focused on pushing rock artists, never mind legacy artists. Now it's 1993 and Mercury's not going to do anything to resurrect somebody's career at that point. It's just about being a distribution company.

Martin: All right, onto the last track, "Network News," which rhythmically and arrangement-wise feels like another *Manic Nirvana*-worthy song.

Todd: "Network News" is one I didn't like so much when this album came out. Calling a song "Network News" gives you an expectation that it's going to be political and it doesn't disappoint. It seems to be anti-violence and about environmental issues. One of the lines is, "Upon the sands such damage done to spoil God's finest treasure." Lyrically it's really good. I like how he closes this album with a couple of quiet songs but then finally this one, which is loud and action-packed and a great closer. Like I say, for most of my life I thought this record was front-loaded. "Calling to You" and "Down to the Sea" are great but I think it stalls a bit with "Come into My Life" and then it just picks right back up.

Rick: "Network News" is a rocker, and its representative of a common trait of his when it comes to choruses, where he makes these oohs and aahs integral to the chorus. You get this in "29 Palms" and "Tie Dye on the Highway." That pure vocalising is used as a hook to get you interested. That's a Robert Plant signature—he owns it, and you can hear it somewhere on most of the albums. Now this is a very political song. It reflects most of the stuff you see photographed in the booklet, about oil and the Gulf War. It's got a bit of a "Heartbreaker" feel to it (sings it). It's not the same riff, but a Zeppelin lick or a Zeppelin attack. It's an original song, but he's winking at the listener, referencing the past. He does that really well. He can keep one foot in the past and one foot in the present and yet he's running toward the future. It's weird, but somehow he can do all of that.

Douglas: I hear "Network News" and I go why? Do we really have to close out this record, which has some really beautiful moments on it, with this dreadful, noisy, horrible message? The whole album thus far is dealing with a search for peace and love and understanding. And this is what he gives us at the end: death, blood, guns, sand and oil. Got it. Still going on in 2023.

Martin: I guess it's a song about the album cover then. And the booklet.

Douglas: Yeah, that's all it really was. It's essentially tapping into what cable news was doing to people at home. You no longer just had ABC, CNN and CBS and PBS sometimes. It was expanding; different information centres were being developed. The internet was developing. All kinds of sources of information were coming at you.

Martin: And actually, you look at the booklet, and those central political images are all chaotic and collaged with the text typed in simple typewriter courier around the edges like they had to figure out how to squeeze it in. And then the rest of the booklet, like the lyrics, has this spiritual calm that you are talking about.

Douglas: Absolutely. I'll say this: What a difference ten years makes in rock. Particularly with "Network News" Plant is sounding more worried and political. You listen to his interviews and he is just completely over with the eighties—wants nothing to do with it, even his own eighties catalogue. He's thrilled that music is more organic and based in guitar, bass, drums and vocals.

But it's 1993 and grunge and hip-hop are kings at the CD store and on MTV. Plant has been on the scene now into his fourth decade. Does anyone, to be blunt, give a fuck? Kinda, sorta. He does a twenty-nation tour and there's a drop-off from arenas. I don't know how that tour made money. This was during the whole Coverdale Page time period as well. And you saw Plant becoming overly snipe-y and sarcastic about that. I'm not saying that he felt his status was threatened. Revisionist history people would say, "Oh well, Coverdale Page, that thing bombed." No it didn't. It sold a million records, which was more than *Fate of Nations* or *Manic Nirvana*. And it was more successful on MTV, it was embraced more by radio, they played arenas. Plant saw that and he didn't like that at all. He always had this thorn in his paw with Coverdale. MTV gave both projects a fair shake in the beginning, airing the videos for those singles, "Calling to You" and "29 Palms," which got to No.4 on *Billboard*.

But yeah, tour-wise, he took this album all over the place. It was insane how much he toured this thing. But he also went out of his way to do a lot of late-night shows globally and in America to promote the record. But the problem is, Plant is no longer an arena act. The people aren't buying the tickets. Robert Plant becomes a theater act. He's playing to 4,000 to 7,000 people, max. I know when I saw the *Fate of Nations* tour in Sunrise Musical Theatre down in South Florida, they booked him two nights, but they weren't sellouts. Previously he was selling out Hollywood Sportatorium, Miami Arena. You're talking 15,000 seats, 16,000 seats, no problem. And that was shocking because you're hearing Led Zeppelin on the radio twenty times a day.

Also shocking, "If I Were a Carpenter," even though it's a cover song—beautiful, beautiful song—didn't chart. He made a video for this song and it was gorgeous. And I'm thinking to myself when I'm watching it, yeah, this is absolutely magical. If this had come out when *Manic Nirvana* came out, when you had Edie Brickell and Sophie B. Hawkins and Sarah McLachlan, that would have fit in. You're missing the boat here by a few years doing that.

Martin: Maybe by the late eighties, he'd be playing Lilith Fair.

Douglas: Yeah. I don't know how much the ladies would have embraced that. I don't know that in terms of sexual politics, they would have been on his side. But yeah, back to 1993, as you know, your boy up in Canada, the late Kevin MacMichael, was the guitarist, founding member of Cutting Crew. And he toured on *Fate of Nations*. I felt so bad for that guy, because I remember seeing them live, and I remember saying to my friend Darren, who I was at that show with, I go, "This guy's not going to have a job." And he's like, "Why?" "Because Page and Plant are getting back together. They're gonna do *MTV Unplugged* and the whole thing." A lot of people tend to forget how the *No Quarter* thing really took off. As soon as Plant's tour was ending, he just moved right into that project. And the success that Plant was able to get off of that—boom!—put him right back into arenas.

I don't know, hopefully Robert Plant as a solo artist gets his due. I know he's in the Rock and Roll Hall of Fame with Zeppelin. I believe he should be in there as a solo artist. And I think it's the same thing with Phil Collins. Phil Collins is one of three artists who has sold 100 million records as a solo artist and 100 million with Genesis, globally. And he's not in the Hall of Fame on his own. That's just unbelievable to me. People say the Hall of Fame really doesn't mean anything anymore, but you know what I'm saying? Plant deserves his due. I think if Robert Plant didn't have a solo career like he had in the eighties, he'd be on the Led Zeppelin tribute circuit. He'd just be playing Led Zeppelin songs 24/7. But he had an adventurous and successful career and I applaud his efforts that he did. He wasn't afraid about trying new things, even with the Honeydrippers stuff, even if that was done partly as a tribute to his mom! Anyway, there's a lot of great stuff that he did. It's not anything that's going to wind up in textbooks, but there was some damn good music pushed out by these guys.

Dreamland

"As far as my voice is concerned, what I do to keep my voice, as far as live shows go, I just keep working. I was joking with Peter Gabriel recently about the kind of workloads and stuff, and a lot of my peers think that I must be absolutely nuts, because I do work lots. But I do have a great time doing it, and I'm in really good company. So my spirits are high, and I don't believe there's anything I can't do. And I can re-adapt. I can visit a career that's pretty long now, so I can modify. Some people get a little bit, shall we say, overtly creative about it, and some people get a little negative. But I have a good time. And I see the way that people like Neil Young work, and the guys that have been around for a while who do the same thing. And I think that's a great place to come from—just keep reinventing. So I sing with optimism."

Robert Plant

Credits

July 16, 2002
Universal 314 586 962-2
Produced by Robert Plant and Phill Brown
Engineered by Phill Brown
Recorded at RAK Studios, London, UK, Moles Studio, Bath, UK and
The Church Studios, London, UK
Personnel: Robert Plant – vocals, Justin Adams – guitars, gimbri,
darbuka, Porl Thompson – guitar, John Baggott – keyboards, Charlie
Jones – bass, Clive Deamer – drums

1. "Funny in My Mind (I Believe I'm Fixin' to Die)" (Bukka White,
Plant, Adams, Deamer, Baggott, Jones, Thompson) 4:44
2. "Morning Dew" (Bonnie Dobson, Tim Rose) 4:24
3. "One More Cup of Coffee" (Bob Dylan) 4:01
4. "Last Time I Saw Her" (Plant, Adams, Deamer, Baggott, Jones,
Thompson) 4:39
5. "Song to the Siren" (Tim Buckley, Larry Beckett) 5:52
6. "Win My Train Fare Home (If I Ever Get Lucky)" (Plant, Adams,
Deamer, Baggott, Jones, Thompson) 6:01
7. "Darkness, Darkness" (Jesse Colin Young) 7:08
8. "Red Dress" (Plant, Adams, Deamer, Baggott, Jones, Thompson)
5:21
9. "Hey Joe" (Billy Roberts) 7:02
10. "Skip's Song" (Skip Spence) 4:45

A *Dreamland* Timeline

May 22, 2002. Robert and his band begin their tour in support of the forthcoming *Dreamland*, starting in Portugal.

July 16, 2002. Robert Plant issues a seventh solo album, consisting mostly of covers, entitled *Dreamland*. Issued as singles are "Morning Dew," "Song to the Siren" and "Last Time I Saw Her." A collectors special edition CD includes an alternate mix and radio edit of "Song to the Siren," two BBC sessions and a video track. A collectors special edition DVD includes a ten-song set recorded live at KLRU Studios, September 15, 2002 plus a spate of radio and TV performance tracks.

July 18, 2002. Robert performs "Darkness, Darkness" on the *Late Show with David Letterman*.

July 20 – September 15, 2002. Robert and the band tour America in support of *Dreamland*.

October 8 – 30, 2002. Robert conducts and extensive UK tour.

November 5 – 14, 2002. Robert tours Europe, closing off with two dates in Russia.

December 31, 2002. Chief guitarist on the *Fate of Nations* album, Kevin Scott MacMichael, dies of lung cancer at the age of fifty-one. A Maritime Canadian, MacMichael's main claim to fame was "(I Just) Died in Your Arms," the smash hit he had with his UK-based band Cutting Crew in 1986.

January 6 – 8, 2003. Robert and Strange Sensation mate Justin Adams perform at the Festival au Desert in Timbuktu, Mali.

June 17 – August 23, 2003. Robert capitalises on the European festival season, performing at sporadic but regular events.

November 4, 2003. Robert issues a two-CD rarities and hits compilation called *Sixty Six to Timbuktu*.

November 29, 2003. Robert plays Cape Town, South Africa.

2004. Viktor Krauss issues an album called *Far from Enough*. On it is a cover of "Big Log," featuring lead vocals by his sister Alison.

January 31, 2005. "Page Plant" album *No Quarter* is certified platinum.

February 19, 2005. Robert performs in support of the Tsunami Crisis in Asia Benefit for Oxfam.

Martin talks to John Clauser, Rick LaBonte and Reed Little about *Dreamland*.

Martin Popoff: Okay, so we get to *Dreamland*, and this certainly wasn't expected. Or was it inevitable? What's the lay of the land that delivers to us *Dreamland*?

Rick LaBonte: I think there are a lot of variables as to how we get here. And we get a taste of it with *Fate of Nations*, where he re-embraced his past with Led Zeppelin. He grew his hair really long and he's gone through Page Plant, where there was lots of Zeppelin as well as world music. But I think also *Fate of Nations* demonstrated again his love for folk music. So he's still this mix of folk and blues and sixties psychedelia. *Walking into Clarksdale* gave us some of that, with "When the World Was Young" and "Heart in Your Hand," where Plant's doing a trippy Jim Morrison thing. It's also similar to something like "What Is and What Should Never Be," where it's really soft and he yells and you get these bombastic, heavy chords. I hear that format in both *Dreamland* and *Mighty ReArranger*. But Plant is not showing off his voice like he would do in the early days. He's more mature. If he's going to play the banshee, he wants it to be occasional and always emotive. He'll make sure he captures your attention and then he'll give you the rebel yell in the chorus.

So there's a good and regular loud/soft dynamic on *Dreamland*, although for the most part, he's doing it with covers—there are only three originals on the album. He's doing a lot of tipping the hat to folk heroes of the past and taking some of the African music ideas he's learned and massaged it all into this new band, Strange Sensation. When Page Plant stopped touring, he did a tour with a band called Priory of Brian, a really psychedelic band, and they are pretty much the building blocks of Strange Sensation. The idea was to grab characters from different walks of life, different backgrounds, young people, who he then would school on all these aspects of his past. Even *Manic Nirvana* was like that, where he had this young cast, but then the idea was to show them the old man still knew how to rock. And with *Dreamland*, he wanted to be contemporary, but even more so apply it to this complex personal history.

But he didn't want to hear Jimmy Page out of these guys. He wanted to hear their own take on this traditional music he was throwing at them. And even if they were to play a Led Zeppelin song, it was going to be a completely different arrangement. He'd be the mighty rearranger. You'd get mandolin, banjo, some of those acoustic instruments, and yet it would still sound dramatic because the band would be so good at dynamics. As a listener you'd appreciate it when they got to a heavy chord, because the band lifted the song up so well. He found the right personalities who could be creative without resorting to hard rock instrumentation, or even if it was electric, as it often is on *Dreamland*, nothing would be played in a hard rock manner. You've got this weird keyboard player in John Baggott who could play psychedelic, and then you've got these acoustic players like Justin Adams who can play blues and rock, and then you've got Pearl Thompson—Porl Thompson from The Cure—who could play noisy electric stuff, even approaching heavy metal guitar. Clive Deamer on drums is really talented, and could play prog, different time signature stuff, and he'd be throwing all sorts of ideas into these songs. And then on top of that, these guys are really thinking like a band.

And what does Robert call it? Strange Sensation. Because it's not just him hiring a bunch of young guns, people trying to deliver on his product. They are now brainstorming and thinking, how can we make this even weirder? How can we stretch the song? How can we give you a taste of Zeppelin and still make it an homage to Lead Belly and two or three other things at once? He presented a strange crew who somehow were able to strike this balance.

John Clauser: Yes, well said, but I think he had a future vision, where he put this band together and a covers album would serve as a feeling-out process. *Dreamland* would be a way for Robert to explore his influences and then watch what these guys would bring to the mix. We get seven covers and three originals. When you get together in a band, what's the first thing you do? You don't just start writing new songs right away; you want to jam on stuff that you're comfortable with and then you kind of explore from there. And I think that's what Robert was doing with these guys.

Reed Little: It's interesting because when *Fate of Nations* came out, he talked about getting back to his roots and paying tribute to bands like Moby Grape, which is a form of nostalgia. And then he gets back with Jimmy Page and does two nostalgia albums, first with a lot of reinterpreting and then with a lot of retro-sounding originals. Now he's back to his own solo work. We're in the 21st century now; it's

2002 and Robert is 54 years old. A lot of time has passed since *Manic Nirvana*, which I also feel was heavy with reflection and reminiscence.

And what I find absolutely fascinating about this album is even though it's so nostalgic and more than half cover songs—it's lot of singer-songwriter stuff, like Bob Dylan and Tim Buckley, plus old blues numbers—it's simultaneously very futuristic in its presentation, or at least au courante. So I think of it as a retro-futurist album. And that is absolutely fascinating to me, this idea of being nostalgic on the face of it, but couching it in this youthful idea generation.

As a result this is my favourite Robert Plant album, which I didn't expect. I do not like old blues and I especially don't like the old Delta Blues that those English guys worshipped so much. I do not connect with it; it does nothing for me. But Robert provides so much sonic interest on this album. I have to put a lot of that down to his new backing band Strange Sensation, featuring none other than Pearl Thompson formerly of The Cure. If I were to describe the general sonics of this album to somebody who had never heard it but was generally familiar with Robert Plant, I would say *Dreamland* sounds like The Cure doing a Doors cover album with Robert Plant singing.

Martin: Any thoughts on this album cover, and how it relates to the contents?

Rick: When I think *Dreamland* and listen to this music, I picture people passing a peace pipe back and forth or smoking a doobie (laughs). But no, the cover relates to "Song to the Siren," because I think they were going to call the album that. But, sure, *Dreamland* is dreamy and slow, kind of like a slumber party album. It's not something you put on to rock out. It's for relaxing and mellowing out. So the title works and so does the cover, with that, I guess, siren, playing a harp, playing a siren song, and the people coming ashore from those ships, which makes you think of distant, exotic lands, dreamlands.

Martin: All right. Let's roll our way through this thing, beginning with "Funny in My Mind (I Believe I'm Fixin' to Die)."

Reed: Okay, "Funny in My Mind" is a half original composition because they credit Bukka White, and the rest of the band gets a writing credit as well, so there's some new musical element to it. Immediately we hear some of these Cure-esque sonic elements.

We get that both in the guitars and in the keyboards, your primary melody instruments. In almost all of the songs, there's what I eventually came to call a disquieting synthesizer pad. There's an underlying sonic layer that goes through the entire song which is just slightly at odds with what you're hearing. There's this constant musical tension to the song. And it's funny, but just that is enough to give even a straight blues cover more interest to me. Because if I never hear another straight-up 12-bar blues, I will not be sad. But this song has interest. And when you get to the guitar solo, you could cut the guitar solo off this and paste it onto a song from The Cure's *Wish* and it would fit perfectly. Now, *Wish* is from the eighties, so that's not exactly a 21st century sound, but as a stew, the idea of this old blues number with that weird, disquieting keyboard and then the Cure guitars over the top of it, that makes for an interesting composition. The lyrics are that of a pretty typical blues lament—they're basically Bukka's—but Robert really knows how to sell this stuff. He clearly loves the material.

Rick: That's a Bukka White tune, but they rearrange it and make it their own little thing and it's really cool. It starts off with that weird keyboard and I think it's nice and heavy and bombastic. It's a good way to start the record and have us get to know the band. The personality of each of them really does shine through. It really becomes a Strange Sensation song.

John: When you read the story about what that was originally written about, that this is something Bukka White saw in prison. It's like, I wonder what that person was feeling like when he was about to die? So you get these really emotional thoughts throughout the whole song. And while it didn't take off for Bukka, when Bob Dylan covered it 20 years later, that gave him a little bit of a resurgence. This is a rousing version. Robert and the band do a wonderful job on this song. Again, Robert is able to take on the voice of the protagonist; he really seems inspired by this rousing arrangement behind him.

Martin: Next we get what is arguably the most popular song on the album, "Morning Dew." I've got covers of this in my collection by both Nazareth and Blackfoot and I'm sure a bunch more.

Reed: Yes, written by Bonnie Dobson but made big by Tim Rose. No offense to Mr. Plant, but I still don't think he's much of a lyricist.

What he gets out of having these cover tunes is much better lyrics. And "Morning Dew" is a song from the 1960s about the nuclear holocaust, about two people having a conversation first thing in the morning after the world has come to an end. Now, growing up in the 1960s, in the Cold War, nuclear holocaust was on everybody's mind. I try and describe this to young people and it's impossible to get across the feeling of what it was like thinking that we were all going to die in a nuclear holocaust. And many of us took it as a given that it was just going to happen at some point. But for Plant to choose that in 2002 is really weird, because you've got an entire generation of people who have never experienced that feeling. And it probably would never have occurred to them to relate this song to nuclear holocaust. But that is back to Plant's retro-futurism. He's singing a song that's about an old topic, nuclear war, and yet presenting it in a way that isn't tied to the time.

There's a singing guitar tone at the start of this song that sounds to me like he's using an EBow. An EBow is a device that creates feedback. You hold it over the strings and it vibrates the string to create functionally endless sustain. It's a very particular sound. But there's no EBow credited, so it's probably one of these other exotic instruments. We also have a wonderful electric piano sound. This is the first song where we get that Doors influence I was talking about. Because it's very much that Fender Rhodes electric piano sound that is all over the Doors recordings.

As for Robert's vocals, he's now fifty-four—he's not a kid. So while there is some higher singing, most of this album is sung in a near conversational range or more of a breathy whisper. That actually suits the music, but I don't know which one came first. I don't know if he chose that because he thought it would suit the music, or if he arranged these cover songs in such a way that it fit that vocal delivery. He certainly is accomplished enough as a musician that he could have done that, but I don't know which was the chicken and which was the egg in this situation.

I will say that for me and probably for many singers, singing well at lower volumes is much harder. That's why most people belt it out, right? In your *History in Five Songs* podcast you've mentioned that with other singers, like occasional singers in bands, that it really sounds like they need to push a lot of air if they were going to hit the notes, and they don't. But Robert Plant is hitting these notes without pushing a lot of air, which is more impressive even than doing those high screams. But it also helps save his fifty-four -year-old throat.

John: With "Morning Dew," here's my thing again. I was not familiar with "Morning Dew" until I heard Robert's version. It's a very sweet, very fragile song about a dark topic, and I think Robert's voice does a good job of maintaining the fragility of the song. It's telling a sad, post-apocalyptic story, where something terrible happens in the world. And then the performance and arrangement is also well suited to the mood of the song.

Martin: Were you dismayed at all that Robert decided to make a covers album?

John: I don't think it's a bad thing. It brings these songs to a new generation. I think he just loves exploring songs that maybe nobody knows. He gives them a new spin, a new lease on life. Other than "Hey, Joe," I didn't know any of these songs. But then I went back and listened to the originals and heard how Robert twisted them and changed them and expanded upon them while still keeping the original melodies as best as he could.

Rick: I'd say that "Morning Dew" was an opportunity for him to bring the mood right down after the activity and volume of the first track. Plus he's always talked about Tim Rose. This was probably one of those bucket list songs for him. But here's another thing about him and this song, and really the whole album and actually, also many things on *Fate of Nations*. He didn't do anything he couldn't pull off live. He sang these songs in a subtle, laid-back manner, one he could pull off on any given day, with nothing too out of his range. So it's in his comfort zone, but he also always made sure to deliver a good amount of what people love and expect out of Robert Plant.

Martin: Next is the Bob Dylan cover.

Rick: Yes, and when he'd do "One More Cup of Coffee" live around this time, he would literally bring a cup of coffee or tea on stage. I saw him open up for The Who in Detroit with this band, and it was informal like that, with couches and chairs around the stage, like he's performing in his living room. But anyway "One More Cup of Coffee" is definitely a Bob Dylan tune that you don't hear too often. He's more about the psychedelic palette on this one, with all the trippy things that are going on. They really made this their own.

Reed: "One More Cup of Coffee" opens with African drumming. By this point in his career, Plant, like many of his contemporaries—Peter Gabriel most famously—has embraced world music. And going forward, world music elements would appear on his recordings more frequently. It provides a great rhythmic foundation for this song. Once again, you hear that weird synthesizer sound. The best way I can describe it is that it sounds like the sound effect from a 1950s science fiction film when the evil monster appears, right? And you've got that going on in the background of the entire song that's a Bob Dylan track. We've got a pseudo-Middle Eastern guitar solo, adding to that world music stew. And then at the end, we actually get a transition to more of a spaghetti western vibe, like an in Ennio Morricone-type film score feel, right to the end of the song. Sometimes all of these things colliding don't work, but for me the parts mesh and it produces a wonderful song.

John: Yeah, more of an electric but almost Middle Eastern vibe to this as opposed to Bob Dylan's original. I like how he handled the harmonies on the chorus—Dylan's original has Emmylou Harris on it. But no, I thought this version was very pleasing to the ear. Again, the moody and atmospheric arrangement went well with the way I would have wanted the vocal delivery.

Martin: "Last Time I Saw Her" is a cool, psychedelic, rockin' tune. Love the textures, love the bass lines, love the drums.

Rick: Yeah, great tune, with lyrics that are weirdly rockabilly, a Stray Cats kind of thing. "Red Dress" is a bit like this too. So it's kind of traditional blues or even outdated, but with a modern twist and some real poetry massaged in there. I would think prog fans would like this one, because even though it's not about time signatures, there's other forms of weirdness, like with the electric and acoustic instruments together and with all the unexpected parts. And the instrumentation is all at the same volume level, which is unusual, with the acoustic things rocking, whereas with Zeppelin they'd be reserved for the quiet passages. I don't know, he's like a modern beatnik. He wants to give you that old acoustic café feel, but I'm bringing a psychedelic and hard rock band to the table at the same time. Depending on the song.

John: I can hear a bit of Zeppelin in this one, maybe the fifties rock 'n' roll of "Hot Dog" meets the funk of "The Crunge," and then lyrically, something sleazier like "Custard Pie."

Reed: "Last Time I Saw Here" is the first completely original song on the album. Again, you've got the evil, fifties sci-fi pad under the song, but it's much more Jimi Hendrix this time. We've moved away from The Doors and we're in Jimi Hendrix territory, and there will be a lot of Jimi Hendrix on this album in the same way that there's a lot of The Doors and The Cure. Not for nothing, but The Doors and Jimi Hendrix were huge influences on The Cure.

Martin: "Song to the Siren" is arguably the centrepiece of the album, the most sober and serious moment.

Rick: Yes, and a beautiful song, with strings, like "Sea of Love" or some of the arrangements on *Fate of Nations*. Even *Walking into Clarksville*, they invited a violinist in. It's very Moody Blues, because it sounds like Mellotron. I think it's really daring for him to do a song like that, because Tim Buckley is a well-respected vocalist, but Plant really shines on this one.

John: The original is kind of based off the Homer story, so there's the tie-in with the front cover. Robert just does a wonderful job with this fragile and tender kind of vocal. It works well on such a sparse arrangement, although there's deceptively quite a lot going on, with the ebbs and flows. Beautiful song.

Reed: I must say, singer-songwriter material is not normally my cup of tea. I can only attribute the fact that I enjoy this version of the song so much to the goodwill that *Dreamland* has built up for me by this point. Because it uses all of the normal singer-songwriter tricks that I find very manipulative, right? Plant's voice is so well suited to the material but he's singing along within a folky acoustic guitar and then these orchestra swells. And that sound is emotionally manipulative. It's making you feel things at certain specific spots, and I dislike being manipulated by my music. But I can let it wash over me because he really suits the Buckley world on this, even though I find Buckley a little maudlin. I find most of that hippie era of singer-songwriters a little maudlin; they rarely sing about happy things. Which is so weird; the flower children are supposed to be happy, but they were so angry at the injustices of the world, right? They were doing songs about coal miner strikes and all this other stuff. So yeah, it's emotionally manipulative, a little melodramatic, but somehow I can find value in it.

Martin: Next is "Win My Train Fare Home (If I Ever Get Lucky)," and Robert's lulled us into a dream state.

Reed: Yes, it's also another original, and even though it's original and credited to the band, we've got some pieces of old blues songs stuck into it, which I think is unnecessary. But maybe that's just Plant's thing. He's done it a lot by this point, so he must like the effect. He's delivering another Doors vibe here. Imagine "The End" but with Robert singing. There's a whooshing, windy sound that pervades through a lot of the song, and the guitar sounds like Robby Krieger's playing on "The End." You hear a very occasionally electric piano in the background and something that I can only describe as a didgeridoo sound. Plant is in that conversational semi-whispered range he has embraced at this point, and then in the back half, we get a long extended instrumental passage, which is something that was missing with *Now and Zen* and *Manic Nirvana*. Those are very Plant-oriented records, and here, he actually steps back and lets his band have a jam. It sounds just like The Doors raving it up back in 1969.

Rick: Again, a marriage between blues and psychedelic rock, with rockabilly, old rock 'n' roll lyrics. It's Strange Sensation at the peak of their powers.

Martin: As for his singing, he's not run away from the Golden God sound; rather, he's slipped away. And everybody's looking around saying, "Where's Robert?"

John: Yes (laughs). He's left the Golden God Led Zeppelin sound and he's in this comfortable, quiet range for him as an older man. Which suits the *Dreamland* collection and other Americana-type things he's about to do. But yeah, another original here, a bluesy song with a speedy electronica vibe to it, like you say, the hipster thing. This is gonna sound weird but there's a sexiness in some of the grooves to the song. And the guitar solo again offers a Middle Eastern vibe, like Reed says, like Robby Krieger. To me, through the process of collaboration, they've made something that flows well and fits well with Robert's range.

Rick: There's a lot of that moaning you get in traditional blues and the whispering, but if you listen to, "And if I say to you tomorrow" from "What Is and What Should Never Be," it's the same personality going on here. And "Take my hand, child" from the same song. The he starts wailing. He wants to lull you, but also at the same time show everybody that he's still got some fire in his belly and gas in that tank. He's got something like that on almost every album, that light and shade, because it's dramatic. It's one thing to sing words, but it's another to deliver with emotion.

Martin: I guess "Darkness, Darkness" was also a pretty important song on the album, along with "Morning Dew."

Rick: Yes, he's always liked this song and often commented on The Youngbloods. I've heard a few versions of this and this is one of my favourites.

John: The original is four minutes long, but Robert and his band stretch it into a seven-minute epic. You certainly feel Robert's despair in the vocal. Basically every time he sings that "Darkness, darkness" line, you feel the pain. I get a bit of a "No Quarter" vibe from it, along with a Celtic vibe.

Reed: Even though it's not a Doors song, they deliver it in the style of The Doors, including the Ray Manzarek-styled electric piano opening. Your primary guitar sound here is acoustic instead of electric. It has a keyboard solo, in addition to guitar, so all of these things, except for the acoustic guitar, are still very Doors. And then we get a musical change in the guitar solo, which is pure Jimi Hendrix, like Jimi Hendrix sitting in on a Doors song.

Martin: Next we're jarred back into combat mode, with the Captain Beefheart guitar that announces the coming of "Red Dress."

Rick: For sure, and the album needs another rock 'n' rolling toe-tapper, and that's what this is. I do find the album a little sober. The next one like this, *Mighty ReArranger*, is better. It sounds like they tested the songs on the road, whereas here, I feel like they recorded it raw and then performed some of the songs later and did better versions then. It feels like they've captured the first or second take or something. It's like the Neil Young approach where you don't spend too much time on it. Get one or two takes and that's good; put it in the bag. I think it's kind of why the album is covers. He didn't spend a lot of time on these songs compared to something like "If I Were a Carpenter," with all that lush production. It was almost like it's coming right off the floor. How they'd play it live, this is how you're going to get it.

And the production speaks to that idea too. It sounds dry, no vocal play, no reverb, no echo, like straight from the board with no ambience from the room. Some of the songs have that, but I think there's room for improvement. When you get to *Mighty ReArranger*, they got it right—that's the best one. Because it's a perfect-sounding album. But *Dreamland* sounds like you're taking it off the stage. For a psychedelic album, it doesn't have much echo or room feel.

John: A slinky, New Orleans-style blues rocker and the last of the originals, with some nice slide moments from Justin Adams, I believe. You get this aggressive but almost junky driving beat and deep groans of harmonica as well as an early Zeppelin feel with the lyrics, plus another fine arrangement.

Reed: I do find it funny that a completely original song is the most straight-up blues song on the album, from the harmonica through to the slide and the Delta blues framework, which screams for slide guitar. Now, of course, the blues man played slide guitar to mimic the voice on the guitar, and when you've got Robert Plant singing, I don't know if that's really necessary. You've got that weird sci-fi synth padding behind the song again, or if it's not fully audible, I imagine I'm hearing it. And that adds interest for me instead of if this was just a straight-up blues song. Otherwise I would skip it every time. But there's just enough sonic interest in it to keep me going.

As for the lyric, it's not bad, it's not deep, it's not profound. You've got a lot of blues clichés about the alluring woman and how life is tough, and maybe a reference to being in jail where he talks about another day in the hole. It's pretty standard blues stuff, but with the Strange Sensation background, clearly they're achieving the effect they want. Because a strange sensation is what I get when listening to these songs. But again, given the strong blues underpinning of both the music and lyrics, he's definitely looking back at his youth.

Martin: Okay, moving on, gotta confess, I find this version of "Hey Joe" to be a bit much.

Reed: Well, it's my least favourite track on the album, a very questionable inclusion. I wonder if this one wasn't Porl Thompson's choice because he's such a big Hendrix guy. You hear that in his guitar playing. Although I don't want to give Porl too much credit either; we don't know how big an impact he as an individual had on this album. Anybody choosing to cover Hendrix is already in different territory. I know that this song was a cover when Hendrix did it—I get that—but this is one of those covers that when Hendrix covered it, it became Jimi's song, like "All Along the Watchtower." Even Deep Purple did a Hendrix cover and it had to be exactly like Hendrix does it.

This rendition is very much not the way Hendrix produced the material. So he's doing a cover of a Hendrix cover in a very non-Hendrix fashion. And then he inserts guitar parts that are played exactly the way Hendrix plays them. So you've got non-Hendrix and then you've got copying Hendrix in the middle of it. The whole song is just continually jarring to me. I don't like the way it works out. And then you've got a genuine Hendrix-styled psychedelic rave-up at the end, right? That's actually the most interesting part of it to me. But somehow this song doesn't hold together. There's too many things that are working at odds and it just never gels.

Rick: Yeah, this version is trippy, a little bit spooky, very dramatic and on the edge of melodramatic. It has these weird, ambient keyboards in the intro, almost like something is wrong. But I really like the eerie soundtrack quality of the thing, and Robert does the lyrics accurately, with respect. Jimi Hendrix did an edited version, where he talked about the .44. But Robert actually talks about the weapon of choice in the song, so he's more true to the original Billy Roberts version. So Robert is more faithful to the very first recording of it.

However, they do put in that ascending Jimi Hendrix riff, near the tail end of the song. But I think it's really dramatic and not something you expect from Robert. It's one thing to say, "Squeeze my lemon," but this is more of a dark, violent lyric, out of character for him. They used to do "Hey Joe" in the Band of Joy when John Bonham was in the band, and you can hear that on the *Sixty Six to Timbuktu* compilation. So I think that's why that song came back. He's reliving his flower power days, striking up the psychedelic hits, and remembering his pal John Bonham at the same time.

John: Again, he and the guys are just harnessing and working with this idea of sparseness, and the song builds and builds and builds until you get that chromatic riff that we all know and love from the Jimi Hendrix version. My goodness, man, this version just sends chills down my spine. I just love this song. It's a chance for the band to let loose and explore all kinds of different vibes in this. Robert did this one justice.

Martin: The album proper closes with "Skip's Song," and man, for the first time we're hearing proper West Coast psych in all its glory.

Rick: Yeah, that's a Moby Grape cover. It's a great song that they should have moved up to the front of the running order. It's also a good way to end an album. But if I was in the producer's chair, I'd say, hey, you should make this one of your singles. I also think it's Robert's best vocal on the record.

John: I hear a little bit of "Thank You" in this, and maybe even a little "Your Time Is Gonna Come" in the organ feel. But comparing it to the original, this felt like the most straightforward cover out of all of them; they don't take much license here. I think you can tell that he was a big Moby Grape fan, and I think he really does a good job of paying tribute to Skip Spence.

Reed: This was a fascinating experience for me. Because my first thought was that this sounds exactly like Led Zeppelin, except it's a cover of a Moby Grape song. And you play the original, and doggone it if it also sounds like Led Zeppelin. Now I know Skip had died a couple years earlier and Robert appeared on a tribute album to Skip. But was it the band's idea to do it so straight? Were they like, hey, let us sound like Led Zeppelin for once? Or was it Robert Plant wanting to do it sounding, as it turns out, almost exactly and faithfully like Moby Grape, when every other cover song on the album is so different than the original?

Martin: Interesting. Not sure. Okay, that's the end of the version I have, but there's this other cool, rockin', shufflin' bonus track song, "Dirt in the Hole" too, right?

Rick: Yes, which is also on the *Nine Lives* box set or the remaster. And honestly, that should have been on the record. It's a hard-rocking song. It's a shame that they only put it on UK and Japanese versions, plus the collector's edition. I would have deleted the Bob Dylan tune any day, because it's a mistake not including this.

Reed: Yeah, most of *Dreamland* has kind of a similar sonic range and this one doesn't sound like the other tracks. But it's about death, and not obliquely about death, but just straight-up about death. It opens up with the preacher throwing dirt into the hole of the grave at the start of the song. I think it's one of Plant's best lyrics ever. And I've always wondered, given Plant's history, he's got this line in there about a precious boy so young and fair. Is he talking about the death of his son Karac? The lyric doesn't necessarily have to be viewed that way. But how can it not be? But yeah, the lyric is really poignant and thought-provoking.

Martin: So, at the end of this exercise, have you come to terms with the idea of getting a covers album from Robert?

John: I think there's a validity, because he's always looking for lost gems to dust off that maybe nobody knows. It's a chance to say, okay, what can we do with this song and bring it back to life? Obviously, that worked well with him and Alison Krauss and the two albums they've done together. If you had the chance to see them on tour, it's just a wonderful mix, especially how they re-engineer some of the Zeppelin songs. But he brings old tracks back and breathes new life into them, which I welcome because it gives me a chance to say, okay, let's learn more about Bukka White. I need to know more about Bonnie Dobson and Tim Rose. I'm not really a Dylan guy, so I really don't want to dive into Bob Dylan, but, The Youngbloods (laughs). It gives me that chance to reflect upon why he's picking these particular people, and then on a more abstract level, why does he keep going backwards with the influences?

Reed: Definitely. And on the purely technical side, I think it's interesting that there's just as much technology on *Dreamland* as there is on *Now and Zen*. It's just as dependent on some pretty expensive technology to produce the sound, and yet I don't listen to *Dreamland* and think that sounds like the early 2000s.

Rick: Doing a covers album is his way of saying he doesn't have anything to prove anymore, specifically as a songwriter. Plus he wanted to take his voice and explore different moods and structures, ones that he didn't write for himself. That's a challenge that most singers look forward to. It's like being an actor. You get to do a character. You take someone else's persona and try it out, on a record or in concert. He's also still trying to stay away from Led Zeppelin and also express his respect for bands that got him where he was even before Zeppelin, bands like Moby Grape and Buffalo Springfield, who he spoke highly about.

So I think he always wanted to scratch that itch. He didn't need to do a Bob Dylan tune, but no one does "One More Cup of Coffee." He did a song that not everybody does. Do we need to hear "Morning Dew?" There are many versions out there, but I think he used that to include something somebody recognised, but also to show that he and his band could really do justice to one of the most famous folk songs. It's an amazing thing. He really didn't need to do this album. But the Page Plant thing, especially *Walking into Clarksdale*, wasn't exactly a ground-shaking moment. I think that album was a bit under-produced, although it still had great songs. Still, I didn't think there were enough ideas on there.

But with *Dreamland*, I think he had every song well thought-out and knew how he and the guys were going to present it. And what's even better, I find the album a little bit on the sober side sonically. Because when you hear him do it live, it's so much better. Maybe because they now own it because they've now played these songs 50 more times. On the record, sometimes I get this sense that he's reading the lyrics as he goes? That he's not owning the words like he would do later on when performing the songs live.

Martin: I like your idea of Robert relishing the idea of inhabiting these different characters.

Rick: Exactly. Let's face it: He had been denying the Percy Plant persona for quite a few years. It took him to *Now and Zen* to finally understand, look, you're a hero and people are mimicking you. When are you going to take ownership of that and go with it? And he slowly welcomed it back. But with *Dreamland*, he was giving direct credit to people he wanted to pay back for making him who he is. It's pretty daring to cover "Song to the Siren" by Tim Buckley, right? That's a powerful song. And for him to show people that side of him is demanding and courageous. And then for him to do it live, well, he's always delivered.

Mighty ReArranger

"Robert's actually singing better than ever. There's more soul in his voice. When I saw him eighteen months ago, I was really impressed on how deep the texture had changed. I thought he was actually getting better. He doesn't have to sing up there anymore, you know? Even on the albums we did together, he wanted to be inventive, change, go forward. That's what we should be doing all the time, really. And I know he's got some stuff happening now that is based on African stuff. That's what's going to come out in the spring. And *No Quarter*, I thought was a fabulous album, which was actually just using the framework and taking it further. Phenomenal drummer, Michael Lee. He's something else, he is (laughs)."

"Robert has said to me, 'Why don't you go and work with Pagey?' And it would've been that simple. 'Here's his phone number, he's doing an album, go do it with him.' And I don't know why I didn't do that. Because I've always been in awe of Page. I think he's the most dangerous and inventive guitarist the world has ever seen. I don't know. It's just one of those things I didn't do. But it's not likely (laughs). It's just one of those things, isn't it? But we have played together, me and Page a couple of times. But that's as far as I ever went. But I really like him. He's a lovely bloke, very gentle, sweet. Have you met him? Very nice guy, very gentle, but a wicked guitar player (laughs)."

"I sent Robert a song a few weeks ago. 'Come on, Robbie Blunt's on this.' Because I've done a lot of recording with Robbie over the last year and I send Robert like two or three things. I'm always trying to get us back together (laughs). Nobody responds. It's like, those days are gone. He doesn't go backwards. I went to see him play at a little place in Shrewsbury, which is a little market town here on the border of Wales, about eighteen months ago, and he says, 'Jezz, I almost asked you to come up here and play with me, but then I thought, that's too long to blast from the past.' I said, 'Okay, that's fine.' I think that Robbie and Robert go back so far that they can't go back again. When Robert first started, he used to pick Robbie up from school and they used to play together. And they basically learned how to do what they do as kids. And then Robert ended up with the Band of Joy. Robbie would've been about 14 when Robert used to go pick him up from school, get his Strat and off they go (laughs)."

"As for Robert, when we do meet, it's always very good. We're very deep friends. We did some amazing stuff together and had a great time. I could pot around there, but I don't. He probably comes past the door, because his farm is just up the road from here. But we don't actually cross paths. He's too busy on his path and my path's here (laughs). We're right in the middle of the Welsh hills. I've got mountains on either side of me and a river in the garden. And this house was built in 1500, and it's got all oak beams in it and stone walls and it's fabulous. Robert has got a place about 20 minutes from here, maybe half an hour. It's just past there where all those Zeppelin songs were written, 'Going to California' and all that."

Jezz Woodroffe

Credits

April 25, 2005
Es Paranza/Sanctuary 06076 84747-2
Produced by Clive Deamer, John Baggott, Skin, Tim Oliver, Teo Miller and Steve Evans ("Recorded by")
Engineered by Steve Evans ("Mixed and manoeuvered by")
Recorded at The Lodge, Bathford, UK, Ellenbury, Bath, UK, Dol Goch, Cwim Einion, UK, Attic Studio, Kingswood, UK, Livingstone Studio, London, UK, Riverside, Bathampton, UK and The Windtunnel, UK
Personnel: Robert Plant – vocals, harmonica, Justin Adams – electric guitar, bendia, tehardant, lap steel, bass, Skin Tyson – acoustic and electric guitars, lap steel, bass, John Baggott – keyboards, electronica, Moog bass, Billy Fuller – electric and double bass, Clive Deamer – drums, bendia

1. "Another Tribe" 3:15
2. "Shine It All Around" 4:03
3. "Freedom Fries" 2:52
4. "Tin Pan Valley" 3:47
5. "All the King's Horses" 4:20
6. "The Enchanter" 5:27
7. "Takamba" 4:04
8. "Dancing in Heaven" 4:25
9. "Somebody Knocking" 3:47
10. "Let the Four Winds Blow" 4:52
11. "Mighty ReArranger" 4:25
12. "Brother Ray" 1:12
All songs written by Plant, Baggott, Deamer, Adams, Tyson, Fuller

A *Mighty ReArranger* Timeline

March 11 – 24, 2005. Robert and the band tour America in support of the forthcoming *Mighty ReArranger.*

April 4, 2005. Robert Plant and the band perform in support of the Teenage Cancer Trust.

April 6 – June 11, 2005. Robert tours Europe.

April 25, 2005. Es Paranza/Sanctuary issue the eighth Robert Plant solo album, *Mighty ReArranger.* Best Buy contracts to sell a special edition, which includes a bonus disc containing a 44-minute interview with Robert. Available in France is a Special Tour Edition that includes a bonus 11-track live disc. The album reaches No.22 on the main *Billboard* chart and No.4 in the UK.

June 15 – July 24, 2005. The band head back to North America for more shows, followed by a handful of festival dates in Europe.

July 5, 2005. "Shine It All Around" is issued as the only single from *Mighty ReArranger.* There is a two-track CD version, a three-track CD version plus a 7" single and 12" single, which are each two tracks. The song reaches No.18 on the *Billboard* Mainstream Rock Songs chart.

September 10 – October 6, 2005. The band play an unusual number of Canadian shows, along with a few more in the US.

October 2005. "The Enchanter" is pressed up and issued as a promo single, i.e. as a suggestion for radio play.

October 27 – December 13, 2005. The band tour Europe once again, with emphasis on France, Italy and the UK.

March 10 – April 7, 2006. Robert and his band tour Europe, with emphasis on France. This is followed by sporadic but regular festival dates through September.

June 23, 2006. Robert performs, using Ian Hunter's backing band, at a benefit concert for Love's Arthur Lee, at the Beacon Theatre in New York.

October 2006. Zoë Records issues a DVD package called *Soundstage: Robert Plant and the Strange Sensation*, capturing the band live for the *Soundstage* TV series in Chicago on September 16, 2005.

November 21, 2006. Robert Plant sees the issue of a massive nine-CD and single DVD box set called *Nine Lives*, thusly named because it's essentially comprised of Plant's first eight solo albums plus the Honeydrippers EP.

March 20, 2007. Rhino Entertainment issues a remastered version of *Pictures at Eleven*. Included are two bonus tracks, "Far Post" and "Like I've Never Been Gone," recorded live at The Summit in Houston, September 20, 1983. *The Principle of Moments* is also reissued and features a non-LP track called "Turnaround," along with three live renditions from that same Houston show. *Shaken 'n' Stirred* is also remastered and reissued this day, adding the Remixed Long Version of "Little by Little." Next is *Manic Nirvana*, which adds the same three tracks featured on the "Hurting Kind" CD single. *Fate of Nations* is particularly action-packed, offering an acoustic mix of album track "Great Spirit," but also non-LP songs "Colours of a Shade," "Rollercoaster (demo)," "8:05" and "Dark Moon (acoustic)." *The Mighty ReArranger*, also remastered and reissued this day, includes "Red, White and Blue," "All the Money in the World" (both non-LP), plus alternate versions of "Shine It All Around," "Tin Pan Valley" and "The Enchanter."

April 3, 2007. Rhino issues a remastered version of *Now and Zen*, which adds live versions of "Billy's Revenge," "Ship of Fools" and "Tall Cool One."

June 29 – August 18, 2007. Robert and the band perform in Europe, with the emphasis on Eastern Europe and Italy.

September 25, 2007. Vanguard issues *Goin' Home: A Tribute to Fats Domino*. Robert appears on two tracks, "It Keeps Rainin'" and "Valley of Tears."

November 27, 2007. Robert's record with Alison Krauss, *Raising Sand*, is certified gold.

March 4, 2008. *Raising Sand* is certified platinum.

August 9, 2008. Robert appears at the Cropready Festival and performs "The Battle of Evermore" with Fairport Convention, in duet form with Kristina Donahue, as a tribute to Sandy Denny.

December 31, 2008. Robert Anthony Plant, singer and songwriter, is appointed a Commander of the Order of the British Empire for his service to music.

January 4, 2009. Famed UK radio station Planet Rock votes Robert Plant the No.1 Greatest Voice in Rock.

April 25, 2009. Robert, Justin Adams and Juldeh Camara perform as part of the Womad Festival, in Abu Dhabi, United Arab Emirates.

Martin talks to John Clauser, Todd Evans and Rick LaBonte about *Mighty ReArranger*.

Martin Popoff: So where is Robert at with *Mighty ReArranger*? Is it an affirmation and underscoring of what he was doing on *Dreamland*?

John Clauser: I'd say so. I think the personality of the record, if you will, is that these guys have gelled together. Now they're saying, okay, we've shown where our influences are. Here's what we can do as a band, as a cohesive unit. Here's what we can write on our own and maybe still capture that vibe of *Dreamland*, with that intriguing Americana-meets-electronica vibe and all the different influences you hear there.

Rick LaBonte: I agree; now the band know each other and are bringing more originals to the table. You'll note that on the cover, the artist is billed as Robert Plant and the Strange Sensation, whereas on *Dreamland* it was just Robert Plant. I think they represent the best characteristics of Robert's music and even Led Zeppelin music while mostly projecting their own personalities and they do an amazing job. They've got this *Soundstage* live DVD where every second song is a Led Zeppelin song. And in fact, *Mighty ReArranger* feels like a concert record—it starts off with a bang and ends with a bang. It has everything you know Robert Plant should be doing, with an acoustic song here and there, so it's a clinic in dynamics.

As for his band, they're personalities drawn from all sorts of different breeds of music. They could deliver the blues when Robert wants it, or they can hang out with him in Timbuktu, like Justin Adams did. Skin Tyson has played in a lot of heavy psychedelic and hard rock bands. So, Robert is finding the right guys for the job, and almost celebrating the fact that these guys are not famous. I got to meet them at Massey Hall. Plant was in the alley outside taking a breather and wouldn't let anybody near him, but the band went through the doors that we were all going through. And I called out "Skin! Skin Tyson!" He turned around and he signed my CD and then I got to chat with him and the other guys. Some of them knew each other before becoming Strange Sensation but they were all hand-picked.

Martin: And what kind of vibe do they put out on stage?

Rick: Well, first of all, they're great performers and play with a lot of passion. They don't get involved in Plant's space, but they're all animated to watch. Justin's really great with the acoustic instruments and he plays a lot of the heavy blues stuff. Your Fender Strats and all that is handled by Skin Tyson. They all play really well, but what I've noticed is that when Plant is holding the fort down, they're all just doing their part. As soon as he takes off and starts dancing, they all start to move. So it's almost like they're reading Robert and his vibe from part to part or song to song. There's this telepathy and they can almost match each other's movements.

Robert Plant still to this day leaves a little room for improvisation live. That's why it was a little bit challenging for him working with Alison Krauss. Now you gotta sing the same thing all the time, if you expect me to harmonise with you. And don't lose your voice, don't get winded on this part or don't speed up on that part because I gotta sing with you. So he has to be tame. But with these guys, they read his singing language and they read his body language. It's great to watch. It's one thing to listen to the albums, but to see him take it to the stage, it's so smart. It's intelligent, almost like a prog band.

Martin: And what do you think of the production here? Phil Johnstone's back in the picture, and is co-producing along with Robert and Mark Stent, who's worked at this point with both Björk and Madonna.

John: Right, production-wise, there are times where I get the feeling he's recording in a nice, tight room. You don't hear a lot of space there. Musically, you have a lot of atmospheric sparseness, you have electronica, you get a lot of great guitar flourishes, there's a good mix of every kind of style in this album.

Todd Evans: Well, I like *Mighty ReArranger* a lot better than *Dreamland*. I didn't like *Dreamland* at all. I continue to this day to not give *Dreamland* a fair chance because I hear it and I think it's too loud. It sounds like it's recorded on vintage equipment. Plus there's a lot of covers from genres that I'm not interested in. And so to me, *Mighty ReArranger* was a step up and back. It's an interesting enough combination of vintage sounds and current sounds. There's some electronic audio mixed in and it's kind of stealthy, the way they do that, which is cool, almost subversive. You'll be listening to something and you'll be like, oh, this has an old music theme or feel to it, and then you'll be like, oh, but there's some synth bass.

Rick: You know what? That surprised me actually, seeing Phil Johnstone back. Because what's interesting is that Charlie Jones from *Manic Nirvana* and *Now and Zen* actually played as part of Strange Sensation, but only on *Dreamland*, not here, where he's replaced by Billy Fuller. Charlie Jones also played with Page Plant. He's Robert's son-in-law—he married one of Plant's daughters. So that keeps the money and wealth in the family by having him on board. But Phil Johnstone is a good friend of Charlie Jones—they were pals. When Robert went on with Page Plant, Phil Johnstone just went and produced other people's records and worked with Alannah Myles. That's all he did. It kind of took the wind out of his sails and he didn't form another band. He died in 2021 and was just sixty-three years old.

But for *Mighty ReArranger*, he was a familiar guy to call, and it gave Phil some work to do, since Robert kind of left the band high and dry. He would do that. He changed personnel in the blink of a second and would move on. You embrace it when you get the moment with Plant but there are no guarantees. He doesn't owe you anything. But I think in this case, Phil would be an old friend who could maybe understand where Robert was going with this. Also, you gotta take into account that Phil had a role in *Fate of Nations*, which contains a few of the gestures or hints as to where he was going with *Mighty ReArranger*. So it's sensible to think Phil might be able to get on the same page with him pretty quickly.

Martin: All right, the album opens with "Another Tribe," which is bright and intimate but yeah, pretty sparse.

John: Yeah, "Another Tribe" begins with simple acoustic guitar over a world music drumbeat. But again, there's this sly layering-in of electronica, and also exotic strings. Lyrically, Robert's immediately getting political, talking about humanity and efforts that get made to justify its actions, whether it's religion or politics. But you can put that aside and just go with the emotion and the vibe of it.

Todd: I'd call that a rootsy arrangement, I guess, with the highlight being that pretty involved and up-front Middle Eastern-sounding string arrangement. It's interesting how Robert's music drifts in that direction after collaborating with Jimmy again. And yeah, even though this is totally a quiet track, the arrangement is more sophisticated than what we generally got on *Dreamland*.

Rick: I get a "Gallows Pole" or "Hey, Hey, What Can I Do" vibe from "Another Tribe," or with those Mellotron-like strings, "Friends." Strange Sensation just had a cool way of suggesting Led Zeppelin music in what they did; there's an underlying sense of humour to it. In fact this song opens with the drum pattern from "Rock and Roll," but they do it with a little bongo or tom or whatever and then they branch off into this little, crazy adventure of a song,

With his vocal phrasing, Plant is all about rhythm. It's like, "Hey hey mama, I say the way you move." A lot of his lyrics are structured around or inspired by the rhythm of the tune, which is a nice approach and a characteristic of his. He doesn't have to hold a note. It's how many notes or words he can fit in. He's not going to do gangster rap or hip-hop, but he'll almost talk it out and create all these rhymes. It's like, if the band wasn't playing, you could still snap your fingers to Robert's vocal because it's very rhythmic. That what's cool about "Another Tribe." Not to mention it's bombastic, but like Todd said, still quiet. All the things we like about *Dreamland* are now done ten times better because they use the room, because of the way it's mixed and produced. I think it's well-produced. Personally, it's what I would have wanted from Robert at that time. Everything's he ever learned from the past is all in this record, in my opinion.

Martin: Nice, okay, traditional drum kit is introduced on the next song, "Shine It All Around," but sonically it's about as rough-hewn and old-timey as you can make a high-hat, snare drum and bass drum sound.

Todd: Yes (laughs), but that makes for a really cool vibe, and one that is still in the same orbit as the first song. The arrangement's kind of sparse but also kind of complete at the same time, and it's a good match for the lyrics, which are really good poetry but also sparse, quality over quantity.

John: "Shine It All Around" was the lone single. I see this one as a call for us to find that love light inside of us. Very catchy chorus, where he delivers those Zeppelin-y kind of oohs and aahs. As for this finicky lo-fi production, I'm just wondering if he's trying to get as far away from the big full band Zeppelin sound as possible; let these guys do their own thing. It's almost like they're using baritone guitars, or really strong detuned or lower-tuned guitars, which provides that griminess I think you're getting at. As a guitar player myself, I was listening closely and trying to figure out what guitars and equipment they were using but it's pretty tough. And style-wise with Justin, there's a Jimmy Page influence—I think that's pretty evident—but at the same time, he's been known for his African and Middle Eastern styles in some of music he's produced and recorded. So he adds a lot of flavours here. He's played with Jah Wobble, and Skin Tyson is from Cast.

Martin: Rick, any thoughts on why "Shine It All Around" might have been picked to be the first and only single from the album?

Rick: It's a catchy, contemporary song and it's got a beat that welcomes you in; it's something you can actually dance to. It got some airplay; I heard it on the radio across the bridge from Detroit quite a bit. There's a hint of Zeppelin to it as well, with the pretty expressive vocal he's doing in the chorus—that's Robert Plant all the way, with those long notes. And just the fact that he's spreading like seeds of kindness and seeds of good positive vibes to his fellow man, that's such a cool hippie thing for Robert to be doing. That's his persona as part of this Strange Sensation band and it's also something that would be appealing in terms of floating it as a single.

Martin: "Freedom Fries" is one of these gritty, lo-fi musical tracks Robert does that reminds me of Tom Waits. But it sure isn't Tom Waits singing, and the lyrics are pure, cutting political Robert Plant, or newly political Robert Plant, I guess.

John: Yes, we get a very fun and funky riff with a busy drum pattern going on. But Robert's taking aim at the American President at the time, Bush II, and especially after 9/11 with war in the Mideast and conspiracy theories about ulterior motives concerning oil. There are oblique references to that regime and who was going to benefit from that supply of oil over there, and its shrouded in religious allegory. So you have a political lyric stuck on a perky song. I agree with your Tom Waits comparison. He's done a good job of replicating something like that.

Todd: "Freedom Fries," I like. I remember liking that when it came out. The riff on "Freedom Fries" is really hooky—a blues lick more than a riff. And the drum track, I think, is really great, groovy even though it has to deal with an odd time signature. The drums are kind of understated on this record. It's another song arrangement that could be described as sparse, as there's a lot of space in it. It's a good example of a song here that sounds rootsy and contemporary at the same time, which doesn't make sense, but he seems to pull it off.

Martin: My favourite Clive Deamer drum fill on the album happens in "Tin Pan Valley," at the 53-second mark, just before Robert starts the second verse.

Todd: Nice, well, "Tin Pan Valley," that's, I think, the best track on the album. It's got a really quiet start, but then gets really busy and explosive. It got nominated for a Grammy for Rock Performance and I think that was really well deserved, even if it didn't win. I'm impressed that they nominated him, but then again, they were probably just gunning for star power, because how many rock stars are bigger than Robert Plant? The Grammy people are thinking, the guy from Led Zeppelin has an album out; let's look at that. But at the same time, it's not the typical type of song that would be nominated for a Grammy and that's kind of impressive.

Rick: Great tune, and what I like about all this is the mishmash of different genres working together, blues, Celtic, trance, heavy rock. It shouldn't make sense but it does. I love the arrangement; I think it's very clever. And it's another dynamic one, where there's this upscale scene he's painting, and then the line "take the hammer to the pearl," followed by "like this!" and it gets really heavy. I think songs like this are more about the show. It's gotta be fun to perform "Tin Pan Valley," where everybody gets quiet and you can hear a pin drop and then they blast your head off like that.

Martin: That heavy riff sounds very much like the main riff in "The Bazaar" by The Tea Party. And Jeff Martin told me once he was working on a project with Jimmy Page. Anyway, John, thoughts on this one?

John: Yes, I feel like in this one, Robert's expressing a desire to move away from the spotlight. But the funny thing is that the chorus is full-on rock god stadium rock, where he proves he can still do it with the best of them, going fairly high-pitched and pushing some air. But yeah, I really feel like the verses are purposefully poignant and quiet, while the chorus is purposely aggressive and heavy, even violent. I like to imagine that the "Some fake the rebel yell" might be a little poke at Billy Idol. Who knows? Maybe he's saying, hey, I've lived that life; y'all can have it now. Because he sees how tough it is.

Martin: All right, next is "All the King's Horses." The Firm did a song called that too, didn't they? On the second one, *Mean Business*.

John: Yeah, they did, now that you mention it (laughs). But no, this is another quiet and quite Zeppelin-esque moment, is how I took it. It's quite beautiful, like a new "Going to California" or "Rain Song," with a touching lyric about discovering new love.

Todd: Yes, "All the King's Horses" is a pretty folk ballad, the first real acoustic track you get here, with a super-simple country flavour. I like the guitar solo. I might have told you this, but when I was growing up, when I got to probably the 12th grade or the beginning of college, I started to rebel against guitar sounds that I thought were typical rock 'n' roll, too meat and potatoes. I didn't like twin lead, so as you can imagine, I wasn't a big fan of Scorpions. And whenever I heard those kinds of rock sounds I would be like, oh, this again. So I've always been drawn towards guitar solos like this one that are kind of understated or sound like something you wouldn't expect. One of my favourite guitarists coming up was Gary Kemp from Spandau Ballet, because all of his guitar solos were at the end of the neck. So yeah, I liked the solo in "All the King's Horses," where a lot of people probably wouldn't even mention it or notice it.

Rick: I also thought of "Going to California." It's your coming-back-down acoustic piece. Almost every album since *Manic Nirvana* has one, like "Liars Dance." On *Fate of Nations*, I guess it would be "If I Were a Carpenter." Just a voice and acoustic guitar dynamic. I love that "I pour myself a brand-new start" line and I love the melody. It's just one of those tunes where if I don't play another tune right away, I hear "All the King's Horses" in my head over and over (laughs). It's a really catchy tune and they should have marketed that one. It would have definitely caught on.

Martin: My second favourite Clive Deamer lick is on "The Enchanter." It's the three whacks we hear right after Robert sings, "Oh, that the stars will light my way." Man, I just love when we get a full set of drums on this album.

Rick: "The Enchanter" is a masterpiece, really. I think every Robert Plant solo album has one of those moments where Plant's deep in thought and the band responds with a majestic and serious music track with a lot of changes. And when they do this one live, it's just in the world.

John: There's some really grimy, buzzing guitar work going on here, almost like they took the tape and just kind of slowed it down to a halt. But yeah, the modern production they're managing here, it's like purposely distressing something to make it look more antique. You've got this moody piece centred around a tribal beat but yet you get this heavily distorted guitar hook. His lyrics seem to be about the mysterious ways of a woman who is casting a spell on him.

Todd: With "The Enchanter," you get the whole Middle Eastern influence again. It starts out slow and kind of develops into a rocker and again is kind of Led Zeppelin-like. I think the synth bass is cool; it's a really interesting choice to put in there. And I like the Fender Rhodes electric piano in it. It's something that doesn't seem like it would fit in a song like that but it works. He takes a lot of chances on this record, a lot of, well, let's just throw this sound in here, even though it might chafe against what we're trying to do and it ends up working. It might be because he liked those guys and enjoyed working with them. I picture them just sitting in the studio going, "Let's try this, let's try that."

Martin: "Takamba" is pretty swampy. Then again, Robert does say "sold me down the river" in it.

Todd: Yeah, this one certainly wasn't the kind of song I expected it to be, i.e. perhaps more world music or flavoured in an ethnic way. It's more of a rock song, great bass line, pretty heavy, big drum sound. It's probably the biggest drum sound on the album, with huge crashing cymbals.

John: "Takamba" is another one that evokes for me early Zeppelin, even a little bit of early Robert solo. It has these tasty and clean fifties and' 60s guitar lines, but again, you get this rousing arrangement. The lyrics poke fun at political aspirations. It's pretty slight on word count, but it's one of these where he makes every phrase count.

Rick: This is another great rhythmic song on the album, and sure, it's hard-rocking, but I'm hearing at least a bit of world music here, maybe mostly in the quiet verses; it's the kind of subtle fusion Strange Sensation does so well, because the sound is all their personalities put together, along with Robert's vision, which is very often drawing from music from all over the world. Most people wouldn't be this daring, so I respect that. In fact the Grammy people recognised Robert both for the creativity and the world music aspect of what he does. It's so artistic, another masterpiece on the album.

Martin: Okay, "Dancing in Heaven" is my candidate for least expected style, with that Paul McCartney bass line. Very Beatles-esque in total.

Todd: Yes, I agree. The bass is kinda like the song, "Rain" and even the drums sound like Ringo, with the drum fills as well as the sixties-harsh production. I don't know if he did that on purpose or not, but that's pretty cool.

John: It's a nice little pop song with an exciting, nostalgic-sounding rhythm section, Beatles-meets-psych, almost, or Beatles when they went psych. Lyrically, this one really spoke to me. It reads like a celebration, as if you were saying goodbye to someone who just died, but in a positive way. I love the folkiness of the verses and the wistful feeling this song emotes.

Rick: "Dancing in Heaven" features just a beautiful vocal. That song should have been a hit too. It's something that could have been marketed. It's a series of hooky parts, so catchy, and it displays the dynamics of the band. What we like about Robert Plant, he was great with hard rock, but he also did great with an acoustic background. You listen to "Hey, Hey, What Can I Do" and his voice stands out over acoustic guitar, even with a rockin' drum track.

Martin: A little off-topic, the lyrics to this one aren't printed in the booklet, but five other ones are. This is something Robert does regularly. What message does that send?

John: *Dreamland*'s got *one*! Although there weren't a lot of originals there anyways "Song to the Siren" is the only one in there and that wasn't even one of the originals. But I guess it's a key song and it relates to the album cover. Yeah, it made it a little hard for me since I'm a lyric guy. I need to read my lyrics so I know what the songs are about.

Todd: You can get around it by referencing it on Google with some of the lyric sites and they're all pretty easy to find. Maybe he just thinks that those are the ones that he wants to showcase. It's interesting; I saw some quotes from him about *Fate of Nations* where he says something like, "Before I made this record, I was listening to Moby Grape and all this sixties stuff that I grew up with, and I wanted to write lyrics that were like that." I know very little about Moby Grape, but I don't think they do sound like that. But maybe he wasn't really sure where he was going with his lyrical content, and then when he found something that really resonated with him, he wanted to showcase it. That's how I always feel when somebody does that. I think, okay, well, they really, really want me to read this one.

Martin: All right, we're up to "Somebody Knocking," which seems to echo a bit of the melody of "Black Mountain Side" from the first Zeppelin album, although this is more a full-bodied song in total, similar to "The Enchanter."

Rick: Yeah, it's another good rocker, short and sweet, get to the point, don't overstay your welcome. The way they sequenced this album, you really can't get bored of it. They're rockin' for a bit and then they give you a minute to catch your breath and then they take you somewhere else.

John: Yeah, "Somebody Knocking" was one of those songs where I could just imagine Robert and his band sitting on the front porch or around a campfire putting this thing together, or just playing it and fortunately somebody hit record. There's a bit of a "Friends" feel to it. Just a rousing, rhythmic acoustic jam.

Todd: "Somebody Knocking" I don't have much to say about. It's kind of mid-tempo and doesn't make much of an impression on me; it's rhythmically similar, loping, to a few songs already on the album. It's just kind of okay but also short. It almost feels like it's transitional, to get us from track eight to track ten. It doesn't seem like a complete idea. It sounds like an old scratchy 1930s record, right? Maybe that's the point. I guess it doesn't need to have much more of a point than that.

Martin: That clean spaghetti western guitar is back, wandering its way through "Let the Four Winds Blow."

John: Yeah, this one is a weirdly modern kind of fifties- or sixties-sounding song, something you could picture in a movie. Lyrically, I see this as the thoughts of a soldier who's trying to get home from the war. It's not a very happy song per sé, but it's certainly deep and emotive.

Rick: Yes, very dramatic, with a great vocal approach and a lot of style when it comes to the singing. I love the arrangement where the band picks up the tempo; it's unpredictable but it has ebb and flow. It flows perfectly, like the wind blowing, I guess. But it's erratic—they take you north, they take you south. I think it's a great song. It feels like an homage to his lyrical approach in Led Zeppelin.

Todd: "Let the Four Winds Blow" is kind of psychedelic and blues rock at the same time, and really steeped in the sixties. When it picks up and gets a little more intense, it sounds like The Doors' "L.A. Woman" to me. There's not much keyboard to it, but what there was reminded me of Ray Manzarek. This one made a big impression on me.

Martin: And that whole Doors thing continues right into "Mighty ReArranger," same key, same tempo, same swing. And with that piano and that beat, we may as well bring "Roadhouse Blues" to the table.

John: Yeah, nice and comfortable and somehow also an energetic shuffle. If you're a Christian, he could be singing about how God does things in the world. If you're following other beliefs, well, this could be whatever belief system you think. Somebody's got their hands on the controls trying to rearrange everything to make everything work, I guess. It's technically not the closer, because there's "Brother Ray," which is a fun, little outro track.

Todd: "Mighty ReArranger" definitely perpetuates that sixties influence, but this time it's more of a skiffle sound. So I don't know, maybe pre-1960s? But it's a really cool track and a good closer, if one doesn't count that one-minute "Brother Ray" jam.

Martin: Maybe that's the Mighty ReArranger on the front cover. Or maybe the graphic artist is the arranger, because it looks like a haphazard arrangement of parts.

Todd: Right (laughs). I think the cover looks pretty much like the album sounds, very much about the arrangement of often quite bizarre sounds. I'm not enough of an art person to know what that particular style is, but it has an organic, nostalgic look to it. And it looks like it's made of wood or like it's a sculpture or something. I think it does a pretty good job of conveying the fanciful mood of the music.

Rick: I listen to "Mighty ReArranger" and the word prog comes to mind, but it's not prog rock, more just properly progressive, right? With all these intimate but strange sounds and arrangements. Like Todd says, "Brother Ray" is just like a short sound collage, I guess. But in this day and age, actually first with the *Nine Lives* box set but now with Spotify and streaming, the bonus tracks are pretty well-known. "All the Money in the World" and "Red, White and Blue" are two powerful Robert Plant songs. It would be a challenge to pick what to remove if you wanted these in. What song would I take out? It's like Led Zeppelin *III* would have been improved with "Hey, Hey, What Can I Do" over "Hats Off to (Roy) Harper."

Martin: Excellent guys, any closing impressions, things you wanted to add?

Todd: One point I wanted to bring up that you talked about earlier is this idea of calling the band Robert Plant and the Strange Sensation. I generally don't like that, but I give Robert Plant a pass. I'm kinda like, well, whatever you want to do (laughs). But I don't think it's necessary. It blurs the lines and I think it's confusing for consumers. But then again, I don't think there's a lot of sameness between this album and the previous album. A lot of people may disagree with that. They may think these two albums go hand in hand.

Martin: Actually, what are your views on where his voice is here in 2005?

Todd: Well, one thing I noticed about this album is that there's nothing you hear where you go, Robert, were you having an off day?

I don't hear anything like that, and I actually do on *Walking into Clarksdale*. But you hear him moving towards that whole Americana thing that he ends up doing later on. He's less in-your-face and bombastic and more understated, which he starts earlier than this, a bit on *Fate of Nations*, more on *Walking into Clarksdale* and even more on *Dreamland*. There was a really good interview I read with Lloyd Cole where he said, "I had this feeling that I had to make adult music, so I started making adult music. And then I realised that all my fans didn't want me to do that." I like that, and I kind of feel it applies to Robert Plant, only he's stuck with adult music. He's going, I don't want to make an album that sounds like the guy who sings in Led Zeppelin.

Martin: I feel like he's happily discovered that even in old age he's got a really good singing voice if he keeps it in first or second gear, kind of thing.

Todd: Yeah, I agree with that. I think that's pretty accurate. You can tell that he's tried this and you can tell that in his head he's going, "Hey, this is working."

Martin: Here's one for you. When he makes albums like this, he's like the rock 'n' roll equivalent of a hipster beard maintenance kit.

Todd: Yes, true (laughs). But then again, I feel like he's pulled off every persona that he's tried. I mentioned this earlier, but, 1982, '83, I heard those albums and went and saw him as pleated pants, jazz shoes, flap shirt Robert Plant and I was totally on board! And then *Now and Zen* and into *Manic Nirvana* Robert Plant, with the Middle Eastern vibe and the wraps and scarves, I thought to myself, okay, well, that's Led Zeppelin Robert Plant. I don't know if I want to go back to that. I'm into urban, sophisticated Robert Plant. I like the idea of him hanging out with different kinds of musicians, and younger than him. I think that's pretty cool. I sometimes wonder if the guys in his bands would be thinking, wow, this is really cool to be making a record with Robert Plant. It's cool that he wants to do this with us.

I feel like one of the best things you could do for your image as an aging rock star is to find some kind of path like that. So you're not the meme of the guy with the skateboard going, "Hey, what's going on, you kids?" You don't want to try too hard to appeal to young people. But at the same time, what he's doing is real. He can totally sell it. He comes out and says, I really like this kind of music and I like this image. This is what I want to do now. You just kind of go, okay. I don't think for one minute of him as a poser who's trying to sound fashionable. If he's a hipster, it's because he's genuinely doing something hip.

Rick: For sure! It's retro, it's contemporary, it's modern, it's weird and sure, it's the kind of thing hipster audiophile vinyl-type guys gravitate to. And it shouldn't be so accessible, but it is. Theoretically, they could make it hard for you like a prog band would do, but instead the progressive spirit in it is subtle. But still, if you study it, it's uncanny and unpredictable. You don't know what you're gonna get, just that somehow there's something Americana about it, or as you keep saying, old-timey (laughs).

Martin: I also wonder if he keeps celebrating music from all these different regions of the world to remind himself of the happiness of his world travels. Or even to share what he's learned with other people, again, to put it crudely, play DJ or to perform the function of what a rock critic does.

Rick: I think it's a little bit of all of that. I think you're right. He's always telling where it comes from. And don't forget, he married an Indian woman and had a kid, so he's already a worldly guy. He's never had any hang-ups about other cultures. I wonder if there's even an over-compensating about wanting to show credit and do covers to make up for the troubles Zeppelin got in earlier with crediting the blues guys. It's like he's rectifying that all later. I think he makes an actual effort to say now, "This is a song we got from here."

But he's long since proven he's a good artist with original ideas too. The last thing he's going to do now is be reticent about credit. Instead, he's doing history lessons, pretty much two whole albums of covers plus the stuff with Alison Krauss. He ended up doing that because he's like me, you and Pete when we go on *Sea of Tranquility*. We're historians. We love to follow the history. And he not only listened to the history of where these songs came from; he knows the dynamics of the culture. Robert Plant still listens to Lead Belly, despite the primitive technology and production, and he still goes and collects rare shit because he's a historian. That's why anything he did with Strange Sensation or The Sensational Space Shifters is going to pay homage to the past. He says to his fans, "You guys love my music. You should hear where we got it from."

And then there's his love of the sixties. That's a whole extra layer to it, which you hear on *Mighty ReArranger* as well. He's the ultimate hippie. He loved Spirit and that song "Fresh Garbage." He was into Moby Grape, Buffalo Springfield, Love, Joni Mitchell. He loved that whole folk side of things and that's why Led Zeppelin *III* had that. They wanted to touch base with that West Coast sixties sound. Because in the Yardbirds period or Band of Joy days, those guys were already collecting all the blues records and then Bob Dylan. Now they're soaking up this San Francisco scene and saying, we've already done this blues and hard rock stuff, let's explore this West Coast American sound. So, Robert has been familiar with a wide variety of music history for decades. They said, "No, but we've already done the hard rock and blues thing. Let's explore that acoustic stuff." And I think that's a very familiar territory for Plant.

And when you've done something like "Battle of Evermore," there's the roots of the duets with women you hear later with Patty Griffin and Alison Krauss, even Toni Halliday on *Shaken 'n' Stirred*. Plant was always moving forward and I think if we're being honest about it, Led Zeppelin was always moving forward too. Plant was always willing to try the next thing, not just stay on a treadmill. So, he's going around the world and picking up things along the way. There was a time when progressive rock bands were in a hurry to get the latest instrument or technology on a record. Well, Plant's doing that all the time on records like *Mighty ReArranger*, but it's almost like it's always subtle, like he wants to keep it a secret or not divulge what part of his travels it came from, if we're talking more about a world music thing than a piece of technology. He's like, "Well, I've never used that drum." Or I like how he gets that one guy in the band, Juldeh Camara, thinking, hmm, I've never had someone who plays like two strings on a guitar. And just for that one instrument, he decides he's gotta change the whole name of the band (laughs). He's like, "Yeah, we gotta do something with that in it. I don't know where it fits, but we gotta find it" (laughs).

ROBERT PLANT
BAND of JOY
ROUNDER

ROBERT PLANT
BAND OF JOY
DECCA
UNIVERSAL
SIDE TWO
1 YOU CAN'T BUY MY LOVE 3:10
2 FALLING IN LOVE AGAIN 3:36
3 THE ONLY SOUND THAT MATTERS 3:43
4 MONKEY 4:58

Band of Joy

"I didn't write lyrics for the previous two records because I was with Alison Krauss and with Patty Griffin and Buddy Miller, doing different stuff, visiting beautiful songs from the North American songbook, if you like. I have a lot to say, and I think a lot and I write a lot, so I guess I was scared, or really, I didn't know how to pick the lock that opened the door that gave me this record. And now our door is open, and everything's flowing beautifully."

"I hate the answer to be a mass of giggles, but I'm always accused of having a very pronounced feminine side. It doesn't do me any harm. I don't think too much is gonna change in my attitude, really, between me and the opposite sex. I'm very happy to be a normal guy, having a great time. I love relationships and friendships, and I'm not very good at keeping them, but I'm besotted by them. And I guess what I did was, I spent a lot of time travelling around using music as a sort of compass. And it's taken me to these various places, with various people. And I write a celebration and a reflection of the journey along the way and basically, that's what you get when you hear my songs, is what I feel. And this is down to the people that I've met, and the instances and the situations that have passed through me since I last wrote my own songs, which is going back like ten years. But the previous two records before this have both been pretty successful, and they were embraced

by large swathes of the public outside of the rock world. And that was an achievement really, because I was able to work with Alison Krauss and work with Patty Griffin, two amazing singers."
Robert Plant

Credits

September 13, 2010
Es Paranza/Rounder 11661-9099-2
Produced by Robert Plant and Buddy Miller
Engineered by Mike Poole ("Recorded by")
Recorded at Woodland Studios, Nashville, TN, House of Blues Studios, Nashville, TN and Clinton Recording Studios, New York City, NY
Personnel: Robert Plant – vocals, Patty Griffin – vocals, Buddy Miller – electric guitar, baritone guitar, 6-string bass, mando guitar, backing vocals, Darrell Scott – acoustic guitar, mandolin, banjo, accordion, pedal steel guitar, lap steel guitar, mandolin (octave), backing vocals, Byron House – bass, Marco Giovino – drums, percussion, backing vocals
Key additional personnel: Becka Bramlett – backing vocals.

1. "Angel Dance" (David Hidalgo, Louie Perez) 3:49
2. "House of Cards" (Richard Thompson) 3:13
3. "Central Two-O-Nine" (Plant, Buddy Miller, Jason Friedman) 2:48
4. "Silver Rider" (Zachary Micheletti, Mimi Parker, Alan Sparhawk) 6:06
5. "You Can't Buy My Love" (Billy Babineaux, Bobby Babineaux) 3:10
6. "Falling in Love Again" (Dillard Crume, Andrew Kelly) 3:36
7. "The Only Sound That Matters" (Gregory Vanderpool) 3:43
8. "Monkey" (Michaeletti, Parker, Sparhawk) 4:58
9. "Cindy, I'll Marry You Some Day" (Traditional, arranged by Plant, Miller) 3:36
10. "Harm's Swift Way" (Townes Van Zandt) 4:17
11. "Satan Your Kingdom Must Come Down" (Traditional, arranged by Plant, Miller) 4:12
12. "Even This Shall Pass Away" (Theodore Tilton, arranged by Plant, Miller) 4:03

A *Band of Joy* Timeline

June 26 – July 31, 2010. Robert and his band tour America.

September 13, 2010. Through Rounder in the US and Decca in Europe, Roberts sees the release of a ninth solo album, entitled *Band of Joy*, with the first single being opening track "Angel Dance." The project will win Album of the Year at the 2011 Americana Music Honors & Awards (*Raising Sand* had won in 2008). *Band of Joy* reaches No.5 on the *Billboard* 200, No.2 on the sub Rock Albums chart, No.7 in Canada and No.3 on the UK charts.

October 14 – November 2, 2010. Robert and his band perform in Europe, with emphasis on the UK.

January 18 – June 25, 2011. Robert and his Band of Joy tour North America.

February 13, 2011. The 53rd Annual Grammy Awards is held at the Staples Centre in Los Angeles. *Band of Joy* is nominated in the Best Americana Album category and "Silver Rider" from the record is nominated in the Best Solo Rock Vocal Performance category.

February 15, 2011. The annual Brit Awards are held, at O2 Arena. Robert Plant is nominated in the British Male Solo Artist category.

July 19 – August 7, 2011. Robert and his Band of Joy mates play Europe, mostly festival dates. At the last show, in Herefordshire in the West Midlands, Robert bids his band "a fond farewell."

October 31, 2011. UK theatre tenor Alfie Boe issues his sixth album, *Alfie*. On it is a cover of Tim Buckley's "Song to the Siren," upon which Robert provides a guest vocal. Plant included a rendition of the song on his own album, *Dreamland*, from nine years previous.

July 2012. Robert Plant lets on that he and singer Patty Griffin are an item and living on and off together in Austin, Texas. However, by the summer of 2014, the union is off.

July 10, 2012. Universal Music group issues a DVD (and Blu-ray) called *Robert Plant & The Band of Joy: Live from the Artists Den.*

July 13, 2012. Issued as a digital download is *Robert Plant Presents: Sensational Space Shifters (Live in London July '12)*.

October 18 – November 12, 2012. Robert and The Sensational Space Shifters play South America and Mexico.

March 21 – April 10, 2013. Robert and his Sensational Space Shifters tour Australia and New Zealand, also playing Singapore.

June 20 – July 27, 2013. Robert and his band play the US, followed by a handful of UK dates in August, September and October.

June 5 – July 19, 2014. Robert and his band tour Europe, with a date at the Mawazine Festival in Morocco preceding the campaign.

August 16, 17, 2014. After playing Glastonbury on August 9th, Robert and his band head to Japan.

September 8 – November 27, 2014. Robert and the guys play a lone London show and take care of some in-studio stuff, followed by a North American tour leg and a return back to the UK (and Ireland).

Martin Talks to Ralph Chapman and Rick LaBonte about *Band of Joy.*

Martin Popoff: Okay, can you give me a little background on *Band of Joy* and explain the concept? It seems like a bit of an outlier in the catalogue, although so did *Dreamland* for similar reasons!

Rick LaBonte: Well, this is an album where, after the experience with Alison Krauss and winning Grammys, Robert is now more than just some old rock god. He's almost some sort of country bumpkin, operating in and appreciated by a world that really would be totally foreign to him. There's the hangover of that whole Americana country bluegrass thing he did with *Raising Sand* bleeding into this. I find it interesting that he uses a similar kind of font that we saw in Led Zeppelin *IV*, for the lyrics and other blocks of text. So, he's embracing the Zeppelin thing, as he does by using the feather symbol that was part of that album. And I remember when I saw Strange Sensation, they actually had that feather on the bass drumhead, so he was embracing his Zeppelin heritage for sure.

As for the name, Band of Joy was a band he had with John Bonham before Led Zeppelin. And I have mixed feelings. Why would he use that? Especially when he did put out some rare music from that band that actually had John Bonham on it. But I think the idea was that this new band would approach these songs in the same spirit that the old band did, and that the original Band of Joy was a covers band too. They would play "Hey Joe" and then play something very folky, something Motown, a variety of music. And that was the only thing different about the Band of Joy—the old band played to the audience, and this is an album concept.

Does that pub concert experience resonate the same here? I don't think so, in terms of this path. But it's cool that he could go and put together a handpicked band that would be able to bring to life some of the things that he learned from working with Alison Krauss and T Bone Burnett. And he dated a woman named Patty Griffin at the time, and played on her album, and she's got a great voice and he loved that whole Alison Krauss experience and her approach on some of the Zeppelin songs. Now Patty can come to the table with that and perform songs like "Rock and Roll" and a few others live with him when he wants to do it. So, when he made this album, he was also thinking about a band that he could take on the road, because he utilised all those players.

Martin: And what's the story on this band? I guess, to put it crudely, it's almost like the *Raising Sand* band 2.0.

Rick: Yes. Unlike Strange Sensation, where he was grabbing people in the UK, this is an American band, Nashville guys, people that he rubbed shoulders with as part of working with Alison and her circle. But it's none of the same people that are on *Raising Sand*. And also in a crude way, the Alison role is replaced mostly by Patty Griffin and also Bekka Bramlett on two songs, although that's just backing vocals. So, they're all new people, major fresh faces for him. And that's what he needed. And on more of an abstract level, that's what Robert does—he doesn't want to get tied down. He's always searching, otherwise no one would let him go from being that Zeppelin guy. He always wants something different. He gets a little nervous about having the same band probably too long before people want to pigeonhole him.

But yeah, the original Band of Joy was a cover band, a bar band basically, and that's why he revived that name. I'm going to put a Band of Joy together and just do whatever I want to do and see what these guy can pull off. And out there live, especially when they did Led Zeppelin songs, they scaled it down to fit their characteristic sound. Their rendition of "Houses of the Holy" was fantastic, and smart. They did "Tangerine," "In the Mood" and "Ramble On" and in such a great way, with that whole bluegrass and little bit of country feel. So, yeah, the covers, including the Zeppelin covers, had that level of consistency.

Ralph Chapman: I look at Robert Plant's career in terms of arcs. The first three records are an arc. The next two are an arc. *Fate of Nations* is a strange kind of sidetrack, because then he falls into the Page Plant thing. *Fate of Nations* is rarely talked about, even though I know Robert himself is a big fan of that record. It doesn't really lead to anything. By the time the Page Plant thing is over, the next thing he does is *Dreamland*, which is a covers record. And that's the moment where, in my mind, he starts another arc. Then we get to *Band of Joy* with a little bit of side-tracking. He does *Mighty ReArranger* in 2005 with his band Strange Sensation. But *Dreamland* is the moment he gives himself permission to be Robert Plant beyond the star, the singer and the songwriter. He gives himself permission to go on a full-on homage to other songwriters. I see that arcing right to *Band of Joy*, where all of a sudden he can do another record where he's not the songwriter.

To go back a bit and flesh out how he gets to this place, I've been known to go on a bit about *Now and Zen* and why I hated it at the time. I saw it as such a deliberate cash-in because *Shaken 'n' Stirred*, to me, was a much more progressive and interesting record, It sold in the dozens and split his band up and then he goes on Live Aid and just regurgitates the past. The next time we see him, he's got the Zeppelin logo and he's back to the hair and he's got Jimmy Page. And that doesn't surprise. Who knows? Maybe at that point, it's kind of like Peter Gabriel saying, "I recorded *So* because I wanted to be a star. I loved being an artist, but..."

And then of all the Plant albums, *Manic Nirvana* is the one I like the least. And possibly because it's the silliest and it's the most pastiched and it's utterly unconvincing to me. But I acknowledge that that's subjective. I can only say that *Now and Zen* was an explicit nod to his past that I found uncomfortable, be it the invoking of a hip-hop sound on "Tall Cool One" to using Jimmy Page on the same song. And maybe it was just for laughs. I felt that he had let go of Jezz, Paul and Robbie and just traded them in for cheaper, younger models for *Now and Zen*. It could have been a great moment of, "I want to work with new people." *Now and Zen* could have been like a *Pictures at Eleven*, where it's, "I'm not really sure where to go now."

But now it's, "So I'm just going to trade on some tropes that are familiar to me with some nods." But the fact that he goes further down that road with *Manic Nirvana*... And I saw the *Manic Nirvana* tour and I just didn't find that the songs were there. And this is so subjective and I'm uncomfortable with it, but I just didn't find his collaborations or his collaborators compelling, I guess. That was the Phil Johnstone era. I checked out of Robert because I didn't know what he was after. I hated the artwork for *Manic Nirvana*. I hated everything about it. I thought it was his midlife crisis record. And that started with *Now and Zen*,

I think there's a reason why he goes into overdrive. He's a guy who steadfastly does not do Led Zeppelin tunes. And then by the time he does the *Manic Nirvana* tour... like I said, I saw him at Maple Leaf Gardens and he's doing "Black Country Woman" and Phil Johnstone is coming out from behind his keyboard and strumming it. And the guy I was with, this guy, Phil—can't remember his last name; I was with a quasi-girlfriend, her friend and her fiancé—they were liking the show. But I think they were liking just what he was putting out there. I was largely indifferent, because I disliked the album so much. But my point is when Phil Johnstone came out from the keyboard with the guitar to do "Black Country Woman"—because that was part of the staging of it—this guy Phil went fucking insane! And he started yelling at me, "Jimmy's here! Jimmy showed up!" He was convinced that that was Jimmy Page. And he wasn't on his own. The whole crowd went bananas. I think partially because it was "Black Country Woman," but I have trouble believing some of them thought what Phil thought. It was more about the whole, again, invocation of the Led Zeppelin myth, spilled out, that I'm sure Plant fed off of.

So, flash forward, I didn't know what Plant was after until *Fate of Nations*. And then I started to understand, again, his lyrics, the production choices he was making, the people he was choosing to collaborate with, the sheer variety that's on that record, including the Tim Hardin cover. And I was much more comfortable with that because it felt that it played to his strong points. I don't count the Page Plant stuff. I find that stuff more satisfying, but that even feels like why Townsend started touring with *Tommy* again, with The Who again, and it was based on the fact that Roger and John appealed to his sense of friendship. When I listen to Page Plant, I feel like that project is as much about friendship and giving Jimmy something to do. Because clearly when Plant's not around, Jimmy does next to nothing. So from my lofty perch (laughs), I love Jimmy Page, and it's interesting when Plant goes in those directions, but they're static moments. They're not progressive moments.

This will lead back to *Band of Joy*; I promise. So why I adore Robert Plant is even if I don't like it, he's moving constantly. And he's tireless in sniffing out talented artists and talented songwriters, which is what *Band of Joy* is partially about. It's largely a covers record, which is an extraordinary move at that point in his career. And the cynical could say, well, it's because he's a spent force. But it's consistent in my mind with who he is, just calling it *Band of Joy*. My understanding of Band of Joy, yes, it had John Bonham and it's part of his youth, but it trafficked in covers too. It was a guy who was exploring great songwriting as an 18- or 19-year-old and exploring his influences more than it was about honing himself as a composer. Because he didn't really do that, as far as I know, until the second Led Zeppelin album. Although there's some talk that because of contracts, his credits are left off the first record. In my mind, knowing what I know, he doesn't step into the role of a songwriter really until 1969, 1970. That's when he starts to hit his stride.

So yes, *Raising Sand* goes platinum, but I think more importantly, it wins Grammys and it's a critical darling. He certainly got pop cred and big royalty cheques from *Now and Zen*. But remembering that era, I don't think he was on the lips of the intelligentsia. Then *Raising Sand*, all of a sudden, I saw that tour, and it wasn't Led Zeppelin fans going to that tour. It was a whole new audience. And again, I brought up Peter Gabriel, *So*. That album introduced him to a whole new audience. You had soul music fans, Kate Bush fans, you had all these different people. All of a sudden he's not only a superstar, but his name is whispered as this incredible artist. *Raising Sand* gave Robert that for the first time and *Band of Joy* is a continuation of that direction.

Martin: Okay, so the first thing we hear, somewhat bizarrely, is Robert covering a Los Lobos song from 1990, from their fifth album *The Neighborhood*.

Rick: "Angel Dance" is a catchy song, but it's not a weird arrangement like Strange Sensation might do. He's more reserved; it's more about accessibility. But again, he's still using instruments of both an acoustic and electric nature. It's still fresh and different but less hippie-trippy than his original material like this and more Americana.

Ralph: I remember you and I were working at Banger Films. I was in the same office with Lisa Ladouceur and she turned to me and said, "Hey, did you hear the new Robert Plant single?" It was "Angel Dance" and I was immediately smitten with it. It was hooky and it was upbeat and I felt it was in the wheelhouse of *Raising Sand*, but it was much more. Or much less. And this is my judgment: I liked the *Raising Sand* thing but I was more intrigued by *Band of Joy*, and I found it more joyful (laughs). And that's how I felt when I heard "Angel Dance." It's an evocative but fun number and an interesting first single. There was nothing ruminative about it or precious about it or too inside, like a lot of the *Raising Sand* material was. I found this whole album accessible. And why that was is, I think, is because I didn't know any of the songs. He wasn't doing famous tunes. He wasn't covering Jesse Winchester. He was drawing on really eclectic sources. And I thought it was a really interesting sequence to start the album with a contemporary Los Lobos cover, which isn't too much of a departure from the original recording.

Martin: Okay, next is "House of Cards," and I'm hearing some of that hoarfrost direction in terms of textures that we're going to get on *Lullaby and the Ceaseless Roar* and on *Carry Fire*.

Rick: Yes, but again, stylistically more accessible and traditional, country even, despite where it comes from. It has a southern gospel flair to it, that kind of vibe you get from a Southern Baptist church. That was something fans of Robert hadn't heard before.

Ralph: A few things about "House of Cards" that I loved is that, first, it reminded you that he has a deep history with Richard Thompson and a deep history with Fairport Convention, with, obviously, Sandy Denny on "Battle of Evermore," and Richard showing up on *Fate of Nations*. But what I loved about this choice is that "House of Cards" is drawn from the *First Light* album, Richard and Linda Thompson, which is often seen as their nadir by Richard. I met Richard Thompson a couple times, once in New York after a Joe's Pub gig and once in San Juan Capistrano, The Coach House. And here I was, he signed my record kind of thing, and both times I asked about *First Light*. And at this point it had been reissued by Ryko but then gone out of print and the rights reverted back to Richard Thompson and he just sat on it. And I asked him; I said, "Some of us want that reissued and it's disappeared." And he looked at me and he echoed what he had said in some other interview. He said, "That's a hackneyed record, don't like it at all, no interest in that. Besides I don't even know where the tapes are." He makes up some horseshit.

So when I saw that Plant had covered this deep cut from that album—like I think it's the ninth track on *First Light*—that was exciting to me. Whatever drama that's infused in that song lyrically, the power of that song had not diminished at all, but he had made it his own.

And what was also interesting about "House of Cards" is that's the first time you hear Patty Griffin. So what I love about *Band of Joy*... how do I say this? I enjoyed *Raising Sand* but I didn't necessarily want to hear Alison Krauss that much with Robert Plant. Or maybe I didn't want to hear a female voice that much with Robert Plant. It may come down to taste. Alison Krauss on her own... I have Union Station records and she is what she is. What I loved about how he used Patty Griffin on this record, how he used the female voice on this record is that he used discretion. It's the same way he used Toni Halliday on *Shaken 'n' Stirred*. Whatever that sound is that is invoked is much more rewarding. On "House of Cards," if you're a rube, you'd think, "Is that Alison Krauss?" Because it's got echoes of that same kind of folk Americana feel to it. Ghostly kind of. But, again, what I loved about *Band of Joy* is he uses it with discretion. He uses it for atmosphere. It's a Robert Plant record, but we get to have this extra element that I think adds a lot of texture and emotion to the record.

Martin: And he's in a relationship with her, right?

Ralph: Well, I think it builds into that, which then collapses, and that leads to one of his records, the next record, *Lullaby*. That's all about the breakup of those two. I don't know; that's pure conjecture. I can imagine that being the terminal romantic that he is, he's got probably a unique relationship to women as people, and as artists. I'm speculating. And so it's kind of a cliché that you record with someone and then, of course, you inevitably end up with them. And maybe that's what made Krauss safe. Because that wasn't going to happen. So they did *Raising Sand*, and then they started recording a follow-up record, and it fell apart for reasons that, as far as I know, are still murky. And it took years later for them to come back again and they did *Raise the Roof* in 2021, again with T Bone Burnett. But it didn't do anything like *Raising Sand* did, which isn't really necessarily a comment on its quality. It's just that the music business has changed that much more since 2007. Anyway, one of the reasons why I like *Band of Joy* is because of Patty Griffin's presence and how, in a way, he does what he did with *Shaken 'n' Stirred*, which is, okay, use that instrument, use that female vocal.

Martin: Next is "Central Two-O-Nine," the only original on the album.

Ralph: Yeah, and of course what makes this record distinct for me as a Plant solo project is how far he's gone down the Americana road, the Richard Thompson song being the exception. He's got Buddy Miller producing with him, who co-writes this song with him, along with Jason Friedman from The Boggs. The song is pure bluegrass blues. But yeah, the album is recorded in Nashville and it's got all Nashville players. Other than *Raising Sand*, which I don't even count as a Robert Plant solo project, I believe *Band of Joy* has the distinction of being the only entirely American piece of work in his catalogue. And just on that it sets itself apart. It's also the only record where he is covering, again, Los Lobos, Low, Milton Mapes, which is this really obscure band, which isn't a criticism of it; it's just a fact.

Rick: This is a catchy but also quite dramatic song for him. It's a nice short one and fits great in the tracking order. And yes, even though it's an original, it's Robert as part of something that is pure acoustic Americana.

Martin: Next we have "Silver Rider," which is from this Duluth, Minnesota band called Low, their seventh album, *The Great Destroyer*, 2005. This is a dramatic vocal showcase. It's like he's discovered all over again that he's this really engaging singer, but you better be prepared to turn him up in the mix if you want to hear him.

Ralph: Yeah, it's funny you mention that, and you're right, this is an extremely whispery and breathless vocal, uncharacteristic. I don't know, because I'm not Robert Plant. And you may be right. My take on that... again, I give him an enormous amount of room because he is a hero of mine, because he's so smart and so funny and so seemingly unaffected by being what he was for so long, which is this larger-than-life, golden god-type creature. So I imagine maybe unconsciously, or maybe, to be a devil's advocate to what you're saying, maybe that's just how he's choosing to interpret the song.

But maybe he's also, on an unconscious level, reluctant to choose material that invokes Robert Plant. Maybe he just wants to do material that is about the song and servicing the song. Because he's not Tom Jones. He's not a guy who's seemingly interested in telling us what range he still has and the power of his pipes at all. I don't think he's done that in years. Even back to *Walking into Clarksdale*, he wasn't particularly interested. I don't think that guy's been around for years.

When your whole purpose of your project here is to celebrate songwriting and songs, I think a shrewd move is to perform them where it's this weird combination of celebrating the songs and getting inside the song but also not making the song about him. And that I guess is what I hear. I hear the honouring of the material at any cost. "Silver Rider", the Low tune, is a very unconventional choice in the sense that it's not by any stretch of the imagination a standard. It's an obscure piece of work, but it's not an obscure blues tune.

But it's tough being Robert Plant. I contextualise everything. So I can listen to this record and really enjoy it because I know I can also listen to *Houses of the Holy* and then I can listen to even *Now and Zen* and it's just part of that story. And I think with Robert Plant, like Neil Young, like Paul McCartney, like a lot of these people, there is the tendency among fans to say, "I like this period" or "I like these people." I've told you this: I like these people as artists;

I'm fascinated by their journeys as artists. It doesn't mean I love everything. Like I said, *Manic Nirvana* is a record that I rarely go back to because I can't get inside it. I don't understand its motivation. Or if I do, it's not a motivation I'm comfortable with exploring because it's out of step.

Rick: With "Silver Rider," I agree, you get one of the most dramatic vocal performances I think I've ever heard out of Robert. But it's also in a specific, almost sleepy, dreamy space. Another great tune—very good. Every album has something like this, although not as extreme, where he's going to cast this spell, almost put you in a state of hypnosis. Sometimes it's only for a line or even a word or two. But yeah, this is a whole song of the most extreme version of that. It's like you're slowly going into a trance—"Keep your eye on this watch" (laughs). It's that kind of approach, barely pushing air.

Martin: "You Can't Buy My Love" represents an entirely different direction for Robert here, more of a sixties' vibe, along with a Bo Diddley beat.

Rick: This is an old song form 1965 that they made really peppy, catchy. It belongs on the record. You kind of trip up over that title, given the similarity to The Beatles and "Can't Buy Me Love," which came out the year before the original version of this.

Ralph: Barbara Lynn is this black guitarist from Texas, from the mid-sixties that I imagine he had heard. Written by two brothers, Billy Babineaux and Bobby Babineaux, this was a single of hers. What I connect to is that the song reminds me of the Paul McCartney album *Run Devil Run*, which was largely a collection of mostly obscure covers. In the promotional interviews, he talked about, "Oh, that's a flipside of the single that I heard in some Liverpool restaurant or whatever." I can imagine Robert saying the same thing. It's a song that one could easily imagine Plant heard back in the mid-sixties, on a single, and it lodged in his brain.

He's an artist completely unconcerned with covering songs of renown. He's actually going out of his way to just do songs that he likes, and to highlight writers and bands that he likes. I can imagine a band like Low is one that someone turned him on to. And again, he doesn't really reinvent the song. It's not like "Blinded by the Light," what Manfred Mann did to that Springsteen tune. It's often going for the same kind of atmosphere. And that's what I discovered when I bought this album too is that I sought the songs out and I thought, oh, this is an homage to these songs. So therefore, it must be an homage to the songwriters. It's not, "That's an interesting song, I'm gonna make it my own." He's going to celebrate it.

And even "House of Cards," rhythmically, although it's American players and it's an American producer, the version on *First Light* is not a million miles away from the original. Now, I haven't heard the original of every single tune on this, but, again, what I thought was interesting is he doesn't seek to reinvent the songs. He seeks to push them into the limelight and give them the respect they deserve. It's a lot easier to do that on a Robert Plant project than to be like a Bob Stanley-type character and put a compilation of all the songs together and put it out on Ace or something. This is Robert's version of saying, "Here's a bunch of songs that I think are great. And I'm gonna celebrate the songs and I hope you dig them."

Martin: "Falling in Love Again" is another one that goes off road in terms of not being based in Americana. This is more of a forties of fifties crooner thing, despite the pedal steel guitar. And it's in three-four time too.

Rick: This is an old classic that has a Honeydrippers vibe to it. Plant does a great job with it, despite it being somewhat of a diversion. But he makes it fit on the record with his voice as well as the way the band sounds, particularly Marco Giovino on the drums. But even here, I'm feeling a gospel-like vocal, which connects it to country, as does that twangy, steel guitar, which is so old country or Grand Ol' Opry country. He's going old school. When Robert Plant goes country, he doesn't do the contemporary country of today. He's like George Jones country, going way far back. It's like when he explores the blues. He goes further back than Muddy Waters. Plant really goes deep.

Ralph: "Falling in Love Again," to me that's one of his most... I gotta attach superlatives. It's incredibly moving, subtle, beautifully phrased, naked but joyous; like, he's really established himself in my mind. But he'd been at it for a while. Like when I listen to "If I Were a Carpenter," I hear that as well. But when I listen to "Falling in Love Again," he reminds me of Bobby Darren or these other master interpreters of songs who are not interested, again, in reinventing a song, but just simply taking that song and singing it, which is a weird distinction.

There's no ego attached. Maybe that's it—there's no Plant. Phil Collins talks about the whole Live Aid experience and why it was so startling for him. He said that he was close friends with Plant, and then once he got into the Led Zeppelin orbit, Plant was no longer Plant anymore; he'd become something else and they couldn't relate. And then as soon as Plant left that orbit, they were kind of friends again and could talk.

I think there's a huge mystique that's well earned with Robert Plant. So to hear *Band of Joy*, which is on this new arc with *Dreamland*, you're getting a Robert who has completely checked his ego, his artistic ego, and is just revelling in the material. And he's reveling in the material in part because he's choosing it, and no one's telling him to choose it. So he's not being dictated to choose it, nor is he feeling any pressure to make it his own. And you can tell when someone makes something their own. Sometimes that ends up great, like the Manfred Mann I mentioned earlier, and sometimes it's like, you've just decimated the song (laughs). With Plant, you get a sense from this record—and you heard it in *Raising Sand* as well— but because this is a solo project, you get a sense of just a master, interpretive, egoless singer.

Martin: Okay, so an Austin, Texas band called Milton Mapes issues an album called *Westernaire* in 2003. On it is a song called "The Only Sound That Matters" and lo and behold, Robert covers it here.

Rick: Again, it's all about vocals. If anything, this is a vocal- and vocalist-happy album, more about that than the musicianship. It's more about that than the arrangement or all that great musicianship you get with Strange Sensation. It's about singer and the voice and only somewhat about the song, even though it's called *Band of Joy*. It's really a singer-songwriter album.

Ralph: I'm grateful that he chose to cover this, because I would have never heard it, in this increasingly fragmented post-Napster era where genres don't exist, where there are seemingly thousands upon thousands of bands that I'll never hear. And they could be great bands. Just the other day, just last night, actually, I heard an Indiana singer, this woman, and I just happened to have heard a song. But it's obscure. My point is, in the post-Napster era, although it's painful for me to admit this, there are probably a similarly high number of extraordinary songwriters to the old days, but there is no industry. There is no meaningful A&R apparatus to find these bands and singer-songwriters and give them the platform that the old bands got.

How the music industry used to work, you were anointed when you were signed. And you were given broad distribution if things went well, and you were given a studio and a budget. And that's how we know so many of these great, great writers. And what Plant does with a song like that is he gives us a window into some of these people who've been, for lack of a better word, ghettoised into obscurity. That's the norm, where it's now acceptable that you can talk to someone and you can say to them, "Who are your favourite bands?" And they'll rhyme off five or six bands that you've never fucking heard of. That's strange and sad. And, again, it's a 21st century thing, I think. And it's a drag. So that's what I think of when I hear him cover that band, and Greg Vanderpool in particular. But I do think that's worthy to know that you have to look at some of this material through a 21st century lens, where if Robert Plant isn't covering it, I would never have heard of it.

Martin: I'm almost arriving at the idea that one of Robert's statements here is that there's a firehose of supply of songs, and that you can throw darts. Honestly, there's hundreds of thousands of songs Robert could have picked, and we'd be no better or worse off. And I'd say that the randomness of his picks underscores that point. This could have been a ten-CD box set rather than a collection of a dozen songs and he would have been no closer to making a specific point, or at least if he chose 100 songs in a similar wide-net fashion. In other words, Ralph, I get that sense of panic about mortality that you are hinting at when you say it's painful and strange and sad and a drag! Anyway, what do you guys think about the back end of this album?

Rick: Well, "Monkey" serves the purpose of having something dark on here, representing the melancholy extreme of the collection, I guess. It's eerie, almost evil, but really cool and one of my favourites. With "Cindy, I'll Marry You Someday," again, he's taking an old gem of a song that was probably never a big hit. Not many people cover that one. But again, this is typical Robert Plant, unearthing an old country chestnut and bringing it into modern times. I think that getting a Grammy for his efforts with Alison made him respect the music of that era just that little bit more. I think he felt he had more to say in this genre or idiom, but that he didn't necessarily have to do it with Alison. It's like, there were a few songs along the way that I liked and maybe I can sing them all on my own. Maybe these are songs that slipped through the net when they were trying to pick songs. And if this song didn't get on the album, he's gonna sandbag it for another day.

Ralph: Both "Monkey" and "Cindy, I'll Marry You Some Day," in two different directions, still conspire to make the point that Robert's working in a different space than some of our other rock 'n' roll heroes. You say this old-timey thing he is doing has a hipster quality to it. What did you say? It's the musical equivalent of a high-end beard maintenance kit? I understand that and maybe this is my point, too. McCartney and Jagger, even if they've lost 70 to 80% of their vocal timbre and all the rest of it, they're still going out there and singing songs comfortably. Now maybe not physically comfortably, but I saw McCartney and he did "I Saw Her Standing There" and "Nineteen Hundred and Eighty-Five" and "Helter Skelter" and yeah, it sounds significantly different. But he doesn't have any problem with it. And he sings them like he takes a certain amount of pride in singing them in the original keys, even if it shreds his voice.

A friend of mine, the same friend who I went and saw *Manic Nirvana* with, Robert Plant just played Toronto and she sent me "Battle of Evermore" just as a video, over the phone. She video'd it on her phone and sent it to me. And it sounded absolutely nothing like the original. It did not invoke the original Zeppelin version at all. I guess my point is—and maybe it's your point—you can hate or not like McCartney because his voice is shredded and, oh, it sounds crap when he does "Helter Skelter." But his modus in that moment is to take you back to 1968. Plant has no interest in that. Plant wants to take you back to 1932. He has no interest in taking you to 1971 because 1971 is loaded. That's the point I'm trying to make. I'm mangling it, but he's locked in a box. Even though that box has a huge amount of frills and toys and joy because he's this hipster dude who's constantly talking about great songs, in execution, it seems often very muted, very mid-fi, very acoustic, very restrained. And it's like, well, that's the rules I play by now.

Martin: And in the main, his rule is—you're right—that we all perform quietly, even me, or in fact, because of me. He's operating often at the level of murmur.

Ralph: I know. But see, when you say murmur or humming, it invokes this idea that it's somehow slapdash or it's limited in its emotional range. And I my point with "Falling in Love Again," which is definitely not a belter by any stretch, but in those muted tones, because he's a master interpreter, what he's lacking in vocal gymnastics, he's making up for in a visceral communication of emotion.

Martin: I like that. Okay, with "Harm's Swift Way," I'm hearing John Hiatt, Joe Ely, Nick Lowe, John Doe, The Del-Lords, even Traveling Wilburys. But of course there's a reason for that.

Ralph: Yes, he's covering Townes Van Zandt. That to me is the heritage part of Robert Plant, his desire to use his notoriety and his fan reach that to this day is still huge. I don't know who buys Robert Plant albums, but in his mind he's taking the opportunity to give another platform for a fairly long-forgotten—in the broader sense— songwriter. Again, that, to me, is a big part of what this project represents, the ability to showcase other people.

Martin: Okay, we wind on down with "Satan Your Kingdom Must Come Down" and "Even This Shall Pass Away."

Rick: "Even This Shall Pass Away" just feels like an upbeat way to end the album. It's a summary or statement of what's just happened and what might come next. Now "Satan Your Kingdom Must Come Down" is dark and almost an "In My Time of Dying" thing. It doesn't sound like that, but it's menacing like that. It's not a place Plant usually goes. First of all, I never thought much about whether he was a Christian or an atheist. He does gospel songs. Maybe he's a believer. So now you're learning something about your singer. In any event, he's challenging Satan and it's eerie and dramatic. It's almost like he's intimidated. He's not singing with conviction. His very vocal seems to say I'm fighting you and I'm scared. I picture David going up against the giant, Goliath. It's definitely an homage to that blues tradition, the Robert Johnson thing, people selling their soul, although it's the flipside of that. It's as spooky as "Crossroads" but it's a gospel song. It's telling Satan you're going down. And you have to be a strong believer to do that. I was very surprised to hear that lyrical content out of him, although the music is entirely expected, all those instruments, that sparse production, the classy use of the female voice, all of it.

Ralph: Yeah, to me, those songs are an extension of the *Raising Sand* project, especially "Satan Your Kingdom Must Come Down," which has that kind of unsettling, eerie American folk feel about it, but very vivid. You paint pictures in your head, even if you're not even listening to the lyrics. It's about mood. I don't know, you could say that the last part of this record is strictly by mood. I'm drawn to the first part of this album, which really ends with "The Only Sound That Matters," which is track seven. There are more moods for me personally in the first part of this record.

I'd love to ask Robert about that. Because this as well: there are still song-pluggers out there; there are still label people. You want to top-load an album, because you have little faith people will stick it out to the end. The album doesn't mean the same thing anymore. I don't know whether I can look at *Band of Joy* and say I want to be there at the end. Although I enjoy it as an album, and Robert Plant is just an extraordinary artist, and you probably could look at it as a complete story, when I listen to it, the story ends with "The Only Sound That Matters" with respect to the journey that is the most satisfying for me in terms of all the moods that this record is going to offer. For the most part, everything that I'm drawn to is done by track seven. That doesn't mean I don't enjoy the rest of the record. But if you hold a gun to my head, really, what I appreciate most are those first seven tracks.

It's funny, I still have my ticket stub from that tour and my original Amazon receipt for the CD—I bought it two weeks after it came out. So yeah, to recap, to me, the thing about this that might be slightly contradictory about *Band of Joy* is that it feels like for the most part, with the exception possibly of "You Can't Buy My Love," which has such a distinct and aggressive bass sound on it, it doesn't sound anything like side two of *Abbey Road* or "Supper's Ready" but it feels like one big melange like those two examples. It doesn't actually feel like individual tracks to me when I sit and listen to that album. It feels like it's one continuous dabbling with atmospheres and textures. And like I say, I've heard most of them by track seven.

But yeah, I feel sequencing is really important. Maybe in the old days he would have ended this record with "House of Cards." Maybe he would have ended it on a more provocative note, sonically. But maybe he'd say, well, "Even This Shall Pass Away" is the perfect closer. I don't know. It's very subjective. But after "The Only Sound That Matters," it's not a fatigue that sets in but the rest feel like bonus tracks on a record, those last five songs. Does that make sense?

Martin: No! (laughs). Because now I can't get out of my head that firehose theory of songs and the vastness and randomness of it all. Now, down to the space of this small and precious selection of songs, his little island of joy, I still feel you'd be singing the praises of each and every one of these songs to various degrees, given a hundred other sequencings. And I know you are a professor of sequencing. You'd probably love that exercise!

Ralph: Okay, maybe so, but I just wanted to address your point about where these songs might come from, or why these songs were picked. I was listening to *Digging Deeper*, which is Plant's kind of quasi-podcast, where he talks a bit about how he has friends send him songs, or send him videos. He's very open. I don't want to couch this in a pejorative sense. But to me, he's always been about great songs. Sounds kind of vague. My vision of Robert Plant is it's much like Peter Gabriel and guys like that, who are always listening to music, who are not trapped in particular areas. Although Robert is renowned for his work in extolling and promoting early American blues music and all the rest of it.

Martin: Still, it's like when people are constantly recommending music to me, or really, sending me YouTube clips of individual songs. I tell them to stop and say it's like you're leading me into a forest and we sit on the ground and blather on about one single fallen leaf. I can't romanticise any of these song choices. There are too many songs in the world. It's more special when the lyrics and music are your own, and new.

Ralph: Okay, fair enough. But you look at *Band of Joy*, where, again he covers contemporary Los Lobos. I don't know how he find songs. I don't know whether it's through publishing, but I like to believe a lot of it is because he's a music fan. And he's always been a music fan. Elton John would be another one, although less. I love Elton John—which is much to your annoyance—but Elton came out with *Songs from the West Coast*, and he said that was from sitting around listening to Ryan Adams records—that's what inspired him. These guys, it's hard to imagine them sitting there with their Macintosh stereos listening to music and going oh, that sounds good. Rather, I think Robert has surrounded himself with people who understand what excites him about music.

I think with *Raising Sand,* that took him into a whole new direction, a whole new different type of American music and an homage to whole different genres of American music that perhaps he wasn't schooled in. But that whole experience with T Bone Burnett and Alison Krauss and that whole *Raising Sand* project, I think, allowed him to do *Band of Joy* seamlessly. It makes sense that he produced *Band of Joy* with Buddy Miller, who was the guitarist on the *Raising Sand* tour. So he had that sense of confidence and security knowing that this was an interesting direction. Like Rick says, I think there were songs they didn't get around to with Alison Krauss that showed up on here. Of course, the similar mindset and direction would have looked attractive, given that *Raising Sand* turned out to be the biggest critical success of Robert's career, in terms of acclaim.

Martin: He wants respect. He wanted that in a Sting and Peter Gabriel frame of mind in the late eighties, but now he wants it with... I guess it's people his age, really.

Ralph: I guess my response to that is that I can't really disagree with it. But my response to that is also, there seems to be among these elder statesmen now of rock 'n' roll, a terror of being parodies or has-beens or some combination of the two.

Martin: At the end of the day, I don't feel any cynicism in what he's doing.

Ralph: No, no, but I think he's partially guided by... reinvention is like a cloak. And all those things that you describe, you couldn't say he was a parody. Like, look at, say Paul McCartney, who's my favourite musician by a long shot. People could attack him because often when he's interviewed, he's got a Lennon story. And he's always promoting something on the back end. When he's promoting his own records, he's always got a Beatles thing. He's still doing the whole shtick he does, which I think is genuine and part of where he comes from or came from, in terms of the type of entertainment he likes. And I think to an extent Mick Jagger is the same way. They both feel entirely comfortable constantly referring to their past, either in how they move or how they sing or how they play. While with Plant, his past is thornier. With McCartney, who I talk a lot about, it wasn't always this way. But I think McCartney's musical legacy is pretty concrete. He is still widely seen as one of the greatest songwriters, one of the blah blah blah. Whereas Plant is legendary for the mystique of him. So I think that made him react, possibly, in his elder years, more defensively or seriously or cognizant of authenticity. But like you say, fortunately for us, there's no cynicism. It's who he is anyway.

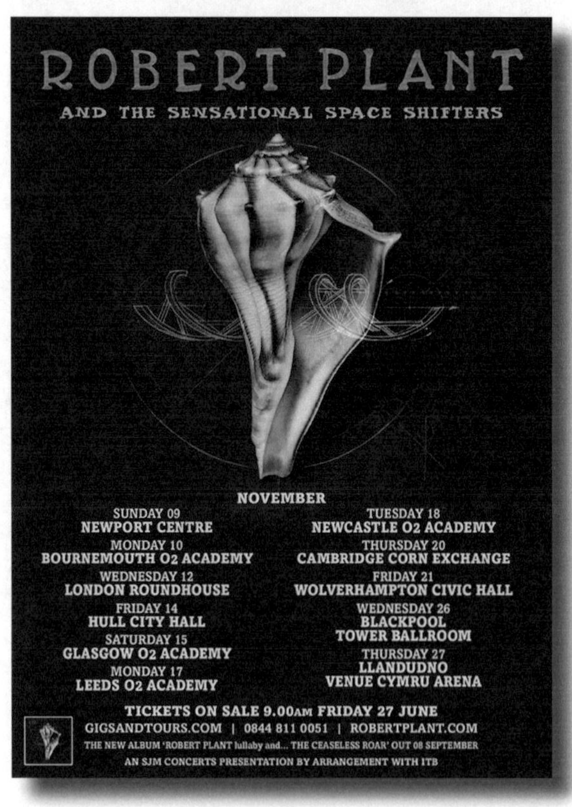

ROBERT PLANT
AND THE SENSATIONAL SPACE SHIFTERS
NOVEMBER
SUNDAY 09
NEWPORT CENTRE
TUESDAY 18
NEWCASTLE O2 ACADEMY
MONDAY 10
BOURNEMOUTH O2 ACADEMY
THURSDAY 20
CAMBRIDGE CORN EXCHANGE
WEDNESDAY 12
LONDON ROUNDHOUSE
FRIDAY 21
WOLVERHAMPTON CIVIC HALL
FRIDAY 14
HULL CITY HALL
WEDNESDAY 26
BLACKPOOL
TOWER BALLROOM
SATURDAY 15
GLASGOW O2 ACADEMY
MONDAY 17
LEEDS O2 ACADEMY
THURSDAY 27
LLANDUDNO
VENUE CYMRU ARENA
TICKETS ON SALE 9.00AM FRIDAY 27 JUNE
GIGSANDTOURS.COM | 0844 811 0051 | ROBERTPLANT.COM
THE NEW ALBUM 'ROBERT PLANT lullaby and... THE CEASELESS ROAR' OUT 08 SEPTEMBER
AN SJM CONCERTS PRESENTATION BY ARRANGEMENT WITH ITB

Lullaby and the Ceaseless Roar

"Having been out in the big wilderness, actually, literally, in the big wilderness, down in Big Bend State Park on the Mexican border across into El Paso, all around Mali, the desert in West African and stuff, it was time to, I guess, come back to the misty mountains from that. Basically, what the whole kind of, if you like, lyrical lean is, it's about coming back and digging in again, and then using a lot of traces of music that could be found in Britain, as opposed to that which might be found in North America. Listen, this band that I'm in, where was I a week ago? Oh, I was in Osaka in Japan. Where am I today? In the misty mountains of Wales. Where was I a month ago? Three weeks ago in the Czech Republic, before I played in Dresden and Berlin and northern Sweden. "

"But I think that I just suddenly embraced my homeland. I think I ran away from it for a while. A lot of my friends were starting to, I guess, close down their lives a little bit sooner than I intended to close mine down. So I took off. I found the deserts of West Africa and maybe South Texas to have a little bit more promise than scouring the neighbourhood after 9:00 PM to see if anybody's got their lights on (laughs)."

"Anyway, this record really gives me the opportunity to write new material with a very prolific and virile group of guys, musically, of course. And that allows me to express myself and go where I wanna go. That has to be the primary driving force behind the whole deal. You gotta knock yourself out before you try to turn anybody else on."

"As for producing it, well, if we go back and think about it, I shared production with Buddy Miller on *Band of Joy*. T Bone produced the one before that, *Raising Sand*. *Mighty ReArranger*, I produced that. But anyway, yes, the thing is, I like to share the blame with somebody, but I got to the point here now where, when I came back from the States and came back to Britain, and I reunited with my friends and added a couple of guys and stuff like that, I really did have a pretty keen perception of what I was trying to do. I wanted to create trance music. I love the whole idea of the hypnotic aspects of music coming out of North Africa, the Gnawa music, which is quite famous. So I wanted to try and put that into a contemporary music setting, despite the fact that I am a mature artist. I want to lean on stuff that really moves me. So I guess I really wanted to hold the reins. But everybody's contribution was strong. I didn't have to kick anybody up the butt to get anything going. This is no criticism about anything; the guys were pretty much conversant and pretty much of a unit, as far as taste and not overcooking the songs. I think we're all kind of united on the way that we want things to sound. I guess somebody's gotta have the last word."

Robert Plant

Credits

September 8, 2014
Nonesuch/Warner Bros. 543973-2
Produced by Robert Plant
Engineered by Tim Holmes and Tim Palmer
Recorded at Helium Studios, Wiltshire, UK, Real World Studios, Box, Wiltshire, UK, Contino Rooms, London, UK and St. George's, Bristol, UK
Personnel: Robert Plant – vocals, production, Justin Adams – bendirs, djembe, guitars, tehardant, background vocals, Liam "Skin" Tyson – banjo, guitar, background vocals, John Baggott – keyboards, loops, Moog bass, piano, tabla, background vocals, Juldeh Camara – kologo, ritti, Fulani vocals, Billy Fuller – bass, drum programming, omnichord, upright bass, Dave Smith – drum set

1. "Little Maggie" (Traditional, arranged by Plant, Adams, Baggott, Fuller, Smith, Tyson) 5:06
2. "Rainbow" (Plant, Adams, Baggott, Fuller, Tyson) 4:18
3. Pocketful of Golden (Plant, Adams, Baggott, Camara, Fuller, Smith, Tyson) 4:12
4. "Embrace Another Fall" (Plant, Adams, Baggott, Camara, Fuller, Smith, Tyson) 5:52
5. "Turn It Up" (Plant, Adams, Baggott, Fuller, Smith, Tyson) 4:06
6. "A Stolen Kiss" (Plant, Adams, Baggott, Fuller, Smith, Tyson) 5:15
7. "Somebody's There" (Plant, Adams, Baggott, Fuller, Smith, Tyson) 4:32
8. "Poor Howard" (Plant, Adams, Baggott, Camara, Fuller, Smith, Tyson) 4:13
9. "House of Love" (Plant, Adams, Baggott, Fuller, Smith, Tyson) 5:07
10. "Up on the Hollow Hill (Understanding Arthur)" (Plant, Adams, Baggott, Fuller, Smith, Tyson) 4:35
11. "Arbaden (Maggie's Babby)" (Plant, Adams, Baggott, Camara, Fuller, Smith, Tyson) 2:44

ROBERT PLANT
RAINBOW

ROBERT PLANT and the
SENSATIONAL SPACE SHIFTERS

ROBERT PLANT
MORE ROAR

A Lullaby and the Ceaseless Roar Timeline

September 9, 2014. Issued through Nonesuch/Warner Bros. is a tenth solo album from Robert Plant, called *Lullaby and the Ceaseless Roar* (stylised as *lullaby and... The Ceaseless Roar*). The album reaches No.10 on the *Billboard* 200, No.4 on the *Billboard* Top Rock Albums chart, No.2 in the UK and No.6 in Canada.

October 9, 2014. Robert performs "Rainbow" and "Little Maggie" on *The Colbert Report*.

March 13 – March 28, 2015. Robert and the band play Mexico and South America.

April 18, 2015. Released for Record Store Day in an edition of 510,000 copies is a 140-gram audiophile pressing 10" EP called *More Roar*. It consists of three tracks recorded live in 2014, namely "Turn It Up/ Arbaden," "Poor Howard" and "Whole Lotta Love (medley)."

April 25, 2015. Robert headlines Lead Belly at 125, a tribute concert at the Kennedy Centre in honour of the blues great. Joining him is Alison Kraus, Viktor Krauss and Buddy Miller.

May 24 – September 23, 2015. Robert and his Sensational Space Shifters play the US, followed by Europe and then back to the US, along with a show in Toronto.

March 4 – 21, 2016. The band conduct a short tour of the American South.

July 1 – August 6, 2016. The band play Europe.

October 11 – 21, 2016. Robert embarks on the Lampedusa Concerts for Refugees tour, along with Emmylou Harris, Steve Earle, Patty Griffin, Buddy Miller and The Milk Carton Kids.

Martin talks to Joe Becht, Tim Durling, Chad Green and Pontus Norshammar about *Lullaby and the Ceaseless Roar.*

Martin Popoff: So what do you think is driving Robert at this point for him to come up with a record like *Lullaby and the Ceaseless Roar*?

Chad Green: Well, you marvel at his skills. He's more than just a singer or a poet. He's a great collaborator and observer. He's insightful and he's had a lot of experience with relationships, both with different musicians as well as love interests. As for how that manifests, this album is incredible, but at the time I wasn't ready to receive it. There's a lot going on texturally, and at the lyric end it's definitely Robert Plant as a more mature man, although it's hard to believe that it's almost ten years ago now. We've got the product of his travels as well, his Middle Eastern influence, and I know he goes to India. One of the reasons I know that is because I have a former boss/friend, that actually encountered him in India on a trip. He was in this bar in the middle of nowhere, some small nondescript bar in India. And he's like, there's this old guy sitting there with all these beautiful women around him. And he's like, what is going on over there? So he got closer and it's Robert Plant. He definitely has a weathered distinctive look, right?

Anyway, I thought maybe this album had influence from that region. And then I started listening to those podcasts of his on YouTube and he started talking about Tunisia in Northern Africa, and how he's very fond of Tunisia. And then you read further and there's lots of expounding upon the music of the deep American south, and so you get banjo but with some extra twang in it, worldly banjo (laugh). It feels more worldly than just strictly Deep South, which is testament to Robert's style, too, this idea of him melding these influences and coming out the other end with a weirdly traditional roots rock song.

Martin: He's a chaser of sounds, right?

Chad: Definitely. I like that point. But like I say, it comes out as a form of pop although not pop, certainly worlds away from *Shaken 'n' Stirred*, which is another kind of pop, not like Madonna but popular at the time, as in the popular sounds of the day. This is world music pop.

Tim Durling: This album definitely represents Robert just doing what he wants to do. And I agree, he really wants to embrace some melding of Americana with Eastern modes of writing and different instrumentation. I think that's always been part of his DNA, because he would do that in Zeppelin every once in a while. But by the time this album comes out in 2014, it's just full-on; he's doing exactly what he wants to do.

Martin: Is there a hipster-with-beard vibe to it? Is he relishing his place in this authentic, critically-acclaimed music?

Tim: Cynically, you could say that but I don't think so. I think very rarely in his career has Robert done what's expected of him or done the commercially viable thing. Maybe *Now and Zen* and *Manic Nirvana*? Those albums might have been, "Hey, you know, you throw in a little bit of that and people go crazy." And they did. But I think once he took that long hiatus after *Fate of Nations* and did the two Page Plant records, I think he said to himself, I'm going to do what I want to do from hereon in. He's referred to himself as an old hippie; I've heard him say that. So I don't think there's anything calculated about this—he's following his muse.

Martin: Okay, and what do you think about this band?

Tim: Well, despite living in small town New Brunswick, I've actually had the pleasure of seeing Robert Plant and The Sensational Space Shifters. My wife and I saw them in Fredericton in 2019—pretty amazing that we got to go. And a lot of these musicians were still in the band at that time. Liam "Skin" Tyson was on guitar and banjo, John Baggott played keyboards and Justin Adams was on guitar and a bunch of stringed instruments. It was basically the same core musicians and they actually did a fair amount of songs from *Lullaby*. This latter-day Robert Plant stuff is not the type of music that I would typically gravitate towards, but having that familiar voice is a way of saying to old-school classic rock guys like me, "It's okay, come on in, you know my voice. Come and take a listen; see what you think."

Joe Becht: Well, 2014 was a weird time in music and I was really searching for albums to get into. But as a completist, I'm buying whatever Robert was doing, I wasn't really into *Band of Joy*, but he has The Space Shifters, who he does that live album with. And that's his backing band here, who help him make a mysterious-sounding album. And I love *Eat the Elephant* by A Perfect Circle, which is not a popular opinion with A Perfect Circle fans or Maynard fans. But I think it's a brilliant album and I wonder if Billy Howerdel was listening to this album at all, because I hear some of that as a precursor to *Eat the Elephant*, particularly in "House of Love." But yes, Robert's voice is soothing and yet haunting and the songs work.

Pontus Norshammar: I must say, I really love *Lullaby and the Ceaseless Roar*. Like Tim, I really believe here is a musician that finally has found what he wants to do and doesn't care whether he was a member of Led Zeppelin or not. I feel like this started on the '93 record, that he wanted to go back even before Led Zeppelin, to the roots of rock music. And both *Lullaby* and *Carry Fire* are on Nonesuch, which is very famous for its roots albums, its country artists, but it's also famous for its avant-garde and new classical music too.

I really enjoy the fact that he works with Arabic and Eastern themes throughout. There's a lot of the stringed instruments from the Middle East. It reminds me of Peter Gabriel's *Us* from 1992, this mixture between rock and folk music from different regions of the world. Robert is the star here but there's also Justin Adams, who plays all these Eastern instruments like bendir and djembe and tehardant. I feel like he is where Phil Johnstone was. He's the guy Robert relates to the most.

But it's also a group album. All the music is arranged by the whole band here and it makes for an exciting record, because he feels like he wants to do this. This is what he wants now. He's found a new niche that has produced a new way of expressing himself, where he's comfortable with what he's saying and the voice he has to say it with. He's older; he's in his 60s. Gone is the high-pitched vocals, replaced by a mature softly singing voice which is middle range but really present throughout the record. I think both of these latest albums have great melodies throughout, and they're as far from Led Zeppelin as you possibly can come, despite the presence of Arabic music in both. He is in this new—but very old—place and he likes it.

Martin: Okay, so into the album and we get its only cover, "Little Maggie," traditional and arranged by the band.

Chad: Right, which sounds Moroccan almost, Morocco being another country Robert likes to visit. But again, there's the influence of the Deep South. It's not exactly a concept album, but there's some kind of concept that emerges with the marrying of these influences—why can't you have both? The main thing you hear is banjo, so that takes us to the blues or bluegrass. However there's this worldly-sounding, slightly out-of-tune fiddle and alien keyboards and frenetic percussion just to confuse the situation. And then Robert chimes in and he's quite subdued, to match the music, which almost has a skiffle vibe or rustic or homemade or something. The band used several unusual instruments on this album. Riti. What is that? I had to look it up. It's a one-stringed fiddle instrument from Africa. What?! So yeah, The Sensational Space Shifters are pretty unconventional.

Pontus: On "Little Maggie" I'm hearing a modern take on rootsy blues, with banjo, some great violin and something that sounds like oud. Plus there's what I call foggy drums, sort of distant, out there in the fog or the haze but somehow modern as well. They almost disappear. Then it moves into a place where you hear these electronic swoops. This is a fresh approach to world music. I really like that track.

Joe: Although he's using banjo and violin for the most part, "Little Maggie" is heavy in its own way, maybe through its murkiness, which definitely describes those drums, which are so processed, I wonder if they're electronic. I don't want to dwell on 2014, but I remember keeping up with my metal bands—like the tenth Sevendust album!—but also finding that with newer bands, you'd get one or two songs and the rest was filler. But I appreciated *Lullaby* because it was so different. Robert Plant's voice is a little off-putting and actually borderline creepy at times, but I enjoy it, especially on "Little Maggie."

Tim: Oh, "Little Maggie" is a really cool song. And yes, it's got this strange combination of musical genres, and yet they manage that with a traditional song. It's got banjo and this light, sympathetic drumming, which at the beginning sounds like it could be done with brushes. It's also got violin, yet at a certain point you start to get this surging, trance-y synthesizer doing this vibrating "wow wow" sound. So it's this strange combination of the very old and the modern and it works incredibly well. I just find myself bobbing my head to this one. It's one of my favourites on the record.

Martin: Yeah, I was making the analogy where it's almost like they're building a modern technological house, a smart house, but it's meticulously designed to look like a heritage home, kind of thing.

Tim: Yeah, it's almost deceptive, but in a playful way. Because you think, okay, well, I'm gonna listen to this Americana album that's going to make me think of old cottages out in the middle of nowhere and sitting on a porch with a banjo and a hayseed in your mouth. But then all of a sudden you get those keyboards coming in and you're sitting on a porch on Mars or something. Or instead of out in the country you're at a rave or some outdoor DJ-set-type concert with thousands of young people. It's a strange combination. On paper it shouldn't work. And if it was a newer act attempting this sort of thing, most record labels would probably say, oh, I don't know about that. You should put that aside. But it's Robert Plant, so they let him do what he wants.

Martin: There's a sense of deliberateness or meticulousness to it as well, verging on preciousness.

Tim: Sure, like, he's very picky on who plays in his band. The last thing he would ever do is hire a guitar player that was like a full-on Jimmy Page aficionado and knows the Zeppelin catalogue inside out. That background might help but you've got to be into stuff that's way beyond the rock standard. And I think that's how he stumbled upon the musicians that he would put in this band. Everything is very much in its place and like you say, I don't think any of it is by accident. There may be happy accidents that happen in the studio, where an extra part of a song gets added, but going into the studio, he has a plan. At least he has an idea of how he wants it to sound coming out.

Martin: "Rainbow" always struck me as bordering on gospel, or at least messiah rock-era U2! What do you guys think of this one?

Pontus: I'm hearing world beat percussion with a prominent guitar played in Arabic tuning, sparse, but full, which is actually the sound of the whole album. In 2007, Robert worked with T Bone Burnett and I think that also influenced him because T Bone Burnett productions are very sparse with lots of space between instruments and stuff like that. And of course *Raising Sand* was a great hit. This one reminds me a bit of "I'm on Fire" by Bruce Springsteen.

Chad: On "Rainbow" I like Robert's wooing and cooing (laughs). I picture him literally wooing after a girl and feeling positive about his prospects. It's a happy, upbeat croon with dominion, like he's on a bit of a mission toward something that he's very much looking forward to. There's a certain confidence in it, augmented by those thumping drums, which sound like two tom-toms hit at the same time. Neil Peart does that in his drum solo and it sounds like cannon fire. Which works here, because it sounds like cannons going off on a hillside or something primal like hunting. I really find this song energising. So yeah, it's melodic and serene yet energised with this powerful percussion, like a rhythmic thumping stomp.

Tim: I agree; it's a mood-lifter of a song, with a simple "We Are the Champions" beat. So not like a Bo Diddley beat, but just something that anybody can immediately start clapping along with. I remember him doing this one live. It just goes to a very standard place. He does a nice falsetto vocal.

Martin: Are you buying my U2 comparison, or no?

Tim: Well, when hear that falsetto, it does sound like something Bono would do. Because he uses his falsetto a lot. Sure. Plus there's that sighing guitar. It's not that you can't pay attention to the lyrics, but if you don't want to, you can drift and just let what he's saying wash over you.

Martin: All right, with the third track, "Pocketful of Golden," the antique-y mood is definitely maintained.

Tim: Yes, and of course the thing that people would zoom in on right away is the opening line: "And if the sun refused to shine." I think Robert does that on purpose, to maybe tease us, to give a knowing nod not just to Zeppelin fans, but the fans that have supported him throughout what is now a solo career that has completely eclipsed the Led Zeppelin catalogue in terms of output and years. This is a slower one, with these amusingly timeless lyrics that could have been written in the 1600s.

Joe: He has a gentleman on his album called Juldeh Camara, who plays his African instruments like the kologo. And I believe that's what you're hearing here. And with the programmed drums and the kologo, and the chord progressions, this song actually really works for me. Again, it's something that I needed, something different, and Robert is bringing that here. But it makes you wonder, is this a direction Robert wanted to go in or is this Sensational Space Shifters saying, hey, we're going in this direction. I'm leaning more towards Robert wanting to go in this direction, because he always likes those mystical sounds. But still, he might not have even imagined going this far without this assembled bunch of people having that vocabulary. In other words, their vocabulary adds onto Robert's. He's saying, hey, can you do this here and do that there? But I feel like these guys are doing things he hadn't imagined. But yeah, he's big into his Welsh heritage and he's always been into mysticism, which is an extra layer added upon his travels in Northern Africa and around the world.

Pontus: With "Pocketful of Golden" you get both acoustic and electronic droning with engaged, forward-pointing percussion. It has a psychedelic feel and there's an Eastern riff that comes and goes. It's very much framed on this Eastern percussion thing, where you don't really miss the traditional drum set. You're in another setting, which is very interesting.

Chad: Very melodic, with Robert doing this mesmerising, hypnotic, monotone humming thing. And I think that's the riti bringing that dull, fluttering, scratching texture. This gives the song that ancient vibe and also being from another world.

Martin: With "Embrace Another Fall," I'm hearing the type of percussion you get from Jerry Marotta in Peter Gabriel, and even David Rhodes guitar, but like it was a field recording down south back in the 1940s.

Joe: Yes, there's those pounding drums, but they're over the hill somewhere, through the mist (laughs). This is where you hear Justin Adams, the guitarist, doing some dirty Jimmy Page stuff. I like the heaviness of it, but again, it's becoming a heavy album that doesn't really have a lot of conventional heaviness. It's more like emotional heaviness, not "Whole Lotta Love" heaviness. It's this heaviness of emotion and of weird, really cool sounds, especially for 2014.

Pontus: With "Embrace Another Fall" you get the hint of a riff along with heavy Eastern production, more recitation than ordinary singing and a nice mix. Yeah, this demands listening. And we also get a female singer in it. Okay, this is really what I feel about this record. This is not background music. *Manic Nirvana*, you can have on in the background and really dig it. But if you put these records on, they might disappear. You have to concentrate and listen to them. You have to sit down and really, really listen. And it pays back in droves, I would say.

I would also say that for fans of Led Zeppelin, the problem is not that Robert Plant's going in a different direction. The problem is those of us who are still stuck in whether *Presence* was a good album or not. I missed out on *Lullaby* when it came out. It was just another Robert Plant album. But when I went back to it, I discovered a great album. And I understand him. He's not in the frame of thinking about what he did 50 years ago. He wants to live now and develop this specific kind of music, where he's picking up signals from Morocco and even Ireland. I think he's in a very good place, but is his audience? Or *where* is the audience?

Chad: "Embrace Another Fall" is just this lovely, beautiful song, which is made even more beautiful when you get this female voice, Julie Murphy, near the end—just stunning. When I heard her sing, I wanted to know more about her. Lyrically I'm wondering if this a call-and-answer type song. Like, is she offering a different perspective to what he's singing about? How there's two sides to a story. But we don't know because she sings her part in Gaelic. But there's definitely a love story of some kind going on here. And I guess if you go with the title, "Embrace Another Fall," they're probably breaking up. It's so well done and so poetic that I feel like this could be expanded into a full-on story.

Tim: It's interesting, because Robert writes, "Embrace another fall/ My year is warm and cold/To you I bare my soul/My summer's almost gone." So is this embracing another autumn or is he falling in love or is he embracing another failure? The lyrics really don't say too explicitly what he's talking about. There's also a bit of Gaelic in here. I don't know, Robert has his Welsh ties, but I think in another life he might have been Irish. As for your Peter Gabriel comparison, I've heard him in interviews say that he's always admired Peter Gabriel for doing the unexpected.

Martin: With "Turn It Up," the guys make a bit more noise, right? It's kind of a rock song.

Pontus: Yes, it's the heaviest track. Plant presents himself as the old desert blues man. It made me think about R.L. Burnside, but made in Egypt.

Chad: Yeah, in short, this rocks. It's a grooving rock song, perhaps even a subdued style of industrial rock. I like this more the more I hear it.

Martin: Bit of a Tom Waits vibe to him at this juncture as well. Again, everything sounds worn-out and lo-fi, old instruments, old tube amps, lots of room sounds.

Pontus: Yes, and compare this with what he was in 1988. It's a totally different place. But I feel this is where he feels at home. That's why I feel that *Now and Zen*, for example, was a bit forced and of its time. Here at 64 or whatever—actually, he's now 75, which is as old as my mom—I think he's in a comfortable place. He can do whatever he wants. They did the Led Zeppelin reunion and everybody was happy and now he can just leave that aside.

Tim: I agree that "Turn It Up" is one of the rockier ones on this album and I believe it was a radio track. And basically, he's talking about listening to the radio and driving somewhere in the Deep South and he's got a really fun line in here: "I'm lost inside America/ I'm turning inside out/I'm turning into someone else/I heard so much about." I don't know if he's looking back and not sure of what he's going to do in the future. There are some references to radio ministries in the line, "The smallest contribution/Will keep me in safe hands/I'm calling 1-800/I ain't leaving it to chance." And the chorus is just "Turn it up." I think he did this one when I saw him as well. Another fun, upbeat song. I gravitate this way anyway, but I'm happy for the variety and range as well.

Martin: What do you think Robert wants from his drummers at this point in time?

Tim: I can picture him saying, "Don't play like a regular drummer, play off the beat, use brushes, leave the cymbals alone." He never wants the expected from any of his musicians. "But above all, keep a beat. Keep a beat people can understand. But at the same time don't do anything stock" (laughs).

I'd say that one of the other requirements of any musician auditioning for his band would be a working knowledge of all that old music. If you don't go back further than the late sixties, chances are you're not going to end up in this band, unless you're just really good and really adaptable. But if you can cut through the, "Hey, have you ever heard of such and such?" and get straight to the point of "What's your favourite song by such and such?" I think that's where he finds a lot of these musicians. You'll notice Robert Plant never ends up playing with someone that used to be in X hard rock band from the seventies. It's never that. And a lot of times it's younger musicians too.

Martin: "A Stolen Kiss" is arranged conservatively, as a straight piano ballad, but it's pretty sophisticated melodically.

Joe: Yes, following "Turn It Up," like you say louder and noisier, with that cool guitar riff but some weird chord progressions, we get a traditional ballad, and quite moody and quiet. But it's my least favourite—I'm not crazy about Robert's vocal.

Pontus: "A Stolen Kiss" is a beautiful piano ballad with string bass and quite tasty backing vocals in places. Although it's a more subdued arrangement, here is a band enjoying themselves. I really felt that. You feel that Robert's in a position where he feels that he is part of a group that likes what they're doing. He's in a new environment with new musicians and they in turn enjoy him for what he is. They're not trying to be the next Led Zeppelin.

Martin: There's an odd duality though, that he likes. When he does covers, he's excited to be showing you old songs that were written by other people. But on *Lullaby*, now he wants to imagine what the writing of "new" old songs would be like, right?

Pontus: Yeah, yeah. I think it was in Mick Wall's book, *When Giants Walked the Earth*, Robert talked about being an avid blues collector when he was very young. He was one of those kids. And I do think he now sees himself as an old blues man or roots music man, as an archeologist trying to dig out old-sounding sounds and see where they can lead or how they can be used on new compositions. I also read in the liner notes to *Sixty Six to Timbuktu* where he said he wanted to try different things that people throw at him. He feels that he can explore whatever he wants now, finally, that he's this old.

Chad: The piano accompaniment is really what makes "A Stolen Kiss" so stunning. This is a good example, once again, of Robert Plant surrounding himself with incredible musicians. I don't know if you're a fan of Mike Campbell from Tom Petty and the Heartbreakers. He doesn't overdo it with the guitar work; usually what he does is just so fitting. This is a similar example of that to me, where the performance fits the lyric and vocal so well. So yeah, that piano is classy and economical, as is the whole thing, allowing the piano to breathe. There's electric guitar, but it's not intrusive. As for the singing, Robert uses that slow tempo to his advantage, sounding both intimate and sincere about it (laughs). Might you actually call this song a lullaby and go so far as to say it inspired the album title in some way?

Tim: There's a wistfulness to this song. As he writes, "I am drawn to the western shore." He sings a lot about that, about being by the waterside.

Martin: And speaking of western shores, he's always been a big fan of San Francisco psych too, right? Not to mention the LA singer-songwriter types.

Tim: Yes, he was highly influenced by those scenes, especially Haight-Ashbury, with Love and Moby Grape and all that. If you listen to enough Led Zeppelin bootlegs, there's one where they're doing some Zeppelin song and he goes into a little bit of the Scott Mackenzie, "If you're in San Francisco, be sure to wear flowers in your hair." And lyrically, if you think about "Misty Mountain Hop," yeah, Robert Plant seems to be someone who's never really where he wants to be. Whether it's geographically or whether it's his place in time, I think he likes the idea of exploring these things that came before.

Martin: "Somebody There" is even more so like a traditional ballad, but this time with wiry Jimmy Page-like guitar. It reminds me a bit of "Ship of Fools" or "Anniversary" without the eighties production of course.

Pontus: Sure, yes, a slow but strong pop song or ballad, with a really accessible chorus and great guitar sounds, uncharacteristically bright. This is very much like the West Coast pop sound we talked about, Moby Grape and stuff.

Chad: I'd say this is basically a jangly, twangy, fun and naive song. As for the message, I'm hearing an enthusiasm and anticipation of seeing someone you are excited about.

Joe: Yes, a much more conventional guitar song, with very cool chords and fairly action-packed drumming and some religious overtones to the lyrics. Works for me.

Tim: I'm struck by how melodic that chorus is, to the point where it reminds you how melancholy much of the rest of it is, even when it's upbeat. I hesitate to say it, but it's quite commercial and extremely accessible—you can latch onto that hook very easily. This one's talking about his childhood, but the wonderful thing about Robert Plant is that you're never really sure if he's talking about himself or not, or if he's creating a character. "When I was a young boy/And time was passing by really slow;" is he talking about himself or is this just something that sounds poetic? The fact that we'll probably never really know is one of the things that keep people coming back and listening to him. This could also be another song that he wrote for his son Karac.

Martin: "Poor Howard" is arranged a bit like the opener, "Little Maggie." As well, it's got a bit of a *Band of Joy* vibe.

Joe: Yes, and with "Poor Howard" Robert's doing what Zeppelin used to do, taking an old song and adapting it, This time it's Lead Belly and "Po' Howard" and he's made it into his own song. It's cool. There's banjo and a great intro. It's got a Led Zeppelin "The Battle of Evermore" kind of weirdness to it.

Tim: Sure, "Poor Howard" is another fun one, accessible, hooky; I really like it. It sounds like a traditional song, but according to the credits, it's a band-written song, even with the Lead Belly connection. This is another one of those successful combos between old and new musics. It's got the Americana, but also something modern about it, maybe in the distressed production. It sounds like something that might have been floating around in his head around the time of Led Zeppelin *III*. And like I say, the hooks are there. Despite the hazy production values, it's Robert Plant—he's not going to be so obscure that you can't latch onto something.

Pontus: I would call this a traditional song, given that it's from Lead Belly and that their arrangement is so old-timey. We have the T Bone Burnett productions values, with lots of space between the instruments. You have banjo and fiddle mixed with Eastern percussion and also the hint of some modern background textures.

Chad: I like this song. It's jangly and positive and energising and it goes together for me with "Rainbow." It feels like he's anticipating a meet-up with somebody that he thinks fondly of, kind of like the last one (laughs). So this one and "Rainbow" *and* "Somebody There," I feel like they're taking on a similar theme. With the Lead Belly derivation, it's kind of a bluesy or bluegrass song, with a Deep South feel but also modern touches. He does the song justice, but it's as much about collaboration with a great band than anything. But you have to hear it if you like adaptations of old folk songs.

Martin: With "House of Love," I feel we're back to some degree of conventional pop, but again with U2 overtones, melodically, rhythmically, arrangement-wise and most definitely with those sighing Edge/Eno guitar lines.

Pontus: Sure, although I consider "House of Love" to be a lesser pop song with a lesser melody. But the instrumental middle section saves it, particularly the guitar. This guy Adams plays a very good guitar, with great tone and this Middle Eastern modal way of playing.

Chad: "House of Love," the rhythm section, the drum and bass here, from that part of The Sensational Space Shifters—so tasteful. Robert's just singing along in his usual melodic way, sounding so close to the mic. But even though he's changing his sound with his advanced age, he's still Robert Plant. He definitely uses significant self-restraint now, and he does talk about that in his podcasts. He talks about holding back and giving other people more space, allowing the songs to breathe and letting the band shine through. He's more mature, mellowed-out, but it's still innovative and fresh. He's in his 60s at this point, when he wrote and recorded this album, and he still has energy, but it's more oblique, more like creative energy.

Martin: The wilful antiquing or distressing continues with "Up on the Hollow Hill (Understanding Arthur)." This sounds like a song before it's put through both the planer and the sander.

Pontus: Yes (laughs), but we get this hypnotic electric guitar line with pulsating drums. Plant is singing long, melancholy notes. Great Eastern scale guitar but it also sounds like desert guitar, a Tex-Mex sound. At the end of the album, these sorts of songs tend to sound quite similar to each other, although they are still good.

Chad: The groove in that song took me back to the *Fate of Nations* album. It's worldly, with the sitar-like guitar. Again, overall, at the time I just wasn't ready for this type of style from Robert but now it's resonating more. The electric guitar part is very pleasing as the notes coincide with Robert's soft and moving pitch. His vocals kind of fade and he leaves space for the percussion to wind up the song.

Joe: There's practically no lyrics, but I take it to be about King Arthur. It has that medieval mysticism to it. There's a cool guitar riff that's very new age, which is something he started evoking in the eighties, beginning with *Fate of Nations*. But this album probably has the most of that.

Martin: All right, the album closes with "Arbaden (Maggie's Babby)," which has even less lyrics, which are nonetheless quite ominous, set to music that is again murky, grimy, and for this one, very African tribal. And if you notice, the lyrics are an excerpt from the opening track, "Little Maggie."

Pontus: Yes, ethnic groove, big drums, although with this sort of production, nothing ever sounds big except in relation to what else is going on. There's percolating electronic backing and African vocals.

Joe: I like the guitar, which is a little funky, but those rhythms I find haunting. Not sure about the synthesizer, which I find a little dated. Again, there's that new age feel, but really not much participation from Robert on this one. As for his vocals, it's like he's trying too hard to be mellow and dramatic. He's trying too hard not to belt anything out. Sometimes when he's whispering, it doesn't even sound like him. It can be annoying. It's like he needs to be artificially cranked in the mix because he's singing so quietly.

Tim: As you say, this one's a callback to the first track, "Little Maggie," even though this one is not a traditional song but one of theirs fully. And the drumbeat behind it is completely different. It's almost like they're playing the music from the opening track, but the drummer is playing a different song. But it somehow works. And there's also an interesting spelling choice here, "babby," which is on purpose. The two songs sort of bookend the album, I guess, which he's also doing on purpose. It's like a reprise but quite altered, although Robert keeps the same vocal melody.

Martin: Okay, and if you look at the booklet, Robert's doing that thing again where he provides some of the lyrics but not all, which goes all the way back to Zeppelin *IV*, where we only got "Stairway to Heaven." *Now and Zen*'s got five lyrics shown.

Tim: Yeah, it's strange. It's only got the middle. *Mighty ReArranger* did this too. To me that reflects the same playfulness and mischief like when you get the title track to *Houses of the Holy* on the next album, *Physical Graffiti*. Which, by the way, on *Houses of the Holy* you get all the lyrics, which is the only time with Zeppelin. It's a wink and a nod and again, very much on purpose. It's not like they didn't have enough money to put them all in or that it's an oversight. It's very deliberate. Maybe they're the lyrics he's the most proud of. But it is strange that you just pick the middle of the album to support with lyrics.

Martin: Any other closing impressions?

Joe: Well, I will say that every interview I hear with him, I detect an underlying bitterness to him. You can't bring up Led Zeppelin. I don't feel a lot of positivity with his interviews. Now here, I know you're gonna shoot some daggers at me. But I'll tell you, when Greta Van Fleet came out, who sounded like Zeppelin, he actually said some positive things about Greta Van Fleet. He's like, "That young guy from the Detroit area has a beautiful little voice," and he's referencing that Joshua Kiszka sounds like him. But Greta Van Fleet delivered what people wanted. I know you're not a fan, but I enjoy them. But I think that they pretty much delivered the Zeppelin-esque riffs we all wanted. Plus he talked about the female cover band Zepparella, who he really liked.

Chad: Well, I'll add that this album comes across as really organic and flowing but also complex, like an aging wine with all the biochemistry that they talk about in wine circles (laughs). I can make some distinctions here and there in the flavours, but mostly I just know I really enjoy every sip. I'm never sure what he's sticking into it as an artist, but I know I like it the more I listen. There's more in these arrangements than I can take in without repeated plays, so yes, it ages well and with distinction and I kinda take it in with gratitude. But yeah, there's no point dissecting it and isolating the parts because it's just a major blend of things.

And it kind of helps that in interviews, his personality is warm and sincere and he is respectful of others. He uses his manners. He's insightful, reflective, sensitive and is really good at recalling past events and telling those stories in an interesting way. He's definitely one of those guys that packs a lot of value into an interview where you're drawn in and want to learn about his perspective on things. But yes, like Joe says, he doesn't want to talk about Led Zeppelin (laughs).

As an artist, he seems like a good collaborator and then for his own part of the job, he's poetic and articulate and pretty often quite mysterious. Plus he's obviously responsive to what's going on and can change quite rapidly. But yeah, each musician is contributing and collaborating. Robert must be a diplomatic collaborator who seeks harmonious relationships with these guys.

Martin: With these late-period albums, is he celebrating his senior years, kind of revelling in the wisdom of old age?

Joe: Yes, but that being said, I always found it interesting that he never really cut his hair. He still wears the long hair, which a lot of older guys will cut shorter. Jimmy let it go all gray and he looks his age. It doesn't work for me with the long hair and the goatee and everything. I think it makes him look older. But that's the thing; you look at the cover of *Carry Fire* and it's like he's proud of looking old. I don't know, it's like he wants to look like Gandalf (laughs), a God-like figure, I suppose.

It's really been something to watch, although I have to admit that in my circle of friends, we were those guys that were always asking, "When is Zeppelin getting back together?" Still, aside from not getting the Alison Krauss stuff, I was a completist with Robert. Maybe I slipped a bit with *Fate of Nations*. I didn't give it much time because there was so much other great stuff coming out. At that time I'm into Soundgarden and even Coverdale Page. There are other bands sounding like Zeppelin and Sabbath out there, and Soundgarden did both (laughs). They just blew me away. Big riff rock was coming back. And I was all-in on the Page Plant reunion. I thought what they did with *No Quarter* was amazing. It was so cool and dark; the down-tuning of the guitar and everything was just haunting. But now, I feel like he has this different passion. Even with all the covers, unapologetically, there he just wants to do his version of what he enjoys and put it out that way. But of course, some of that key Zeppelin material consisted of covers reworked. It's in his DNA. He wants to put his mark on songs that he likes.

Martin: And another general question. Why do you think Robert is constantly replacing band members?

Joe: That's a good question, because there's a creative angle as well as the business angle that people don't want to talk about but is a reality. Sometimes people ask for too much money or maybe this guy is already costing too much. Or maybe somebody has their own creative aspirations and wants to do something else. Or maybe it's a combination. Maybe Robert's not paying them enough and they want to go on their own way and do something else. It's Robert Plant, and we know from seeing it for ourselves that he's generous with song credits, so I tend to think it's more purely creative. He always wants to move forward. He always wants to stay inspired.

But yeah, do these records sell? I texted a huge Zeppelin fan buddy of mine the other day. I'm like, "Did you ever get *Lullaby*?" And he's like, "No, I never got that." And I couldn't believe it. And he loves the Alison Krauss stuff too, but he never got *Lullaby*. So I was the only guy in my circle who had it. But man, I still think about the aftermath of the O2 show. I'm like, why did they leave all that money on the table and not go on tour?! We were ready to go to Soldier Field and see them (laughs). But for him, it's all about being creative and not living in the past.

But it's interesting. I remember when *Lullaby* came out, 2014, he did an interview saying my schedule is open; 2014 is open for me. Because Zeppelin was toying with the idea of having Myles Kennedy sing with them, or maybe Steven Tyler, and going on tour. And then he makes the comment that 2014 is open to him. And then he releases this album and does an interview saying, "Well, I'll do an album just with Jimmy and it'll just have to be acoustic." So I don't know. I really wonder why he doesn't just go full-on Zeppelin.

Martin: Well, O2 was really good, that's for sure. And I get in trouble for this, but at this point I get more value out of Jason Bonham as a drummer than I get out of his dad. Tim, anything you want to add?

Tim: The travel thing is important too, to his modus operandi. Whether he's somewhere where he can play soccer or whether he's in Memphis or Clarksdale or some other birthplace of the blues, or in Morocco, he finds a way to bring that music in. He always talks about Morocco. He's traveled there several times throughout his life, and he's been a sponge with that music, or Algerian music or Turkish music. He's a transmitter for picking up sounds that for most classic rock vocalists, it's just not in their wheelhouse. But Robert has worked very hard to make it part of his musical DNA. To an uncommon degree, he doesn't trade on his past glories and I think that's very admirable. Now, I don't know how these recent albums have sold. Albums don't sell the way they used to, but he's still putting them out, and I admire that too. They shall remain nameless, but there are lots of classic rock artists that don't make records simply because they can't stand watching them not sell.

Martin: Is he acting somewhat like a DJ or even a rock journalist?

Tim: I think so, yeah. I think the hope is that if someone asked him where some song he was covering came from, he would delight in telling them all about them and their records, including the B-sides (laughs).

Pontus: And the reason he can do this is the same as with McCartney—he has a financial backbone to fall back to if his current record doesn't sell. You can do the experiment, whether it's with originals or with covers.

Martin: I imagine he appreciates being critically acclaimed as well. This music is seen as greatly authentic by the chattering classes.

Pontus: Yes, definitely, plus I do think he enjoys his fame. But I don't know if the Led Zeppelin audience is listening here. Or is the Nonesuch audience even listening? The people who dig roots music, Americana, world music, enthusiasts of that. Fans of Lucinda Willams, Neil Young, alt.country, jam bands… I call them the *Mojo* crowd, those really "serious" music fans that see *Mojo* magazine as The Bible. I feel he's more upper echelon even than that, like jazz. I have to stress this again. If you don't actively listen to this record, it might just disappear. It's so intricate. You have to listen because it's quite slow. You have to really take a seat and get comfortable and really dig in.

Martin: And in terms of the vocals, I feel like he's been pleased to discover that even at this age, he has an interesting and very likeable voice and that he can use it accurately, but only in this specific low gear. If he drives in first gear, he will still get to the promised land, but it will just take a little longer.

Pontus: He understands his age as a musician. And it goes back to those old blues records. He realises he can't be the rocker of his past and nor does he want to be the rocker of the past. He wants to be in this position now, an explorer. And if you want to follow him, you follow him. And if you don't, he will go there anyway. And he still has a certain natural charisma that lends himself to that process. He's Robert Plant. He's like Midas—whatever he touches turns to gold. This is not unique to Robert Plant though, this this idea of doing these traditional songs. Mark Knopfler and Eric Clapton both do tons of traditional stuff, and many artists revisit traditional songs from their home country, or you have British artists that immerse themselves in the history of American blues. It's possible that some of his inspiration to be this way is from some of his peers who have done something similar. Or maybe he just did it on his own accord.

Chad: You bring up his singing. That's one of the things he talks about, including how Alison Krauss was such a big influence, and just the process of doing duets with Alison and working out songs with her. She helped teach him how to, I guess, work with someone else on the framework of a song. That project had happened a few years previous to this album and he's taken that to heart.

As for his lyrics, I find him to be more personal and introspective on the early albums, yet he writes in a way that's universal. He doesn't necessarily reveal what he's referring to, but he must have had some personal experience. He expands that in his later years to more general human condition stuff, talking about other people's experiences, their reflections and perspectives. So the lyrics are more broad, as are the spaces in the arrangements. I don't know for sure if that's intentional, but I feel like with Robert, everything's intentional.

He's absolutely embracing where he's at in life. He doesn't need to do any of this. Why is he working so hard? Maybe he isn't working that hard. Maybe he's just doing what feels natural. And maybe he's inspired by the fact that he gets to get his own way. That's something I notice as I get older. I'm happier because I get to do more of what I want to do. There are less outside pressures, my kids are grown up and my bills are paid and stuff like that. I'm on more solid ground and able to do things that I enjoy and not do things I don't enjoy. Whereas when you're younger, you're trying to make your mark and you're more easily influenced and you're under pressure. So maybe he's feeling less pressure, more relaxed. It's amazing there are still artists like him that have already made it so many years ago and they're financially independent. Like, he's still doing it for the love of it. He's not doing it to try to make a living at this point. He's trying to make a statement. He probably would go crazy if he wasn't doing this.

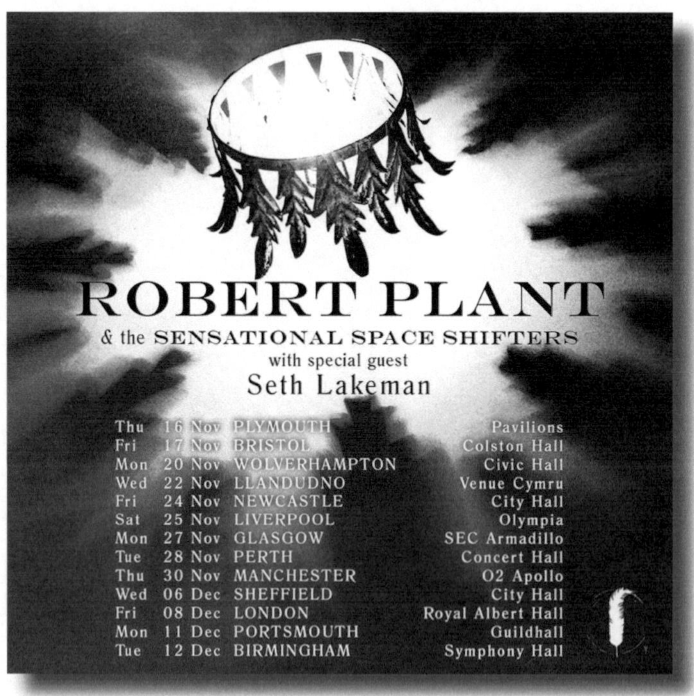
ROBERT PLANT
& the SENSATIONAL SPACE SHIFTERS
with special guest
Seth Lakeman
Thu   16 Nov PLYMOUTH   Pavilions
Fri   17 Nov BRISTOL   Colston Hall
Mon 20 Nov WOLVERHAMPTON   Civic Hall
Wed 22 Nov LLANDUDNO   Venue Cymru
Fri   24 Nov NEWCASTLE   City Hall
Sat   25 Nov LIVERPOOL   Olympia
Mon 27 Nov GLASGOW   SEC Armadillo
Tue   28 Nov PERTH   Concert Hall
Thu   30 Nov MANCHESTER   O2 Apollo
Wed 06 Dec SHEFFIELD   City Hall
Fri   08 Dec LONDON   Royal Albert Hall
Mon 11 Dec PORTSMOUTH   Guildhall
Tue   12 Dec BIRMINGHAM   Symphony Hall

Carry Fire

"This is the most prolific and freethinking bunch of guys I've worked with. Maybe it's time that's done this. Maybe it's an air of a sense of maturity or experience, travel, other cultures, playing through West Africa with the Tuareg into Morocco, and across, down into Mississippi, around. Everybody's on the move and these guys come from... I would say, the kind of Bristol urban scene with Roni Size and Massive Attack, moving into Jah Wobble and Sinead O'Connor and moving into the Womad Festival. It's a very fluent and very, I suppose, light-footed assembly of spirits, really. And it just dances through everything. The great thing is to pillage and to take the stuff of value, and to turn it and twist it and craft it into something that isn't expected, I think. Or actually, most importantly, to knock oneself out before you start trying to knock anybody else out."

"But people are coming from other environments, coming together to bring their gifts and to make a melange. It's a masala of musical themes coming from throughout the British contemporary music scene. So it's a very kind of fertile and virile place to be coming from, and it allows me a really good tapestry and a great canvas to work my side of the deal."

"And what I do is, I pillage, not in the hotel room sense with unidentified members of the public so much, really, but just musically.

I move through the spheres. But as I do, I am drawn to the same scales, musical scales, that exist, in Africa and in Arabic music, that slightly end up in the Mississippi Delta, the music of West Africa, particularly. There's something quite mournful about a lot of the modal scales that draw me in. It has an effect on me; it encourages me to write. But I don't think I'll be, hopping on a plane to Beijing and recording with some guys out there."

"I mean, my band, they're all seekers too. I'm just talking the talk, because I've got the... the name is bigger on the tin than theirs. But they all come very creative backgrounds. Some people are stuck in some kind of group that says outside of rock we don't go. Well I don't live in that world, and neither did Led Zeppelin, neither did Jimmy Page, neither did Bert Jansch, neither did Sandy Denny. Like I say, we just move through the spheres and we gather stuff as we go, and they allow me a really great canvas from which to operate. Which gives me a great deal of spirit. The answer to anything and everything is being prolific and having a large and benevolent heart. And I think I'm in that kind of company. My spirit is high and I will write the way I feel, in the company that is the most spirited."

Robert Plant

Credits

October 13, 2017
Nonesuch/Warner Bros. 563057-2
Produced by Robert Plant
Engineered by Joe Jones, Oli Middleton ("Recording assistants") and Tim Oliver
Recorded at The Attic Studio, Bristol, UK, The Bee Barn, Bala, Gwynedd, UK, Billy Fuller's Home Studio, Bristol, UK, Black Earth Studios, Bath, UK, Real World Studios, Box, Wiltshire, UK, Rockfield Studios, Monmouth, UK and Top Cat Studios, Wiltshire, UK
Personnel: Robert Plant – vocals, Justin Adams – guitar, acoustic guitar, oud, E-bow quartet, percussion, snare drum, tambourine, Liam "Skin" Tyson – dobro, guitar, acoustic guitar, pedal steel, 12-string, John Baggott – keyboards, Moog, loops, percussion, drums, brass arrangement, T'bal, snare drum, slide guitar, piano, electric piano, bendir, Billy Fuller – bass, keyboards, drum programming, Dave Smith – bendir, tambourine, djembe, drum kit
Key additional personnel: Chrissie Hynde – vocals on "Bluebirds Over the Mountain," Redi Hasa – cello on "A Way with Words," "Carry Fire" and "Bluebirds Over the Mountain," Seth Lakeman – viola on "The May Queen," "Carry Fire," "Bluebirds Over the Mountain," Richard Ashton – drums on "Bluebirds Over the Mountain"

1. "The May Queen" (Plant, Adams, Baggott, Fuller, Tyson) 4:14
2. "New World…" (Plant, Baggott, Fuller, Smith, Tyson) 3:29
3. "Season's Song" (Plant, Adams, Baggott, Fuller, Tyson) 4:19
4. "Dance with You Tonight" (Plant, Adams, Baggott, Fuller, Smith, Tyson) 4:48
5. "Carving Up the World Again… A Wall and Not a Fence" (Plant, Adams, Baggott, Fuller, Tyson) 3:55
6. "A Way with Words" (Plant, Adams, Baggott) 5:18
7. "Carry Fire" (Plant, Adams, Baggott, Fuller, Smith, Tyson) 5:28
8. "Bones of Saints" (Plant, Adams, Fuller, Smith, Tyson) 3:47
9. "Keep It Hid" (Plant, Adams, Baggott) 4:07
10. "Bluebirds Over the Mountain" (Ersel Hickey) 4:58
11. "Heaven Sent" (Plant, Adams, Baggott, Fuller, Smith, Tyson) 4:39

A *Carry Fire* Timeline

October 13, 2017. Robert sees the release of an 11th solo album, entitled *Carry Fire*. *Rolling Stone* ranked the album the 37th best of 2017. It ranks No.14 on the main *Billboard* 200 grid, No.4 on the Top Rock Albums chart, No.3 in the UK and No.12 in Canada.

November 16 – December 12, 2017. Robert and the band conduct a UK tour, with one date in Dublin, in support of *Carry Fire*.

February 9 – March 2, 2018. Robert and his band tour North America in support of *Carry Fire*.

March 23 – April 8, 2018. Robert and The Sensational Space Shifters conduct an extensive tour campaign in Australia.

June 8 - 29, 2018. After a few shows in England, Robert and the band conduct a short North American tour, followed by European dates in July and August.

September 9 – October 1, 2018. The band tour America again, with emphasis on Texas.

April 13, 2019. It's Record Store Day, and Robert has ready for the festivities a remastered version of *Fate of Nations*, with proceeds going to Greenpeace.

June 13 – July 4, 2019. With only sporadic dates over the previous ten months, the band tuck into the European festival season.

September 13 – October 5, 2019. The band return to North America for shows until the worldwide epidemic closes things down. This is it for the official solo situation to this point, with Robert Plant going on the road again with his low-key acoustic act Saving Grace in 2021 and then Alison Krauss in 2023.

October 2, 2020. Es Paranza issues a two-CD companion compilation to Robert's *Digging Deep* podcast called *Digging Deep: Subterranea*.

May 31, 2021. Important Plant collaborator Phil Johnstone—*Now and Zen, Manic Nirvana, Fate of Nations, Mighty ReArranger*—dies at the age of 63, after a long illness.

July 19, 2021. Robert plays live for the first time since the Covid pandemic, appearing with his acoustic act Saving Grace in Worthing, England, after which a small UK tour ensues.

November 19, 2021. Robert Plant and Alison Krauss issue a second album together, called *Raise the Roof*.

January 2, 2023. *Rolling Stone* magazine names Robert Plant the No.63 Greatest Singers of All Time, down from No.15 in the 2008 ranking. However in 2011, readers of *Rolling Stone* put Robert at No.1.

Martin talks to John Clauser, Tim Durling and Pontus Norshammar about *Carry Fire.*

Martin Popoff: Okay, so articulate for me how Robert's changed for *Carry Fire*? What is the personality of this album versus *Lullaby and the Ceaseless Roar*?

Tim Durling: I find these albums to be quite similar, without sounding like these are leftover songs. Lyrically, there's a definite shift; he's very topical on some of the songs on *Carry Fire*. As far as the personnel goes, it's the exact same band.

Pontus Norshammar: It's not so focused on folk music and odd instruments, shall we say? It's a more straightforward sort of record, with the same ancient sound, but it hasn't got all the trappings of the banjos and violins and things like that. It has a dark sound. Like *Lullaby*, you have to really sit down with this record, otherwise you will miss out because it demands listening. I'd say that the band, The Sensational Space Shifters, has played more so they are more integrated with each other. Justin Adams is just playing guitar and oud here. So everything is scaled down instrument-wise. I think this is a more Celtic album.

Martin: Is a lot of it about one's final years? He seems to be revelling in the crags in his face with that front cover shot.

Tim: Yeah, I'd say purposely, it's not a bright shot. You can tell who it is, of course, but's all very traditional and in muted colours. I've heard him say if he had his way the cover would not have any text on it at all. I believe he's also said that he'd have been happy putting The Sensational Space Shifters on it, but commercially, there's more marketability when it has Robert Plant emblazoned on it. And the opening track, "The May Queen," sure, maybe he is talking about his mortality, where he repeats "the dimming of my light" versus, say, "surrender to your light," which comes earlier. As well he says he's "so long into my night." Not exactly an upbeat sentiment for an opener, but musically, it kind of sets the pace rather well—it's actually quite joyful. The title represents a nod to "Stairway to Heaven," but in the lyrics, he never says "the may queen." Which is a well-travelled trick of his. Essentially, though, it's a love song.

John Clauser: The album builds on the foundation of *Lullaby*, and by the time he gets to *Carry Fire*, I think the material is even stronger. It's still Americana mixed with current sounds, just building upon that with this same particular band and with their new songs. "The May Queen" is a perfect example of that, where you get this nice little bluesy kind of acoustic intro, but somehow the feel of electronica. Solid opening track to the album. I get a wonderful feeling of lost love, looking for love, a mystery woman maybe, that person you're seeking. But yeah, I just love all the guitar work in this song and that simple intro.

Martin: Later in the song there's fiddle, which strikes different than something you'd hear in a Celtic song. And then there's some Eastern modalities. Robert strikes me as a guy at this late stage who's done all or most of his world travel and one of his missions is to report back on the music he's heard, possibly right up to his death.

John: I like that; I would agree with that. But here's a question: do we call it world music? Or do we just say Americana? Because I don't know if I would put him in the world music department. Peter Gabriel is closer to that versus what Robert is doing. Maybe it's a little early to call him world music yet. Maybe we need more albums that go even further (laughs). But yeah, that cover, it's indeed fiery and pretty deep. I imagine Robert looking off to the distance to a sunrise, or even a wildfire.

Martin: Pontus, anything to add on "The May Queen?"

Pontus: It's got this Celtic and yet Eastern feel, acoustic guitars, violins, world acoustic percussion and surging, hanging rhythm guitars. It reminded me a lot of "Friends" by Led Zeppelin, actually, with those lush guitars.

Martin: I can almost picture "New World..." on *Walking into Clarksdale*, Those guitars are pure Jimmy and I dare say I hear a drum set, although approached from a glance.

Pontus: "New World..." is a slow but very potent rocker; I really like that one, with, yes, those rumbling, ringing Jimmy Page guitars, simple tribal drumming, great vocals, echoey, pure singing. It rambles on quite nicely (laughs). Throughout both these records, you can easily follow the melodies. It's regular and simple and then reinforced by Robert's ooh-ooh-ing, this non-word singing he's always done.

Tim: "New World…," yeah, dot dot dot, playing around with the grammar. This one is about immigration. And even though it's in a language that's rather traditional, it's topical, "With songs we praise a happy landing/On yet another virgin shore" and then "Embrace the new world." Might be a little reference to "Immigrant Song" there. But then it's "Uneducate the noble savage" and "Subjugate them to liberate them." So it's very, very topical. If you listen to it here in Canada, you think about the residential schools or just any part of history where settlers had come and displaced the people that already lived there. It's obvious from his tone that he's not singing about it as if this was a good thing. Musically, it's a good pick-up from "The May Queen," an increase in volume as you ease into the album.

John: Straight-ahead melodic rocker, no bones about this one. Lyrically, as Tim says, he invokes a different kind of "Immigrant Song." This obviously tells the dark side of immigration, or emigration, the plight of immigrants coming to these different countries. Just a side note, Martin. What are your thoughts about *Walking into Clarksdale*? I've just listened to it for the first time in I couldn't tell you how long just the other day, and something about that, oh, it was a tough hour to get through for some reason. I don't know why. Maybe it's just because it's Jimmy Page. Maybe it was just too Zeppelin, which Robert had been trying so hard to get away from. Maybe I just need to listen to it some more but, boy, it was a tough hour for me to get through.

Martin: Interesting. Yeah, I've never had a problem with it. In fact, next to Robert's first two solo albums, and maybe even more so, I consider it the stealth Zeppelin album, or like the closest thing to a ninth album. It's a little rough and ragged, but I'm pretty happy with the songs, and certainly Michael's powerhouse drumming. I got to meet him backstage at Massey Hall when he came to Toronto with Thin Lizzy. Super-nice guy, and just tragic we lost him so young. Alright, sorry, onto "Season's Song." Thoughts?

John: Gosh, this is just another example of Robert's voice just taking the theme of the song and singing it in such a fragile and caring way.

He emotes this beautiful story of a couple that's aging and maybe coming to their next season of life where they're about to pass away or something. It's this couple growing old together and moving onto the next season. Such a pretty song. The band create a perfect piece of music to go with his words.

Pontus: This is a beautiful ballad, great mix of guitar—acoustic forefront and electric background. Sometimes this is with keyboards and sometimes with electric guitar, but there's often this wall of sound built in the background, almost subtle, like a vibration or rolling tone, and then the acoustic instruments in front.

Tim: Yeah, these next two are love songs lyrically, but again, it's mixed with musings about mortality, "Oh my love/What is there left to do?" Then it's "The nights grow long/The snow upon the hill" and "Summer's slow farewell." Robert sings about the seasons a lot, and of course, you did an episode of your *Contrarians* YouTube show where you constructed a Led Zeppelin double album about the seasons (laughs). So, yeah, it sounds like a lament, and I think the music backs that up; it's introspective both musically and lyrically.

Martin: I like that—a lament, which leads us to "Dance with You Tonight" which even more so feels that way.

Pontus: Yes, meditative modern soundscape, slow, rolling along, not as immediate as the others. It builds with a fuller arrangement in later parts. This was a composition I felt took a while to get into because it really it took some time to develop as an arrangement.

John: "Dance with You Tonight" picks right up where "Season's Song" leaves off, but it's different because you get more of a tribal rhythm. To me, it paints the picture of maybe a little earlier in the life of that couple that's nearing the end of their lives in "Season's Song." "And if there's one more time I can dance with you." Somehow I found this song playful and positive and uplifting. The band did a great job with it, reflecting Robert's words, although texturally it's quite murky.

Tim: What I've noticed about this one is that when Robert writes a love song, it's very traditional. He's not trying to be clever; it's very plain speak. And again, you're never really sure if he's writing about himself, but he sure makes it sound like he is. "Out in the land of never ending/The rich parade the roar of life." Then there's another Zeppelin reference with "Through dancing days and wondrous nights," again, very much on purpose. "'Til time conspired to steal our crown"—there's looming death, fate. It's ever-present in a lot of these lyrics.

Martin: What kind of singer is he now?

Tim: I really like the way he's embraced his advancing years. He's using his voice very effectively. It's not an unknown voice; it still sounds like him. He's not singing baritone. He's not shrieking like he did in the early days, and even in some of the eighties. He's writing songs that are in keys that he can sing very well. I think his voice is as good as it ever was. And that's the thing that catches up to every singer, is your vocal cords. They're not designed to belt out rock for 50-odd years. Some of these guys still do it and it's killing them. And I think Robert just said, "I can't do that." Even though I think he did quite well at the 2007 Zeppelin reunion. He sang those songs as well as could be expected. But for his own work, I think he wants to be comfortable. He doesn't want to be comfortable musically, and rest on his laurels, but I think he wants to be able to deliver the songs to the best of his ability, so he doesn't write them in really high keys or surround the songs with a pile of loud noises. Many of the songs, he can sing almost conversationally, and that's by design.

Martin: Well, that's the point. More important than the keys, it's like he's singing them in such a non-pushing-of-air whisper that he could just be vacuuming his house while singing them. He's literally almost murmuring the songs, or like you say, speaking them, right?

Tim: Yeah, it's almost like you're in a very small room listening to him sing. You're not going to scream in somebody's face if you're in a small room. But it makes for some of the most direct communication I think we've ever gotten from him. It's not the rock god far removed from reality. It's as plain speak as someone like him can get.

Martin: He's wily about it, or smart. It's like he's discovered that he's an excellent singer, still, at 68 years old here. But he's an excellent and accurate singer, with a good voice, only if he uses it a specific way.

Tim: Yeah, he's someone that understands the instrument that is his voice very, very well, and doesn't want to risk losing it. He wants to preserve it and keep doing what he's doing as long as he possibly can. If you're going to come up with an album that pushes too much air and demands too much of the vocal cords, if he loses his voice, that's it. Nobody wants to listen to an album of somebody whispering (laughs).

Martin: With "Carving Up the World Again… A Wall and Not a Fence," we're back to that Irish or Newfoundland kitchen party Celtic music rhythm, and also a melody here that's pretty joyous.

John: Yes, you get those layered tribal beats, which are then complemented by the electric guitar, which takes a funky rhythm guitar role. It's a song that pokes at big government and how they hide behind their walls, instead of a fence where you can see through, perhaps (laughs). I know I keep saying "tribal beat" but it's hard to ignore because it's so high up in the mix.

Martin: It's funny, and not for the first time of course, but there's this balance between sounding old-timey and historical and then modern and even hip at the same time, or hip to a young roots rock fan.

John: Pretty much. And maybe this kind of started when they did the *No Quarter Unledded* thing, right? Because there was a lot of that Moroccan and Middle Eastern stuff there. Of course, there was a lot of that in Zeppelin too, with "Kashmir" and stuff like that. So as he puts it, I think his proclivities were there from the start. Now he's been given more of a chance to explore them, and to dig deep into those influences and pull them together, and perfectly aligned with these guys he's playing with. Like I say, his band has done a good job of bringing that sound and vision in his own head to life.

Pontus: "Carving Up the World Again," this is a political song; it's about the world in 2017. It's a reflection about the Trump administration and the trappings of America being America but also the world and even the Brexit thing. And then you had Scotland wanting to leave Great Britain and all that stuff. There were all these discussions going on, and I think he wants to express this in a song and it's a great one. Love the snaky guitar solo, the way it ignores the beat, great melodies, acoustic historical percussion. But if there's any criticism, it's all a bit middle-paced at this point.

Tim: Again, here he goes with the dot dot dot, the ellipses. Musically interesting, and lyrically I find this one is not quite so traditional, but very, very literal. He says "The Russians, the Americans, the British and the French," and although this is nothing new, it's also very, very topical. Then he gets into an area that I think is closest to his heart, "The Irish and the English and the Scottish and the Welsh," to which he ascribes "a damp and misty history." Then he talks about China, and we get a direct reference to the wall in the title. Wow, it's extremely topical and I'm kinda surprised by that. But there's no techno-speak here. Years from now, I think someone could look back on this and think, oh well, he must have been talking about the present day, not 2017, which I think is what he's talking about here.

Martin: Next is "A Way with Words," which is quite haunting. It reminds me of Peter Gabriel or Kate Bush.

Pontus: It's really just piano and the bass guitar and him singing, as you say, whispering in this hushed voice.

Martin: And like all over the last album, there's these foggy, distant drums. Robert loves that sound for some reason. What do you think that means to him? Why does he do that?

Pontus: I'd say that's the influence of T Bone Burnett. It's a modern sound that works with this music. It creates a reflective mood and you hear it in a lot of Americana records.

Martin: You call it reflective, but it almost evokes more of a dream state or fugue state or hypnagogic state, between being awake and sleeping.

Pontus: Yeah, you're correct. You're in a special place when you listen to those types of recordings, and I really feel that with this album. While I think of this record having a dark sound, it's not exactly bleak; you're not in a world that's bleak. It's dreamy, which goes with that album cover, with him in that dark red background, looking old (laughs).

Martin: Is he preparing for death?

Pontus: Maybe. The last song I think is about aging and about making amends with what your life has been, stuff like that. He has done one record after this, the Alison Krauss record, the second one, but I don't know if he's going to do another solo album. I don't know where he is, his state of mind. As I say, he's just as old as my mom. She's also born in 1948. And I think those people are at an age where they start thinking about the past and how the end will be, how it will happen. He has lived a good life. He has definitely made a mark for himself and he's in a place where he wants to be now. I don't expect we're going to have a Led Zeppelin reunion again, or whatever, because he doesn't want it. He wants to stand and sit in this world. He wants to do this production where we're in this dream world of his. He doesn't want to go back and do "Kashmir." If he wants to do it, he wants to do it the way this band would want to do it.

Tim: This one's different because there's only three writers credited. Again, "The seasons turn." You could do a study on how many song lyrics Robert's written that talk about the seasons and the changing of the seasons. He's had loss in his life; he's lost family, he's lost friends. And I think that he's just very realistic about the fact that sooner or later they'll be talking about him resting in peace. This one is more of a love song but again there's a lamenting feel to it, and the music feeds into the lyrics very well. "Are we built but falling down/ Holding you and hit the ground." That's kind of the hook of the song.

John: "A Way with Words" starts off with an almost Talk Talk-like sparseness in the arrangement. If you're familiar with those later Talk Talk albums, there's not much there. Musically there's very little going on but their songs go on and on. "A Way with Words" doesn't go on and on, but it's got that sparseness. Co-written with Justin and John Baggott, it's got a fragile vocal from Robert, and I guess fragile in the way that he delivers the vocal as someone who is longing to reconnect with someone that he lost touch with over time. There's a lot of water that's passed under the bridge in this relationship. And it's one that is met with a lot of regret that it came to that point. The seasons are used as a metaphor here for the lost time that continues to march forward. Is there a desire and a warmth from this person he's longing to reconnect with? It's like, words can lift people up and when used properly, the power of communication can mend bridges that have been torn down. I think musically, the song is perfectly complemented with the topic of reconciliation, and I think by making it so spare, the message naturally goes to the forefront.

Martin: True, and there are a lot of lyrics, but we're back to Robert saying things obliquely. You can tell a rainbow of emotions has gone on with whatever he's talking about, basically his lifespan, I guess, but we don't really get any concrete stories. That's another thing he regularly does and it's kind of cool. All right, how about the title track?

John: With "Carry Fire," you get a Middle Eastern vibe in the guitar, or I guess, the oud, played by Justin Adams. And you get a matching Middle Eastern vibe in the vocal melody, which again, Robert always had a love for that, and the song showcases it. Lyrically, this is about the depths of how far one is willing to go and what one is willing to do for someone, whether it's the love of another person or something along that line—what they are willing to do? I'm willing to carry fire for you here with my naked hands. That's pretty hardcore. I'm not sure I'd be willing to carry fire for somebody but again, it's just what the person's willing to do.

Pontus: "Carry Fire" really works. The music is very well thought-out and arranged for this setting, with the Arabic tones. They know what they're doing. Here's where we are and here's what you get—you're in this world. And the mystical sound, Led Zeppelin had that, so maybe that's why these albums sound so mysterious and dreamlike. In the *Song Remains the Same* film, Robert's dressed as a Viking trying to save the princess or whatever it is, during "Rain Song." They were into Aleister Crowley and all that, although I don't know how much of that was Robert. You've got the hermit in the gatefold of the fourth album, and the *Houses of the Holy* cover, front and inside, and I do know he was into Celtic history and legend. But now the mythology centres around Middle Eastern and African rhythms and instruments, and even what he finds magical about American blues. He's always trying to find new ways to connect the past to the present and dig deeper.

Martin: Also, in the making of these records, he's reminding himself about his fond memories of his travels, right? And he wants to make those travels productive by saying, "Look what I brought back. There's a lot more out there in the world than Led Zeppelin fans think there is."

Pontus: Yes, you hear interviews with him; he's one of those people who thinks, "Why are people still living in 1969?" Because as I said before, we, the audience, we also get a bit stuck. I remember the eighties. I remember that it was records that sounded like *Now and Zen*. Not just *Now and Zen*, but let's say the Bryan Adams records or modern Elton John. He's a very famous person and here is a new record. It's called *Leather Jackets*. And you put it on and it was shit. Here's the new Paul McCartney record. It's called *Press to Play* and it's another record that went nowhere. So you started going backwards, and then someone played you some older records. That's what happened with my stepfather. He played me Led Zeppelin *II*; he played me *Band on the Run*. Someone else played me *Goodbye Yellow Brick Road*. And then you realise that the seventies was the golden age. So you started going backwards. The problem with us is that we're stuck there because the newer music wasn't good (laughs). So we never went back; but we never went forward either. And I do think that is a problem now. You've talked about this many times, how Deep Purple have done a ton of good records with Steve Morse, maybe on some level, their best records. But listening to them, who's gonna hear them? There's no radio for it. Who's gonna find them?

Tim: "Carry Fire" was the advance single. It's got that Eastern modality from the oud or whatever stringed instrument makes the dissonant sounds that are not found on the Western scale; it's very intoxicating. When you first see the title of the album and the song you think, "carry fire," that's an odd choice of words. But then he says, "I'd carry fire for you." Oh, okay, I get it—pretty interesting. I really like this song a lot. I wouldn't say that it rocks, per sé; I guess I'd say that with an asterisk. But it does have more of an upbeat tempo feel to it, which is probably why it was the focus track. But as he talks about carrying fire, it's basically the idea of doing anything for someone. But then he says, "Just like I scarred you." So it's almost like he's atoning for something. I think the superior version of this song is on a BBC appearance he and his bandmates did when this first came out. They go into an extended jam at the end, and that actually does rock. There's some very cool stuff that happens there. But it's a good song in its own right as the recorded version.

Martin: Again, the arrangement is such that it doesn't compete with his vocal.

Tim: Yeah, it wouldn't make sense to have big, loud, bombastic drums and completely saturated guitar sounds. Certainly in the studio you could do some trickery to make his voice punch through, but live it would be just about impossible to play in pretty much any size of venue. It would look like he's moving his lips on stage but you wouldn't hear anything.

Martin: But even on these records, it's almost like his vocals are an instrument that is in the same wheelhouse as the rest of the instruments, versus what happens with a guitar, bass and drums hard rock band, right?

Tim: Yeah, I can imagine that. It certainly sounds like most of the songs would have been performed live in studio. And I think that if there was a problem with the vocal being drowned out, you'd know it right away. And they'd say, okay, what's the offending sound? Let's dial this back or dial that back. Again, very deliberate choices on all fronts.

Martin: With "Bones of Saints," we're back to something resembling rock 'n' roll, or at least rambunctious Tom Waits music. I suppose Bob Dylan makes music like this sometimes too.

John: I got a bit of a *Now and Zen*-era feel from this one. It's another upbeat rocker, and it has ties with "Carving Up the World." I like how he references Robert Johnson in this one with the "When the best fair deals come down" lyric. Robert Johnson has a famous song called "Last Fair Deal Gone Down" and that brings that old influence into the mix. This lyric really spoke to me. I don't know, this one raises a lot of important questions and thoughts. All through the lyrics of the song, the message of oppression is prevalent, and it all seems to surround itself with firearms, and then the money found in the use of and selling of firearms to gain control over those less fortunate. There's the building of fences to keep people away and there's walls coming down. In the bridge part of the song, you get this reference to the Garden of Eden, when everything was perfect and there were no problems in the world until evil came in and the fight between good and evil becomes the song of ages thing. And again, he's using the Robert Johnson song title, "Last Fair Deal Gone Down." The land of those who use oppression to weigh down those less fortunate, their Garden of Eden becomes increasingly corrupt, right? And musically, you have touches of sixties folk but brought forward into the current electronic landscape, along with backing vocals from Plant that take me back to Zeppelin. I don't know, the song has a smoothed-over, electronic rockabilly feel to it.

Tim: "Bones of Saints" is another one about immigration, or maybe slavery or war, definitely exploitation. There's another wall reference, and there's ships, plans, guns, bullets and money. It's almost a blues type of lyric, but much more poetic. And it certainly doesn't sound like a blues song musically. It's another band-written song. "So much of me is broken/The servants of a lie;" some of the lyrics on this album, this song included, you could almost say they're angry, but he never sings any of them angry. It's a consistent delivery no matter what the emotion or message. It's almost like, I'm putting this out here—you decide for yourself. What do you think it means?

Pontus: "Bones of Saints" sounds like a political song about the geopolitics of today. I understood it as a gun control song or maybe an anti-war song. Again, I'm Swedish, not English, so I may miss out a bit on nuance. But I felt he had something he wanted to get off his chest and he tries to sing in a higher register at the end. You hear the "No no no" part and you can picture the old lemon-squeezer guy.

Martin: Wow, and then "Keep It Hid," here's Robert really straddling time, creating—or with these guys, sculpting—a blues song, but with really modern sounds. And as John says, I guess "Bones of Saints" does this too.

Pontus: Yes, for sure. "Keep It Hid" is quite a bit more electronic, with this swinging, almost samba-like rhythm and great electric guitar sound.

John: Agreed, bluesy chord changes and bluesy vocal with prominent programmed synth and kind of sparse. That's pretty much what drives this whole song. I guess it asks the question of a woman who is dealing with life struggles, and she doesn't let it show. There's a hope for someone to let it out and find that person who will comfort her when her man is no longer around. The sea plays a role here, calming her, almost helping her devise her next move. The silver key and a golden cup references, I imagine, are when she finally finds that peace and happiness that she's been longing for. The wine from the loving cup is referenced in the second verse. Like I say, musically, very sparse with repetitive programmed beat. I feel like the guitars are there to add to the mystery of the situation of this woman.

Martin: Like I said earlier, sometimes it's like he's got a house that's a completely new build, but designed to look like an old cottage out in the woods. In other words, it's in touch with old styles, but it's got all the modern conveniences.

John: But he's making it work. And I don't know of anybody else who is doing this kind of stuff.

Tim: "Keep It Hid" is out of character in that the lyrics are much more traditional. "Take the wine from the loving cup/Momma, take your time, don't you spill a drop" and "Who you gonna rock when your mother's gone?;" this could be a Led Zeppelin lyric. And there aren't many times across this album that I would say that. Musically it doesn't sound like Zeppelin, but he's got it in his toolbox to write these types of lyrics. And I think once in a while, it just comes out. Okay, let's not be quite so cerebral; let's bring it back down to earth for this one.

Martin: "Bluebirds Over the Mountain" underscores the idea on the previous track, where technology gets applied to old-timey music. This one's legitimately old-timey, coming from 1958, but "Keep It Hid" doesn't sound any less vintage.

Pontus: Yes, true (laughs). We've got the album's only cover here, performed in a duet with Chrissie Hynde. And the interesting thing here is that I had heard "Bluebirds Over the Mountain" with the Beach Boys beforehand. And it's written by Ersel Hickey, who had a hit with it. But here the rhythm almost sounds like "Are You Experienced," the Jimi Hendrix song. It has the same military rhythm and big drums. And it has this backwards thing going on in the background. So it's like a mash-up between this folk song and a homage to Jimi Hendrix and psychedelic times.

John: I really like that languid, marching beat, with that Jimmy Page, Echoplex-type guitar line going on in the beginning. The Chrissie Hynde duet—I'm like, yeah, can we get more of this? I thought they worked very well together.

Tim: I'm not familiar with Ersel Hickey, but Robert's such a musical scholar, this could've been an independent artist of our time—or it could be someone from the 1700s, because it's almost like a sea shanty. That one kind of sneaks up on you, because if you haven't read the credits, all of a sudden you think, that voice sounds familiar. It works. He's done two albums with Alison Krauss, so he likes this idea of having the female vocal to play off of, all the way back to "The Battle of Evermore." It's not one of my favourites on the album, but again, it's him doing exactly what he wants to do.

Martin: Why do you think Robert's so comfortable with doing covers, to the point where he'd just wade right into it and make a whole album of covers?

Tim: I think the main thing is that he really wants to share this music with people. I don't think there's anything more to it than that. Certainly it's not for commercial purposes, because if it was for commercial purposes, he would do songs that everybody knows, which is usually never a good thing. So he puts out a covers album like he did with *Dreamland* and you might as well call it a brand-new album because most people don't know those songs. And I think he's hoping that there are enough members of his fan base that think the way he thinks in that they want to find out more about this kind of music and where these songs came from. That they might now want to hear the original versions. He's obviously capable of creating great music on his own and writing really thoughtful lyrics. I think there's a part of him that thinks, well, I've done that. When *Dreamland* came out, I was like, is this all we're gonna get from him now, are covers albums? So I'm glad he didn't stick with that. But throwing one in once in a while, especially if it's as obscure and thoughtful as *Dreamland*, not a big deal.

Martin: Okay, *Carry Fire* closes with "Heaven Sent," and man, if that's the last solo song we ever get from Robert, he's left us on an ominous note, inscrutable with the lyrics, and almost disturbing at the music end.

John: Yes, a dreamy and very dramatic closer to the album, with a jazzy feel but with buzzing atmospheric instrumentation. Certainly an ethereal way to close the album. Moody, electronic loops with a quiet, reflective vocal by Plant. Things that sound easy to do but are not. It's this journey of finding new things and carrying them forward. People get taken on the journey and come out as different people and sometimes that's a good thing and sometimes not. In the end we must carry on with our lives. There are things in life that continue on, I guess, whether we're here or not. But yeah, with the electronic sparseness of the loops, it gives you a feel like you're listening to Talk Talk a little bit, who I mentioned before. But with the lyrics, it works so wonderfully. It leaves the listener with a satisfying—and questioning—feeling. I think it's a perfect album closer.

Tim: He bows out with "All the long goodbyes/All the goodbye songs/Spend the time forgiving/Never really done." Wow. He closes the song with that and also the album and maybe his career, although this album is now from quite a long time ago. It feels like this is another example of him looking back on his life. He's had a crazy life and he's taking stock of it. It feels well-placed as the closer because musically and lyrically it does sound like he's taking a bow.

Martin: Robert seems to be one of the most comfortable artists of his vintage in terms of writing from an old person's point of view, right?

Tim: Yeah, that's another great point. Because most of my favourite bands, they put out a new album and you want to like it, but every once in a while there'll be a song that sounds like, God, when did you write this? When you were 14? And Robert is definitely not writing from the point of view of the younger man that he was. It's almost a grandfatherly point of view, the voice of wisdom, the wise old sage. Not that he's preaching, but he's just saying, "This is what I'm observing; this is what I'm feeling."

Martin: And it's reflected in the music too. The last time he tried to keep abreast of the competition, or take aim at the competition, was *Manic Nirvana*. Across a long expanse of these latest records, he could be entertaining royalty or a benefactor back in medieval times.

Tim: Yeah, almost like a bard of the court. And if you look at his band, they could almost show up as they look now and they wouldn't look out of place. I guess we'd call it timeless, but with his aesthetic, Robert and his band are almost like time-travellers.

Martin: Space Shifters! There is one other album that I feel is very much like what Robert's doing, at least on a lyrical level, with this idea of an old man who's seen almost too much life, reflecting on it all, and that's Roger Waters with *Is This the Life We Really Want?*, which is actually from the same year, 2017. Roger would have been 73, so five years older than Robert at the time. Man, and I worship that album; I think it's my most played album from the last 20 years. Anyway, Pontus, any closing thoughts, I guess beginning with this last song, "Heaven Sent?"

Pontus: Well, yes, coincidentally, this is a song about aging. Love the guitar tones. If you look at the lyrics here, you asked me about lyricism in the eighties and eighties, I think he has matured. And now he wants to express himself more, both as a bluesman but also with more reflective writing about what he's going through, what he's witnessed. It's not "Baby, baby, baby." That is still present on *Manic Nirvana*, the mannerisms that he had in Zeppelin, the ooh-ooh-ing and all that. But they're gone here. Ultimately, he's a very interesting person. He always was, but significantly more so in his old age.

Martin: I know I keep coming back to this theme but given that here we are at the end of the story, I think the most poignant and dramatic theme here is the stock-taking he wants to do in his twilight years.

Pontus: In Sweden we call that death cleaning. It's said tongue-in-cheek. You sell all your stuff, before, so you have very little when you get old. As you say, you take stock and you go through your house and then you just part ways with the stuff that you don't need. That's what Robert's doing across both these last two albums—he's death cleaning.

Contributor Biographies

Joe Becht
Joe is a music aficionado and avid Chicago rock historian who has worked at several radio stations including KRUI in Iowa City and WSCR in Chicago. He currently hosts the *Wasted Some Time with Average Joe* YouTube channel and the *Logical Logistics* podcast. He currently works in the logistics industry and services the largest concert promotion company in the world. He has published articles for many music web sites and fanzines and well as logistics industry publications. Led Zeppelin and Robert Plant are extremely important to him as artists. He has seen Plant in concert three times, most recently in 2015.

Ralph Chapman
Ralph's most recent project is scripting the very first official feature documentary on that "little ol' band from Texas," ZZ Top, in collaboration with Banger Films. Previously, he served as writer and associate producer on the VH1 series *Rock Icons*. Prior to that, he served the same roles on the critically acclaimed 11-part series on heavy metal, *Metal Evolution*. Ralph was also part of the creative team behind the Juno award-winning documentary, *Rush: Beyond The Lighted Stage* which took the Audience Award at the Tribeca Film Festival in 2010. Ralph also continues to work with Iconoclassic Records as a project producer notably overseeing the reissue campaign of The Guess Who catalogue. He continues to develop projects with Banger Films, and on his own with his production company, Wesbrage Productions, while contributing to various music-related websites in his spare time.

John Clauser
John is a Pennsylvania boy living in Alabama. He's a long-time music fan, wrestling fan and Steelers fan. When he's not at work, he likes to talk music, wrestling, movies and faith on his YouTube channel, *My Music Corner*. It also goes without saying that John remains a long-time Led Zeppelin fan, as well as follower of Robert Plant's solo work.

Tim Durling
Tim has worked in radio in various capacities, from on-air to commercial writing since 1993. His DJ career started back far enough to include spinning a few "gold" songs on actual 45s, then CDs, all the way up to digital, and he's played many a Led Zeppelin and Robert Plant ditty, even songs by the Honeydrippers. Tim is also the namesake of *Tim's Vinyl Confessions* on YouTube. Since 2014, he's talked passionately about the music he loves and collects. Speaking of collecting, Tim also has a peculiar habit of seeking out rare 8-track tapes from the later eighties, so much so that he wrote a book called *Unspooled: An Adventure in 8-Tracks*, on the subject. He's also been known to poke his head in on the author's *The Contrarians* YouTube channel from time to time. Despite living in off-circuit New Brunswick, Canada, Tim and his wife Sarah had the privilege of seeing Robert Plant live in September 2019 on a rare tour through the area.

Chad Green

Chad is a Calgary-based Gen Xer, music fan, environmental scientist in the oil industry, dad of adult-aged kids, hiker, motorcyclist and terrible guitar player. He enjoys rambling on about various topics, including the universe, the human condition and Robert Plant.

Sean Kelly

Sean is a Canadian guitarist, educator, and author who has performed with Nelly Furtado, Lee Aaron, Coney Hatch, Alan Frew, Helix, Gilby Clarke, Honeymoon Suite, and Crash Kelly. He is the author of two books, *Metal on Ice: Tales from Canada's Hard Rock and Heavy Metal Heroes* (Dundurn Press) and *Don't Call It Hair Metal: Art in the Excess of eighties Rock* (ECW Press). In 2015 he performed in Twisted Sister frontman Dee Snider's *Rock N Roll Christmas Tale*, and also has played guitar in the Toronto production of the hit Broadway musical *Rock of Ages*. Sean is a Music Teacher with the Toronto Catholic District School Board.

Rick LaBonte

Rick is a singer/songwriter from Windsor, Ontario. He has been collecting music and studying rock history since the eighties. As a vocalist and multi-instrumentalist, he has been performing in the music scene since the eighties. He was inducted in Windsor's Musician's Hall of Fame in 2017. He has released albums that are available on Spotify, iTunes, and on his website, ricklabonte.com, namely *On a Mission* (2016), *The Blues Side* (2021) and a double album called *Living It Up* from 2022. He is a regular guest on the *Sea of Tranquility* YouTube channel discussing all things classic rock. He has appeared in *519* magazine and *Windsor Life* magazine several times. As part of his storied music career around the Windsor/Detroit area, he has performed on stage with Uriah Heep, The Tea Party, Jody Raffoul, God's Joe Konas, Powder Blues Band's Tom Lavin, Detroit's Queen of the Blues, Thornetta Davis, Larry McCray and Scott Holt, current vocalist for Foghat.

Douglas Maher

Douglas is a well-known and highly regarded music historian and archivist who also spent nearly two decades working as a music columnist for Yahoo! Entertainment and journalist for *The Lakeland Ledger, Naples Daily News, All Headline News* as well as stints working at WSHE-FM in Fort Lauderdale, WJNO-AM in Palm Beach and WAMI-TV in Miami. His history includes contributing to numerous publications and documentaries including *Rush: Beyond the Lighted Stage, Rush: Album by Album* and *Rush: Merely Players*. Doug has amassed an inventory of over one million items in radio, music and film-related advertising pieces dating back from 1890 to 2023. He is repeatedly sought after for help by artists filling in gaps for biography and documentary projects with his arsenal of entertainment history. Doug has attended a dozen Robert Plant concerts dating back to 1988 and continues to expand his large ephemera collection covering Plant's post-Led Zeppelin career.

Pontus Norshammar

Pontus is a Swedish journalist based in Stockholm. A music geek and a major record collector since childhood, Norshammar contributes regularly to the YouTube channel *The Contrarians* and has appeared on the British music podcast *The Epileptic Gibbon Music Show*. He is also involved with the Swedish concert scene. When it comes to the music of Robert Plant, Norshammar says "My stepfather had an original copy of

'The Brown Bomber' (Led Zeppelin *II*) and it was love at first listen when I was 14. In 1990 I was introduced to Robert's solo work through the *Knebworth: The Album* 2CD set. Recorded at the Silver Clef charity show, it featured everybody from Tears for Fears through Cliff Richard and The Shadows to Pink Floyd! Robert and his band were featured with four tracks, with Jimmy Page joining in on two of them. It is a must-have. I have always admired Plant's vision of looking forward and trying new adventures. I was lucky to see Page and Plant in 1995 with The Black Crowes opening. It was a fantastic outdoor show in Stockholm in the summer sun overlooking the water."

Special Thanks

A hearty appreciation goes out to Agustin Garcia de Paredes who applied his eagle eye to a copy edit of this book. Agustin is also the moderator of the *History in Five Songs with Martin Popoff* podcast Facebook page.

About the Author

At approximately 7900 (with over 7000 appearing in his books), Martin has unofficially written more record reviews than anybody in the history of music writing across all genres. Additionally, Martin has penned approximately 120 books on hard rock, heavy metal, classic rock, prog, punk and record collecting. He was Editor-in-Chief of the now retired *Brave Words & Bloody Knuckles*, Canada's foremost heavy metal publication for 14 years, and has also contributed to *Revolver, Guitar World, Goldmine, Record Collector*, bravewords.com, lollipop.com and hardradio.com, with many record label band bios and liner notes to his credit as well.

Additionally, Martin has been a regular contractor to Banger Films, having worked for two years as researcher on the award-winning documentary *Rush: Beyond the Lighted Stage*, on the writing and research team for the 11-episode *Metal Evolution* and on the ten-episode *Rock Icons*, both for VH1 Classic. Additionally, Martin is the writer of the original metal genre chart used in *Metal: A Headbanger's Journey* and throughout the *Metal Evolution* episodes.

Then there's his audio podcast, *History in Five Songs with Martin Popoff* and the YouTube channel he runs with Marco D'Auria, *The Contrarians*. The community of guest analysts seen on *The Contrarians* has provided the pool of speakers used across the pages of this very book. Martin currently resides in Toronto and can be reached through martinp@inforamp.net or martinpopoff.com.

A Complete Martin Popoff Bibliography

2024: Pictures at Eleven: Robert Plant Album by Album, Perfect Water: The Rebel Imaginos

2023: Kiss at 50, The Who and Quadrophenia, Dominance and Submission: The Blue Öyster Cult Canon, Wild Mood Swings: Disintegrating The Cure Album by Album, AC/DC at 50

2022: Pink Floyd and The Dark Side of the Moon: 50 Years, Killing the Dragon: Dio in the eighties and 2000s, Feed My Frankenstein: Alice Cooper, the Solo Years, Easy Action: The Original Alice Cooper Band, Lively Arts: The Damned Deconstructed, Yes: A Visual Biography II: 1982 – 2022, Bowie @ 75, Dream Evil: Dio in the eighties, Judas Priest: A Visual Biography, UFO: A Visual Biography

2021: Hawkwind: A Visual Biography, Loud 'n' Proud: Fifty Years of Nazareth, Yes: A Visual Biography, Uriah Heep: A Visual Biography, Driven: Rush in the eighties and "In the End," Flaming Telepaths: Imaginos Expanded and Specified, Rebel Rouser: A Sweet User Manual

2020: The Fortune: On the Rocks with Angel, Van Halen: A Visual Biography, Limelight: Rush in the eighties, Thin Lizzy: A Visual Biography, Empire of the Clouds: Iron Maiden in the 2000s, Blue Öyster Cult: A Visual Biography, Anthem: Rush in the seventies, Denim and Leather: Saxon's First Ten Years, Black Funeral: Into the Coven with Mercyful Fate

2019: Satisfaction: 10 Albums That Changed My Life, Holy Smoke: Iron Maiden in the eighties, Sensitive to Light: The Rainbow Story, Where Eagles Dare: Iron Maiden in the eighties, Aces High: The Top 250 Heavy Metal Songs of the eighties, Judas Priest: Turbo 'til Now, Born Again! Black Sabbath in the Eighties and Nineties

2018: Riff Raff: The Top 250 Heavy Metal Songs of the seventies, Lettin' Go: UFO in the eighties and eighties, Queen: Album by Album, Unchained: A Van Halen User Manual, Iron Maiden: Album by Album, Sabotage! Black Sabbath in the Seventies, Welcome to My Nightmare: 50 Years of Alice Cooper, Judas Priest: Decade of Domination, Popoff Archive – 6: American Power Metal, Popoff Archive – 5: European Power Metal, The Clash: All the Albums, All the Songs

2017: Led Zeppelin: All the Albums, All the Songs, AC/DC: Album by Album, Lights Out: Surviving the seventies with UFO, Tornado of Souls: Thrash's Titanic Clash, Caught in a Mosh: The Golden Era of Thrash, Rush: Album by Album, Beer Drinkers and Hell Raisers: The Rise of Motörhead, Metal Collector: Gathered Tales from Headbangers, Hit the Lights: The Birth of Thrash, Popoff Archive – 4: Classic Rock, Popoff Archive – 3: Hair Metal

2016: Popoff Archive – 2: Progressive Rock, Popoff Archive – 1: Doom Metal, Rock the Nation: Montrose, Gamma and Ronnie Redefined, Punk Tees: The Punk Revolution in 125 T-Shirts, Metal Heart: Aiming High with Accept, Ramones at 40, Time and a Word: The Yes Story

2015: Kickstart My Heart: A Mötley Crüe Day-by-Day, This Means War: The Sunset Years of the NWOBHM, Wheels of Steel: The Explosive Early Years of the NWOBHM, Swords and Tequila: Riot's Classic First Decade, Who Invented Heavy Metal?, Sail Away: Whitesnake's Fantastic Voyage

2014: Live Magnetic Air: The Unlikely Saga of the Superlative Max Webster, Steal Away the Night: An Ozzy Osbourne Day-by-Day, The Big Book of Hair Metal, Sweating Bullets: The Deth and Rebirth of Megadeth, Smokin' Valves: A Headbanger's Guide to 900 NWOBHM Records

2013: The Art of Metal (co-edit with Malcolm Dome), 2 Minutes to Midnight: An Iron Maiden Day-by-Day, Metallica: The Complete Illustrated History, Rush: The Illustrated History, Ye Olde Metal: 1979, Scorpions: Top of the Bill - updated and reissued as Wind of Change: The Scorpions Story in 2016

2012: Epic Ted Nugent, Fade To Black: Hard Rock Cover Art of the Vinyl Age, It's Getting Dangerous: Thin Lizzy 81-12, We Will Be Strong: Thin Lizzy 76-81, Fighting My Way Back: Thin Lizzy 69-76, The Deep Purple Royal Family: Chain of Events '80 – '11, The Deep Purple Royal Family: Chain of Events Through '79 - reissued as The Deep Purple Family Year by Year books 2011: Black Sabbath FAQ, The Collector's Guide to Heavy Metal: Volume 4: The '00s (co-authored with David Perri)

2010: Goldmine Standard Catalog of American Records 1948 – 1991, 7th Edition

2009: Goldmine Record Album Price Guide, 6th Edition, Goldmine 45 RPM Price Guide, 7th Edition, A Castle Full of Rascals: Deep Purple '83 – '09, Worlds Away: Voivod and the Art of Michel Langevin, Ye Olde Metal: 1978

2008: Gettin' Tighter: Deep Purple '68 – '76, All Access: The Art of the Backstage Pass, Ye Olde Metal: 1977, Ye Olde Metal: 1976

2007: Judas Priest: Heavy Metal Painkillers, Ye Olde Metal: 1973 to 1975, The Collector's Guide to Heavy Metal: Volume 3: The Nineties, Ye Olde Metal: 1968 to 1972

2006: Run for Cover: The Art of Derek Riggs, Black Sabbath: Doom Let Loose, Dio: Light Beyond the Black

2005: The Collector's Guide to Heavy Metal: Volume 2: The Eighties, Rainbow: English Castle Magic, UFO: Shoot Out the Lights, The New Wave of British Heavy Metal Singles

2004: Blue Öyster Cult: Secrets Revealed! (updated and reissued in 2009 with the same title; updated and reissued as Agents of Fortune: The Blue Öyster Cult Story in 2016), Contents Under Pressure: 30 Years of Rush at Home & Away, The Top 500 Heavy Metal Albums of All Time

2003: The Collector's Guide to Heavy Metal: Volume 1: The Seventies, The Top 500 Heavy Metal Songs of All Time

2001: Southern Rock Review

2000: Heavy Metal: 20th Century Rock and Roll, The Goldmine Price Guide to Heavy Metal Records

1997: The Collector's Guide to Heavy Metal

1993: Riff Kills Man! 25 Years of Recorded Hard Rock & Heavy Metal

See martinpopoff.com for complete details and ordering information.